Leibniz

Classic Thinkers

Daniel E. Flage, *Berkeley*
J. M. Fritzman, *Hegel*
Bernard Gert, *Hobbes*
Dale E. Miller, *J. S. Mill*
A. J. Pyle, *Locke*
Andrew Ward, *Kant*

Leibniz

Richard T. W. Arthur

polity

First published in 2014 by Polity Press

Polity Press
65 Bridge Street
Cambridge CB2 1UR, UK

Polity Press
350 Main Street
Malden, MA 02148, USA

ISBN-13: 978-0-7456-5374-7
ISBN-13: 978-0-7456-5375-4 (pb)

A catalogue record for this book is available from the British Library.

Typeset in 10.5 on 12 pt Palatino
by Toppan Best-set Premedia Limited
Printed and bound in Great Britain by T.J. International Ltd, Padstow, Cornwall

The publisher has used its best endeavours to ensure that the URLs for external websites referred to in this book are correct and active at the time of going to press. However, the publisher has no responsibility for the websites and can make no guarantee that a site will remain live or that the content is or will remain appropriate.

Every effort has been made to trace all copyright holders, but if any have been inadvertently overlooked the publisher will be pleased to include any necessary credits in any subsequent reprint or edition.

For further information on Polity, visit our website: www.politybooks.com

Contents

Acknowledgements

Many people have helped to make this book better than it might otherwise have been. It is a pleasure to acknowledge Barry Allen, who co-taught a graduate seminar with me on Deleuze, Spinoza and Leibniz, and the students in that seminar who read early drafts of some chapters; and also the students, undergraduate and graduate, in my course on Leibniz and English Philosophy, for whom the manuscript was a set text. Their reactions to it and excellent weekly comments and discussions helped me to frame my treatment of many points. I also benefited greatly from the comments and suggestions of Ohad Nachtomy and a second (anonymous) reader for Polity Press, and am much indebted to my sons Alexander and Thomas Arthur for advice on how to frame chapter 1, to my colleagues Stefan Sciaraffa, Violetta Igneski and Stefan Rodde for feedback on chapter 8, to Liam Dempsey and David Wright for comments on the whole draft, to Stephan Meier-Öser for supplying me with the latest edited versions of some passages from Leibniz's writings, and above all to my wife Gabriella Colussi Arthur for her encouragement and critical advice. To all of you, and to Emma Hutchinson, Pascal Porcheron and everyone at Polity Press, many, many thanks!

Note on the Text and Translations

Leibniz wrote mostly in Latin, somewhat less in French, and occasionally in German. All translations here are the author's own translations from standard editions of Leibniz's original Latin and French (except where explicitly noted otherwise). For the convenience of the reader wishing to see a given passage in fuller context, references are also given to available English-language translations where these exist, e.g. (A VI iii 518/DSR 75).

The titles of Leibniz's books and papers are all given in English; for ease of reference, the original-language titles are also given in the Chronological Sketch.

Abbreviations

A   Akademie der Wissenschaften der DDR, ed., G. W. Leibniz, *Sämtliche Schriften und Briefe* (Leibniz 1923–); cited by series, volume and page, e.g. A VI ii 229, etc.

AG   Ariew and Garber, eds, G. W. Leibniz, *Philosophical Essays* (Leibniz 1989).

AK   Akademie der Wissenschaften, ed., Immanuel Kant, *Gesammelte Schriften*, ed. (Kant 1910–); cited by volume and page, e.g. AK viii 138.

AT   Adam and Tannery, eds, *Oeuvres de Descartes* (Descartes 1964–76); cited by volume and page, e.g. AT viii A 71.

C   Couturat, ed., *Opuscules et fragments inédits de Leibniz* (Leibniz 1903).

CSM   Cottingham, Stoothof and Murdoch, eds, *Philosophical Writings of Descartes*, vols 1 and 2 (Descartes 1984–5).

CSMK   Cottingham, Stoothof, Murdoch and Kenny, eds, *Philosophical Writings of Descartes*, vol. 3 (Descartes 1991).

D   Dutens, ed., G. W. Leibniz, *Opera omnia . . .* (Leibniz 1768); cited by volume and page, e.g. D iv 279.

DSR   G. W. Leibniz, *De Summa Rerum*, trans. Parkinson (Leibniz 1992).

GM   Gerhardt, ed., *Leibnizens Mathematische Schriften* (Leibniz 1849–63); cited by volume and page, e.g. GM ii 157, etc.

GP   Gerhardt, ed., *Die Philosophische Schriften von Gottfried Wilhelm Leibniz* (Leibniz 1875–90); cited by volume and page, e.g. GP ii 268, etc.

Grua   Grua, ed., G. W. Leibniz, *Textes inédits* (Leibniz 1948).

L	Loemker, ed., G. W. Leibniz, *Philosophical Papers and Letters* (Leibniz 1969).
LDB	*The Leibniz–Des Bosses Correspondence*, trans. Look and Rutherford (Leibniz 2007).
LDV	*The Leibniz–De Volder Correspondence*, trans. Lodge (Leibniz 2013).
LoC	G. W. Leibniz, *The Labyrinth of the Continuum*, trans. Arthur (Leibniz 2001).
MP	G. W. Leibniz, *Philosophical Writings*, trans. Morris and Parkinson (Leibniz 1995a).
NE	G. W. Leibniz, *Nouveaux essais sur L'entendement humaine*, translation in Leibniz 1981, which has page numbers keyed to A VI vi.
PW	G. W. Leibniz, *Political Writings*, trans. Riley (Leibniz 1988).
T	G. W. Leibniz, *Théodicée (Essais de Théodicée sur la bonté de Dieu, la liberté de l'homme et l'origine du mal)*, page numbers keyed to the Huggard translation in Leibniz 1985.
WFT	Woolhouse and Francks, eds, G. W. Leibniz, *Philosophical Texts* (Leibniz 1998).

Chronological Sketch

1646   1 July: Gottfried Wilhelm Leibniz born in Leipzig, Saxony.

1652   death of Leibniz's father, Friedrich Leibnutz; a year later Leibniz enters Latin school in Leipzig.

1661   April: begins studies at the University of Leipzig; awarded bachelor's degree in philosophy in December of the following year.

1663   June: discussion of bachelor's dissertation at Leipzig, *Disputatio metaphysica de principio individui* (*Metaphysical Disputation on the Principle of Individuation*); enrols in summer school at the University of Jena.

1664   February: Leibniz earns a master's degree in philosophy at Leipzig; nine days later his mother dies of a respiratory infection; December: discussion of master's dissertation, *Specimen quaestionum philosophicarum ex jure collectarum* (*An Essay of Collected Philosophical Problems of Right*).

1665   July, August: discussion of dissertation *De conditionibus* (*On Conditions*) for bachelor's degree in law at Leipzig, granted in September.

1666   March: discussion of the first part of dissertation *Dissertatio de arte combinatoria* (*Dissertation on the Combinatorial Art*) for habilitation in the faculty of philosophy; September: leaves Leipzig for Nuremberg, where he enrols in the law faculty at the University of Altdorf in October; November: discussion of the thesis *Disputatio inauguralis de casibus perplexis in jure* (*Inaugural Disputation on Ambiguous Legal Cases*) for a licence and doctorate in law at Altdorf.

1667 secretary of alchemical society in Nuremberg; meets Baron Johann Christian von Boineburg in Frankfurt and publishes *Nova methodus discendae docendae jurisprudentiae* (*New Method for Learning and Teaching Jurisprudence*).

1668 enters the employment of Johann Philipp von Schönborn, Elector and Prince-Archbishop of Mainz, to help reform the judicial body; begins collaboration with Boineburg, writing *Confessio naturae contra atheistas* (*Confession of Nature against Atheists*) and a conspectus of the *Demonstrationes Catholicae* (*Catholic Demonstrations*) for his employer.

1670 new edition published of the nominalist Mario Nizolio's *Antibarbarus: seu de veris principiis* (*Antibarbarus: or on the True Principles and True Reason for Philosophizing against the Pseudo-philosophers*), including an introduction by Leibniz and a revised copy of his 1669 letter to Jakob Thomasius stating his philosophical views.

1671 works on a proposed treatise, *Elementa mentis* (*Elements of Mind*); completes *Theoria motus abstracti* (*Theory of Abstract Motion*) and *Hypothesis physica nova* (*A New Physical Hypothesis*), which are sent to the Académie Royale des Sciences and the Royal Society.

1672 March: arrives in Paris on a diplomatic mission for Boineburg; will live there for four years, despite Boineburg's death in December, establishing contacts with Christiaan Huygens, Simon Foucher, Antoine Arnauld, Edme Mariotte, Claude Perrault and Nicolas Malebranche; writes *Confessio Philosophi* (*A Philosopher's Confession*) and *Propositiones quaedam physicae* (*Certain Physical Propositions*).

1673 January–February: first visit to London, where he meets Henry Oldenburg, secretary of the Royal Society; March: demonstrates his calculating machine to the Society; April: elected to the Royal Society. His employer Johann von Schönborn dies as he and Melchior Schönborn return to France.

1675 invents the differential and integral calculus, and composes a treatise, the *De quadratura arithmetica circuli . . .* (*On the Arithmetical Quadrature of the Circle . . .*), which he submits the following year in an effort to get elected to the Académie Royale des Sciences; begins exploration of Spinoza's philosophy with Walther von Tschirnhaus in Paris; writes notes on philosophy (the *De Summa Rerum*) between December and the following summer.

1676   summer: composes *De Arcanis Motus et Mechanica ad puram Geometriam reducenda* (*On the Secrets of Motion and Reducing Mechanics to Pure Geometry*) and *Principia mechanica* (*Mechanical Principles*); October: leaves Paris for London, where John Collins shows him some of Newton's manuscripts; November: writes the dialogue *Pacidius Philalethi* (*Pacidius to Philalethes*) while waiting in the Thames estuary for fair weather to sail for Holland; extended conversations with Spinoza in The Hague, and with Swammerdam and Leeuwenhoek in Amsterdam; December: finally arrives in Hanover to take up appointment as court counsellor and librarian to Duke Johann Friedrich.

1678   January: composes *De corporum concorsu* (*On the Collision of Bodies*), in which he outlines his new notion of force as proportional to mv^2; works on plans for a *scientia generalis*, including a demonstrative encyclopaedia, and proposes the creation of scientific societies and research groups to work on it; sketches a binary arithmetic and writes a paper laying the foundations for the theory of probability; Autumn: begins involvement with improving the mines in the Harz mountains, where he spends at least 165 weeks until the collapse of the project in 1685.

1679   April: composes a series of logical papers laying the foundation for a logical calculus; sketches plans for a *characteristic geometry* or *Analysis Situs*, which he sends to Huygens for his reaction; December: death of Johann Friedrich, who is succeeded as Duke of Hanover by his younger brother, Ernst August, who is married to Sophie von der Pfalz.

1684   January: invention of determinants and discovery of their properties; June: his biting attack on the Sun King, Louis XIV, *Mars Christianissimus seu Apologia armorum Regis Christianissimi contra Christianos* (*The Most Christian War-god, or an Apology for the Arms of the Most Christian King against the Christians*), appears in print anonymously; October: publication of his first paper on the differential calculus, the *Nova methodus pro maximis et minimis* (*New Method by Maxima and Minima*) in the *Acta Eruditorum*, as well as *Meditationes de cognition, veritate et ideis* (*Meditations on Knowledge, Truth and Ideas*) in November.

1686   July: his second paper on the calculus appears in the *Acta Eruditorum*, as does his attack on Cartesian physics, the *Brevis demonstration erroris memorabilis Cartesii et aliorum circa legem* *naturae* (*Brief Demonstration of a Notable Error by Descartes and Others Concerning a Law of Nature*); he writes four other treatises, the *Discours de métaphysique* (*Discourse on Metaphysics*), the *Specimen inventorum de admirandis naturae generalis arcanis* (*Specimen of Discoveries of the Admirable Secrets of Nature in General*), the *Generales inquisitiones de analysi notionum et veritatum* (*General Investigations in the Analysis of Notions and Truths*) and the *Examen religionis Christianae* (*Examination of the Christian Religion*), and initiates his correspondence with Antoine Arnauld on the topics of the *Discourse*.

1687 Publishes a letter *Sur un principe général utile à l'explication des loix de la nature par la considération de la sagesse divine* (*On a General Principle Useful in Explaining the Laws of Nature through a Consideration of Divine Wisdom*) in the *Nouvelles de la république des lettres*, in which he states his Law of Continuity and shows how Malebranche's laws of motion are in violation of it.

1688 April: finds proof of the connection between the Este and Brunswick families in a codex in Augsburg, and continues touring Germany and Italy to do further archival research; May: arrives in Vienna, and after reading a review of Newton's *Principia Mathematica Naturalis Philosophiae* (*Mathematical Principles of Natural Philosophy*) (1687) in the *Acta Eruditorum*, gets hold of a copy, on which he makes notes and marginal comments, composing a number of draft manuscripts in quick succession in which he tries to derive Newton's results in conformity with the mechanical philosophy, using his invention of the differential equation.

1689 February: the *Tentamen de motuum caelestium causis* (*An Essay on the Causes of the Celestial Motions*) is published in the *Acta Eruditorum*; leaves Vienna for Italy to consult the Este archives in Modena, visiting Venice, Rome, Naples, Florence, Bologna and finally Modena in December; composes his major works on dynamics, the two dialogues *Phoranomus seu de potentia et legibus naturae* (*Phoranomus, or on Power and the Laws of Nature*), and begins the treatise *Dynamica de potentia et legibus naturae corporeae* (*Dynamics: On Power and the Laws of Corporeal Nature*).

1690 February: discovers the exact connection between the Este and Guelph houses, and writes drafts of *Brevis synopsis historiae Guelficae* (*Brief Synopsis of the History of the Guelphs*); May: *De causa gravitatis* (*On the Cause of Gravity*) is published in the *Acta Eruditorum*; discussions with Michel Angelo Fardella in Venice; June: returns to Hanover.

1692 Leibniz's efforts to establish Duke Ernst August's electoral claim meet success when Emperor Leopold I grants the status of ninth electorate to the territories of Calenberg (Hanover) and Celle; declines an invitation to join the court of Louis XIV; composes the *Essai de dynamique* (*Essay on Dynamics*) for the Paris Academy.

1694 March: publication in the *Acta Eruditorum* of *De primae philosophiae emendatione et de notione substantiae* (*On the Emendation of First Philosophy and the Notion of Substance*); December: finishes, but does not publish, the *Protogaea*, his treatise on geology.

1695 publication of the first part of *Specimen Dynamicum* (*Specimen of Dynamics*) in the *Acta Eruditorum*, and the *Système nouveau de la nature et de la communication des substances* (*New System of the Nature and Communication of Substances*) in the *Journal des sçavans*, and comments on Foucher's objections.

1697 completes a treatise on the German language, *Unvorgreiffliche Gedanken betreffend die Ausübung und Verbesserung der Teutschen Sprache* (*Novel Thoughts on the Use and Improvement of the German Language*); writes *De rerum origine radicali* (*On the Ultimate Origin of Things*).

1698 death of Ernst August, Duke of Hanover, who is succeeded by his son, Georg Ludwig; Leibniz begins a correspondence with the Dutch thinker Burcher de Volder which will last until 1706; publication of *De natura ipsa* (*On Nature Itself*) in the *Acta Eruditorum*.

1700 February: elected to the Parisian Académie Royale des Sciences; March: founding of the Berlin Society of Sciences, with Leibniz appointed President in July; October: summoned to Vienna by Emperor Leopold for talks on reunification of the Catholic and Protestant churches.

1703 begins writing his *Nouveaux essais sur l'entendement humain* (*New Essays on Human Understanding*), intended to initiate a dialogue with John Locke, but decides not to publish after Locke dies in October 1704; writes the *Méditation sur la notion commune de justice* (*Meditation on the Common Notion of Justice*).

1705 February: death of Queen Sophie Charlotte of Prussia, one of Leibniz's closest confidantes; May: publishes *Considérations sur les principes de vie, et sur les natures plastiques* (*Considerations on Vital Principles and Plastic Natures*) in the *Histoire des* *ouvrages des savants*; begins his *Discours sur la Theologie naturelle des Chinois* (*Discourse on the Natural Theology of the Chinese*), which he works on until 1716.

1706 January: begins a ten-year correspondence with the Jesuit Bartholomew Des Bosses, centred on the possibility of adapting his philosophy to the articles approved by that Order.

1707 brings out the *Novissima Sinica* (*Latest News from China*), an edition of writings by missionaries about China, for which he wrote a famous preface, extolling the virtues of that culture and of a multicultural approach to knowledge, and supporting Ricci's stand on the rites of ancestors.

1710 publication of *Essais de théodicée sur la bonté de Dieu, la liberté de l'homme et l'origine du mal* (the *Theodicy*), written in response to the good-natured criticisms of Pierre Bayle in his *Dictionnaire*.

1712 November: after audiences with Peter the Great during the previous year, nominated Russian privy counsellor of justice and adviser to the Tsar on mathematical and scientific matters; December: leaves for Vienna, where he will stay until September 1714; appointed Imperial Court councillor in Vienna. Returns to work on *Analysis Situs*, composing many new drafts in the next four years, as well as a treatise on etymology, *Epistolica de historia etymologica dissertatio* (*An Epistolic Dissertation on Etymological History*).

1713 January: publication in England of the *Commercium Epistolicum*, the supposedly neutral report by the Royal Society on the priority dispute over the calculus, in fact largely composed by Newton himself; on seeing it, Leibniz writes a quick anonymous response (the *Charta volans*), as well as his own account, *The History and Origins of the Differential Calculus*, which remained unpublished.

1714 composes the *Principes de la nature et de la grâce fondés en raison* (*Principles of Nature and Grace Founded in Reason*) for Prince Eugene of Saxony, and the essay that came to be called the *Monadology*; June: death of dowager Electress Sophie, Leibniz's friend and protector in Hanover; writes the *Initia rerum mathematicarum metaphysica* (*Metaphysical Foundations of Mathematics*), summarizing his mature views on space and time; 14 September: returns to Hanover from Prague, only to find that Georg Ludwig and his court have left for London without him three days before; Georg becomes George I, King of England.

1715 November–October 1716: correspondence with Samuel Clarke, mediated by Princess Caroline; Newton's 'anonymous' account of the *Commercium Epistolicum* appears in the *Philosophical Transactions*.

1716 Summer: meetings with Tsar Peter the Great in Lower Saxony; 14 November: Leibniz dies in Hanover of complications arising from self-administered treatment of gout; funeral one month later.

1

Introduction

Gottfried Wilhelm Leibniz was one of the most prolific thinkers of all time. 'Often in the morning when I am still in bed,' he wrote, 'so many thoughts occur to me in a single hour that sometimes it takes me a whole day or more to write them out' (quoted from Mates 1986: 34). These thoughts might have included designs for a new wind pump to drain the mines of the Harz mountains or for a calculating machine based on binary arithmetic, sketches for a treatise on geology or etymology, another draft of a logical calculus that was two hundred years ahead of its time, or a new derivation of Newton's law of gravitation on strictly mechanical principles. Even before getting up, Leibniz would usually have written lengthy letters on such subjects to one or two learned correspondents. He might also have penned a proposal to his employer the Duke of Hanover for a universally accessible state medical system, a legal brief in support of the Duke's electoral claim to certain territories, a deposition aimed at church reunification, or tried to mediate in the dispute among the Jesuits over the interpretation of Chinese religious rites. In short, Leibniz was an indefatigable one-man industry.

Yet all this worldly activity seems at odds with the usual understanding of Leibniz as a philosopher. He is perhaps best known for his *monads* or unities of substance. These he conceived as enduring entities constituting what is real in bodies and their motions. But although in those respects they are like material atoms, Leibniz characterized monads as 'possessing something analogous to perception and appetite' (NE 318), where perceptions (or states) of monads are representations of the whole of the rest of the universe, and their appetites are tendencies toward future states, governed by a law specific to each individual. Consequently, Leibniz is usually understood as an idealist who wished to reduce the whole of reality to mind-like entities and their intentional states: each monad is a world apart, constituted only by its own perceptions, sequenced according to its own internal law. On the usual understanding, moreover, these monads do not even exist in space and time. For, as Leibniz famously argued against Isaac Newton (1642–1727) and Samuel Clarke (1675–1729), space and time are relations; but he also held that relations, far from being independently existing entities, are supplied by a perceiving mind. On this reading, then, Leibniz's philosophy appears as a thorough-going idealism.

This presents a perplexing contrast. Leibniz was a 'natural philosopher', making active contributions to geometry, mechanics, dynamics, optics, geology and the life sciences. But why would someone on the cutting edge of both theoretical and empirical developments in these fields have developed a philosophy apparently so hostile to the physical world? We know that Leibniz understood himself to be attempting a rapprochement between the new 'mechanical philosophy' of Descartes, Gassendi and Boyle, and the Aristotelian philosophy taught in the universities. But both parties understood the physical world to exist in an unambiguous way: for the mechanical philosophers, it was constituted by bodies in motion, bodies being understood as parts of matter extended in length, breadth and depth, whose motion could be treated geometrically; for the Aristotelians, bodies or 'corporeal substances' possessed 'substantial forms', which they used to explain all types of goal-directed behaviour: plants tending to face the light, heavy bodies tending to fall to Earth, and so forth. Now what kind of rapprochement would Leibniz have achieved if he was asking both parties to deny the existence of matter and motion, and of the corporeal substances that they took to be the very stuff of the physical world?

Interpreters have generally answered that question by an appeal to a distinction between Leibniz's public and private philosophies: the 'optimistic, orthodox, fantastic, and shallow' philosophy 'designed to win the approbation of princes and princesses', as Bertrand Russell puts it (Russell [1946] 1972: 604), and the 'profound, coherent, largely Spinozistic, and amazingly logical' philosophy he had developed in his unpublished manuscripts. On this view, Leibniz was happy to promote his philosophy in public as solving such problems as the interaction between body and mind by proposing that both bodies and minds unfold their states independently and perfectly in step, like two clocks that keep perfect time; and generally to speak of bodies and corporeal substances in a realistic vein. But in his private philosophy bodies are no more than the coherent appearances of perceiving substances.

I see no such schism between private and public in Leibniz's philosophy, but only differences in presentation, resulting from his cooperative approach to building knowledge. Although Leibniz worked hard to produce general principles that he thought could promote science and its application, as well as heal religious rifts, he knew this could only be achieved through dialogue with others. And in order to promote dialogue, he would bend or colour his views to maximize the chances of productive exchange.

A big difficulty in trying to present Leibniz's philosophy, however, is the sheer profusion and ambitious scope of the projects in which he was engaged, either at the bidding of his employers in court or on his own account, which virtually guaranteed he would bring few of them to completion. As a result of this almost permanent distraction, Leibniz produced no definitive masterwork, such as Spinoza's *Ethics* or Kant's *Critique of Pure Reason*. He did publish a long book on the problem of evil in 1710, the *Theodicy*, but, like his posthumously published *New Essays*, the work is too discursive and polemical to serve as an introduction to the main themes of his thought. Consequently, his philosophy is usually introduced through the study of two summaries he gave of his metaphysics, the *Discourse on Metaphysics* of 1686 and the *Monadology* of 1714 (both these titles are the creations of later editors). The first presents his views in a context heavily conditioned by his desire to engage Antoine Arnauld in correspondence. Arnauld (1616–98) was a co-author of the famous Port Royal Logic, and a leading Catholic theologian and critic of Descartes, whose approval would aid Leibniz (a tolerant Lutheran) in his ambition to bring about a reconciliation of faiths. But for a modern reader unfamiliar with this context, it is hard to understand the *mélange* of issues from theology, logic, metaphysics and physics that Leibniz chooses to stress. The second work, the *Monadology*, although in many ways an admirably succinct summary of Leibniz's metaphysics, by and large fails to give much argument for his views, the contexts in which they were generated, or the problems they were designed to resolve. As a result, Leibniz's philosophy comes across, in Hegel's words, 'as a string of arbitrary assertions, following one upon another without any necessity in their connection, like a metaphysical romance' (Hegel 1836: 454).

The usual reception of Leibniz is also conditioned by the need to fit him into a simple narrative about the history of philosophy, where he is seen as one of the 'great rationalists' along with Descartes and Spinoza, whose dogmatism is opposed by the British empiricist philosophers beginning with Locke. But Leibniz was not an academic with an allegiance to any one school. He was a court diplomat, who thought that a political career would better enable him to achieve his goals of reforming scientific knowledge and helping to bring about the reunification of the Church. Seen in this light, his contributions to science, such as his correction of Descartes's law of the conservation of force, were not side-issues, but an integral part of his programme for the advancement of learning which he hoped would repair the theological rifts that were dividing seventeenth-century Europe. Leibniz was not trying to undermine the mechanical philosophy by reducing things to ideas and intentions, but rather trying to improve it by providing it with a proper foundation that could lead to new discoveries and advancements, as well as reconcile it with accepted articles of faith.

Accordingly, I shall approach Leibniz here in a way that I think is in keeping with his philosophy, although it will be an unusual methodology for a book of this kind. Instead of beginning with the themes and principles of his mature philosophy, and then structuring his philosophy around them, I take a genetic approach, trying to show how Leibniz's views arose by reference to the problems he was trying to solve, in their own historical context. In so doing, I will concentrate on his youthful writings, most of which are scattered Latin drafts that do not exist in any convenient compilation, and all of which I have translated. This genetic approach courts some obvious dangers: a reader encountering Leibniz for the first time might remember him more for views he gave up, or confuse his earlier attempts with his mature solutions to some of these problems, or simply rue the fact that not much space is left to discuss developments in his mature writings. And of course, it is more difficult to understand anyone in historical context: the various scientific, political and theological problems that occupied Leibniz, such as the correct measure of force or church reunification, will seem remote from today's philosophical concerns. But the reward is to see Leibniz at his best, as a profound and creative thinker always pushing the boundaries of knowledge, anticipating and engendering new approaches, many of them of surprising contemporary relevance.

Another advantage of this genetic approach is that it allows me to tackle some of the issues of interpretation obliquely, rather than head on. Instead of assuming that Leibniz had a definite metaphysical system, consisting in certain dogmatically asserted premises that were more or less impervious to his scientific and political pursuits, I will try to show how his metaphysics developed through the attempt to solve various more specific problems in the life sciences, theology, physics and mathematics. From this perspective it will emerge that Leibniz never intended to deny that substances have real bodies, but he meant rather to convey a deeper appreciation of what it is to be a substance or to be a body. Nor did he intend to deny that things exist in spatial relations, or that states of substances really succeed one another in time; rather he wanted to show how a correct understanding of space as an order of situations and time as an order of successive things would rule out a metaphysics in which extension is taken to be a substance, or space and time are depicted as existing independently of the things in them.

This results in a picture of Leibniz's metaphysics very different from the idealistic interpretation described above, and it may be worth briefly stating it to orient readers familiar with the issues. On my reading, Leibniz's corporeal substances simply are his embodied monads, whose bodies are aggregates of subordinate substances.[1] A corporeal substance is a unity by virtue of what is substantial in it, namely the form which gives it a unity of function and purpose through time. The body it has at any instant derives its reality from the substances presupposed in all its parts, although it is not itself a substance, and has at any time only a perceived unity. Similarly, motions derive their reality from an underlying instantaneous force existing at any instant. Thus Leibniz's commitment to corporeal substances is quite genuine, although by that term he means something different from what either the Cartesians or the Aristotelians understood by it. 'It is really not surprising that the Cartesians have failed to understand the nature of corporeal substance,' he tells his correspondent Burchard de Volder in June 1704, 'since they consider extension as something absolute, ineffable, irresolvable, and primitive' (GP ii 269/LDV 305). Extension, Leibniz insists, must be the extension *of* something, and what that something is he explains in terms of his new concept of force: it is the diffusion of a *passive force* of resistance. This passive force is complemented by an *active force*, which is his reinterpretation of the 'substantial form' or 'first entelechy' that Aristotle claimed to be the active principle of perfection in a body. Together the active and passive forces constitute corporeal substance. But more on these matters below.

Now let us turn to the context in which Leibniz's views were formulated. How did he come by his ambitions, and how did he seek to achieve them?

Historical Context

The political world into which Leibniz was born in 1646 was one riven with conflict. The German nation at that time was the Holy Roman Empire, an entity created already several hundreds of years before as a result (on two separate occasions) of a German king coming to the aid of a Pope in need of protection. In the seventeenth century the Empire included most of central Europe, including Burgundy, Bohemia and northern Italy. It was comprised of hundreds of imperial states ruled over by various dukes, counts, margraves and princes subservient to the Emperor, and at the time of Leibniz's birth had been at war – the Thirty Years War (1618–48) – for almost three decades. Peace negotiations were under way, but war did not cease until the Peace of Westphalia two years later. Hostilities had begun with the Bohemian revolt of 1618, in which Protestant estates rose up to defend their religious liberties against an attempt to impose Catholicism on them by the Habsburgs. When the Calvinist Palatine Elector came to the throne in Bohemia, the war widened along confessional lines, with Leibniz's state of Saxony entering into the fray, later to be joined by the fellow Lutheran states of Denmark and Sweden. Although military hostilities ceased in 1648, the truce, in recognizing the rights of Lutherans to practise their religions in Lutheran territories, and Calvinists in Calvinist territories, only confirmed the division of the Empire into three unreconciled religious confessions.

The intellectual world, too, was in turmoil. Leibniz lived in the heyday of what we now call the 'Scientific Revolution', when the Aristotelian philosophy of the Schools (the European universities) was under sustained attack from modern thinkers. After the demolishing of the older Aristotelian cosmology by Galileo Galilei (1564–1642) and Johannes Kepler (1571–1630) in central Europe, the Copernican worldview was widely accepted, even if in the Catholic countries it was theologically dangerous to embrace it as literal truth. Still in a state of flux, however, was the natural philosophy that would support Copernicanism: by what means did the planets stay in orbit around the Sun? If heavy bodies do not fall to the ground because of their natural motion to the centre of the Earth, as Aristotle and the Scholastics had taught, then what explains terrestrial gravity?

René Descartes (1596–1650) had famously exhorted his contemporaries to make a clean break with Aristotle's conception of the natural world. Where Aristotle had populated the world with individual substances modelled on living creatures, each with its own form or soul, acting in accordance with ends appropriate to its nature, Descartes introduced a radical dichotomy between the material and the mental. For him, created substances are of two kinds: corporeal substances or bodies; and mental substances or minds (a human being, of course, as a mind with an associated body, is a kind of composite of the two). Since matter is identical with extension, there can be no vacuum: the material world is full (a *plenum*). Bodies, or material substances, are simply divisible portions of this continuously extended plenum, distinguishable by their different motions. As such, they are entirely passive. They can react, as when one body is moved by the impact on it of another, but they cannot initiate any action. God has imbued all the matter in the world with a certain quantity of motion, and this gets redistributed among the bodies as they mutually collide, subject to the three laws of motion that Descartes expounds. Mental substances, on the other hand, are immaterial, and not divisible into parts. They are characterized by completely different qualities, such as willing, perceiving, believing and thinking. Mind, in fact, is essentially a thinking thing, a conclusion Descartes derives through his famous *cogito, ergo sum*, 'I think, therefore I am'.

Thus on Descartes's austere philosophy, it is simply anthropocentrism to think of the planets as having souls (as Kepler did); he was highly sceptical whether any organisms apart from humans were animate, or contained souls. Just as the appearance of a force for resisting motion could be explained in terms of a redistribution of quantity of motion of the bodies (without assuming that they had an inherent inertia or laziness, as Kepler had proposed), so the motion of the planets could be explained entirely mechanically in terms of the actions on them of the matter of the fluid heavens without assuming planetary intelligences. Descartes's definition of bodies as quantities of extension, on the other hand, possessing a certain quantity of motion at each instant, facilitated the replacement of the qualitative Aristotelian physics with one in which mathematics, the science of quantity, would have immediate purchase. All natural phenomena were to be explained in terms of the motion, shapes and sizes of particles subject to mathematical laws, in accordance with both atomism and Plato's privileging of geometry; but matter was strictly incapable of initiating any action, so that the behaviour of animals and other substances could no longer be explained by analogy with human behaviour, or ascribed to the teleological (goal-directed) workings of a substantial form.

This new 'mechanical philosophy' of Descartes caught the imagination of his contemporaries, even if they reserved judgement on his denial of souls to animals and his identification of matter with movable extension. His main rival, the French scholar Pierre Gassendi (1592–1655), conceived matter as consisting in atoms moving in an otherwise empty space, drawing his inspiration from the atomist philosophy of Epicurus of the third century BC, and moulding Epicureanism, Stoicism and other ancient heathen learning into a grand synthesis compatible with Christianity. In England, Henry More (1614–87) initially welcomed Descartes's philosophy as a kind of modernized Platonism, but later became virulently anti-mechanist, balking at the Frenchman's denial of extension to spirits and of souls to the higher animals. Other leading lights of the age maintained a neutrality between atomism and the plenum. Robert Boyle (1627–91), for example, sought to extend the application of the mechanical philosophy into chemistry, showing how much of what had been discovered in the alchemical tradition could be understood in terms of collisions of corpuscles. As to whether these corpuscles should be understood as Gassendian atoms or as divisible Cartesian corpuscles, though, Boyle was agnostic, declaring the question empirically undecidable.

Above all, what appealed to Descartes's contemporaries about his philosophy was the rejection of substantial forms and the promise of successful explanations of natural phenomena using mathematics. Descartes, of course, was by no means the first to propose either. But the appeal of his philosophy was much enhanced not only by its rigorous formulation and presentation, but also by its own successes in achieving new knowledge, particularly his ground-breaking *Geometry* and novel contributions to optics and meteorology, to which his famous *Discourse on the Method* (1637) served as an introduction.

Beyond that, however, there was much controversy. Descartes maintained that once God had freely decided upon the laws of nature and created the world, all the possible states of the universe would eventually come to pass in a determined order. This seemed to commit him to a version of necessitarianism, since there would be no possible states of affairs that did not actually come to pass.

After Descartes's death, the issue became acute when Baruch Spinoza (1632–77) endorsed the Cartesian position on the necessity of the sequence of states of the universe, but dismissed the attribution of a will to God as anthropomorphism, rendering the Divine Being as a non-creating, non-judging intelligence – to the horror of his Christian contemporaries.

A second theological difficulty with Cartesianism was its rejection of all teleology in the physical world. How could material things, acting out of mere mechanical necessity, possess the means to reproduce and display the optimal forms, designs and behaviours mandated by Divine Providence? These designs and behaviours, especially in the biological sphere, suggested there was more to nature than Descartes's version of the mechanical philosophy would allow. Third, there was trouble for Descartes in making his philosophy fit with the Catholic interpretation of the sacrament of the Eucharist as transubstantiation. Although Lutherans interpreted this in terms of Christ's 'real presence' in the bread and wine, Catholic orthodoxy required that when the bread was converted into Christ's body and the wine into his blood, in each case its substance was literally changed, despite its remaining the same in appearance. This was hard to reconcile, to say the least, with Descartes's insistence that the substance of body is simply extension. As Leibniz wrote to Duke Johann Friedrich in 1679, 'if a body's nature consists in extension, as Descartes claims, it would without any doubt involve a contradiction to maintain that it might exist in many places at once' (A II i 487/L 261). In these latter respects, Gassendi's philosophy appeared as an attractive alternative to Cartesianism, for Gassendi did not deny teleology in the natural world. Moreover, since his atoms were not simply lumps of extension, but contained active principles, there was scope in his philosophy for maintaining that the different substances of Christ's body (or blood) and the bread (or wine) could give rise to the same appearances.

Leibniz's Schooling

The young Leibniz was not immune to the attractions of the mechanical philosophy in its Gassendian guise. In a letter to Nicolas Rémond of July 1714, he confided that he had held Gassendi's philosophy in high esteem 'when I was starting to abandon the opinions of the School, while still myself a schoolboy', and that 'I gave myself over completely' to atoms and the void (GP iii 620/L 657).

In another letter, to Thomas Burnett in 1697, he recalled how when he was 'not yet fifteen' he had spent days wandering in a grove on the outskirts of Leipzig called the Rosenthal deliberating on whether to keep substantial forms, before finally deciding in favour of the mechanical philosophy. These accounts tally, as Leibniz graduated from the Latin school in his home town of Leipzig to go to university there in April 1661, when he would still have been a few months shy of his fifteenth birthday.

That someone so young could be 'seduced by the flattering ease with which things could be understood' in the new philosophy (Leibniz 1991: 809) is perhaps understandable, if we can get past the sheer precociousness of Leibniz's considering questions like this at such an age. It becomes all the more remarkable, though, when his early education is taken into account, for few thinkers of his time had been so thoroughly immersed in Scholasticism. Leibniz's father was Friedrich Leubnitz (or, as he sometimes spelled it, Leibnütz) (1597–1652), a name Leibniz later held to be of Sorbian (Lusatian) origin, tracing his ancestry to Lubeniecz, a family of Polish nobles.[2] Friedrich had held the chair of moral philosophy at the University of Leipzig, where he was by all accounts a very conservative Lutheran scholar, deeply immersed in Aristotle's *Nicomachean Ethics* and the study of theology. A pillar of Leipzig society, Friedrich Leubnitz had represented the university in his capacity as actuary in the surrender of the city in 1633, and also served as dean of the faculty and notary. He anticipated great things from his precocious son, to whom he was in the habit of reading histories. But he was not to see the fruits of this parental tuition, for he died at the age of only fifty-four, leaving two children by his first wife, and two more, Gottfried himself (aged six) and Anna Catharina (aged four), by his third wife, Catharina. Nevertheless, before his early demise he had instilled in the boy a love of history, which was only heightened two years later, when Leibniz gained access to his father's library. This had been kept under lock and key by family and teachers wary of the heterodox views young Gottfried might find there, until a visiting nobleman scholar had managed to persuade them to give him access.

This episode is significant in itself, for it highlights a certain tension between the extreme religious orthodoxy of Leibniz's immediate environment in Leipzig and the attractions of the more tolerant attitudes to religion that he was to find in the books in his father's library. Leipzig was anything but tolerant, and any hint of Catholicism, or, even worse, of the rival Protestant sects of

Calvinism or Zwinglianism, was met with outright hostility. Leibniz's mother Catharina, daughter of the prominent Leipzig jurist Wilhelm Schmuck, was a pious and fervent Lutheran, and raised her children accordingly. There is a reflection of this family piety in the stern warnings Leibniz received from his siblings years after his mother's early death in 1664 not to abandon his faith, and to return to the fold in Leipzig – first from his half-brother in 1669 when he had left Leipzig to take a position in the Catholic court of Mainz, and then from his younger sister in 1672 when he had arrived in Paris. Yet these warnings fell on deaf ears: by then Leibniz had long been committed to the less provincial world he had found earlier in the books of his father's library. Quickly mastering Latin with the help of the pictures in Livy's illustrated Roman history, the boy had progressed from history to philosophy, managing to orient himself by identifying some conceptual landmarks, and then comparing and contrasting different positions taken on them. As he advanced in his teenage years to weightier tomes, he devoured the classics of Plato, Aristotle, Archimedes, Cicero, Seneca and others, and then works by mainstream theologians, Luther, Calvin and their followers, as well as Roman Catholics, and even writings of unorthodox sects such as the Jansenists and Arminians. But what appealed to him the most among the theological writings, according to his later testimony, were the writings of Georg Calixt (1586–1656), a Lutheran professor of moral philosophy based in Helmstedt, who had advocated the reconciliation of Lutheranism not only with Calvinism but with a reformed Roman Catholicism. Calixt, it should be noted, was anathema to the theologians at his father's university, who had led the opposition to his conciliatory position.

There is more to be said, of course, about just how Leibniz managed such astonishing progress in wading through what was hardly normal reading matter for an adolescent. What he appears to have done is to have applied an innovative learning method inspired by Ramus (Pierre de la Ramée 1515–72) that was percolating through the German schools as well as into the tomes in his father's library. According to this method, as outlined in various handbooks, the way to approach a new subject is as follows: first, you assemble lists of categories or topics that appear in the reading; then you set them in a logical order, by making divisions and subdivisions of categories; then you collect a wide variety of opinions on these topics, and compare and contrast them, looking for points of agreement and disagreement, and ways of reconciling contradictions. This enables you to master the subject in an orderly way, but also makes it easier to recall what you have learned. Writing later about his adoption of such methods as a boy, Leibniz reports that it gave him two decisive advantages: 'first, that I did not fill my head with empty assertions (resting on learned authority rather than an actual evidence); second, that I did not rest until I had penetrated to the root and fibre of each and every doctrine and reached its very principles, from which I would be able to discover by my own efforts everything that I needed to discuss' (GP vii 185).

The result of this approach to his early self-education was Leibniz's lifelong preference not only for a comparative and ecumenical approach to received doctrines, but also a desire always to try to refine and improve upon what he was presented with, rather than remaining content with merely understanding it. In fact, the influence of this Ramist (or 'semi-Ramist') method of learning explains a great deal about his approach to philosophy, as we shall see. Ramus himself had offered a set of basic categories (the so-called *praedicamenta*), but these were improved upon by Bartholomew Keckermann (1571–1609) and writers of the Herborn school, Alsted, Bisterfeld and Comenius, whose works Leibniz had eagerly devoured in his father's library. In addition, as we will discuss in chapter 2, these authors also tried to improve upon the Aristotelian logic on which this method was based by giving combinatorial methods of combining simple concepts into complex ones. In this way they transformed the method from one that merely aided in learning to one in which the ordering of concepts was supposed to reflect the order of things themselves. The exposure to neo-Ramist methods bred in Leibniz a lifelong respect for Aristotelian logic and the possibility of improving it, as well as planting the seeds for his idea of a universal language based on logic.

University and Scholastic Studies

In fact, Leibniz's break with Scholasticism was not as complete as might be supposed from his remarks about his schoolboy conversion quoted above. This is made clear in his exchange of letters with the prominent jurist Hermann Conring (1606–81) in 1678. For when Conring takes exception to Leibniz's firm commitment to mechanism, and jibes that he might have obtained a better opinion of the Schoolmen's metaphysics if only he had read them (Conring to Leibniz, 26 February 1678: GP i 191), Leibniz responds (19 March) that when he began his university studies he 'did in fact read them, more immoderately and eagerly than my teachers approved', to the extent that 'they feared I would cling too tightly to these rocks' (GP i 197/L 190). One of the fruits of these studies was the dissertation Leibniz wrote for his bachelor's degree at Leipzig in 1663 on the Principle of Individuation, under the supervision of his professor, Jakob Thomasius (1622–84). This was a traditional problem of the schools: what is it that gives each substance its individuality? In his thesis Leibniz gives a traditional solution indebted to the influential Spanish Jesuit, Francisco Suárez (1548–1617), that it is the 'whole entity' of each individual substance (not just its matter and form treated abstractly) that makes it distinct. But by the time he writes to Conring in 1678, his view has undergone some radical changes, and he now favours the Scholastic idea that it is the substantial form itself that is the principle that individuates corporeal substances. As he writes to Conring, 'Who would deny substantial forms, that is, essential differences between bodies?' (196/189).

But this is no retreat from mechanism. In his previous letter to Conring, Leibniz had firmly declared that *'everything in nature happens mechanically'*, to which Conring had replied trenchantly, 'if you want this to be understood in a Cartesian sense, I for my part do not hesitate to pronounce it a most absurd statement' (Conring to Leibniz, 26 February 1678: GP i 191). Leibniz's response is uncompromising, one of the most eloquent statements of the mechanist creed ever made: 'I recognize nothing in the world but bodies and minds, and nothing in mind but intellect and will, nor anything else in bodies insofar as they are separated from mind but magnitude, figure, situation, and changes in these, whether partial or total. Everything else is merely said, not understood' (to Conring, 19 March 1678: GP i 197f./L 189).

So how could Leibniz say in the same letter that he accepted substantial forms? The answer lies in a careful attention to his words. He has said that, apart from geometric properties and their changes, there is nothing in bodies *'insofar as they are separated from mind'*. And by 1678 (indeed, as early as 1668) Leibniz considered mind, or at least a mind-like principle involving memory of its body's past states, to be the key to individuating bodies. Over the next few years he will build this idea into his new conception of substance and the 'rehabilitation of substantial forms' announced in the *Discourse on Metaphysics*. The idea that each individual substance is individuated by a concept implicitly containing its whole history will develop into his predicate-in-notion principle, and the uniqueness of each such actually existing substance will be enshrined in his Principle of the Identity of Indiscernibles, according to which no two created individuals are exactly alike.

In addition to individuation, there were two other Scholastic problems Leibniz studied in his university days on which, he assured Conring, 'you would have been seen me making some singular and profound comments', namely 'the composition of the continuum and the concurrence of God' (GP i 198/L 190). It will be worth saying something here about these two issues too, for they also continued to dominate Leibniz's thinking into his maturity. They are, as Leibniz describes them in the preface to his *Theodicy* of 1710, 'the two famous labyrinths in which our reason very often loses its way' (GP vi 29/T 53). The 'concurrence of God' concerns the issue of the compatibility of human freedom with divine foreknowledge of human actions. It is the 'great question of freedom and necessity, above all in the production and origin of evil' that is the topic of the *Theodicy* itself. In the preface to that work he writes:

> Even if God did not concur in evil actions, one would still find difficulty in the fact that He foresees and permits them, despite His being able to prevent them through His omnipotence. That is why some philosophers and even some theologians have preferred to deny Him detailed knowledge of things, above all of future events, rather than admit something that they believed clashed with His goodness. The Socinians and Conrad Vorst incline toward this opinion. . . . They are without doubt very much mistaken. (34/58)

But equally mistaken, Leibniz continues, are those who fall into the opposite extreme associated with the great Islamic philosopher Averroës (Ibn Rush'd, 1126–98) and his followers, namely that of believing that God is responsible for all the human actions He determines, thus compromising divine goodness. In keeping with his aversion to extremes, Leibniz follows Suárez in trying to delineate a middle way between these poles, to explain how it is that 'God concurs in all the actions of His creatures . . . without being the author of sin' (37/61). Leibniz's distinctive solution, as we shall see, depends on his articulation of the notion of uncreated possible worlds, whole worlds of individuals each of whose existence is compatible with the others', but which God chooses not to create. For given His goodness and omnipotence, God is bound to create the best of all these possible worlds. He foresees all the consequences of all the actions of humans in such a world, including free ones, and chooses to create the world in which goodness is maximized.

The other labyrinth 'consists in the discussion of continuity and the indivisibles that appear to be elements in it, which necessarily involves consideration of the infinite' (29/53). Here Leibniz has in mind a cluster of problems that was exercising his contemporaries: if matter is continuously extended as the Cartesians claimed, then it appears to be just parts within parts, with no smallest units out of which it could be composed; but then, so critics objected, it cannot be a true unity, or even a collection of such, and therefore cannot be substantial. Similarly, if motion consists in the tendency of each body to continue moving at an instant, then a body's motion over time should consist in an infinite sum of such instantaneous tendencies. But no matter whether these tendencies are considered finite, zero or infinitely small in magnitude, this leads to contradiction, and one can say the same about the composition of matter from indivisibles. Leibniz devoted his considerable talents to this cluster of problems throughout his career, making contributions to the understanding of the infinite and the infinitely small that very few other thinkers have matched. Also, as we shall see below, it was as a solution to the above difficulties of the continuum that his theory of substance was largely designed. But he never managed to find the time to write a treatise on this second labyrinth, and as late as 1710 we find him still hoping to find the opportunity to give a full account of his solution to this labyrinth by pointing out how the insurmountable difficulties result from 'a lack of a true conception of the nature of substance and matter' (29/53).

As we shall also see, guiding Leibniz in his devising of solutions to these three problems is a very intimate knowledge of traditional views on substance that he learned from his immersion in the Scholastic literature, not only the works of Suárez and other Iberian scholars like Pedro de Fonseca (1528–99), but especially the tomes of now forgotten authors like Julius Caesar Scaliger (1484–1558) and Jacopo Zabarella (1533–89), whose interpretation of Aristotle had greatly influenced the Lutheran scholars whom the young Leibniz was lapping up.

Leibniz's Early Career

Despite his obvious talent for philosophy, however, Leibniz chose not to become a professor like his father. How much this had to do with his being snubbed by the University of Leipzig after his habilitation in the faculty of philosophy in 1666 is not clear. But by then he had in any case opted for a career in law rather than philosophy. After enrolling in summer school at the University of Jena in 1663 to hear the mathematical lectures of Erhard Weigel, by February 1664 Leibniz had obtained a master's degree in philosophy, with his thesis *An Essay of Collected Philosophical Problems of Right* – although any feeling of satisfaction at this achievement would have been crushed by the loss of his mother to a respiratory infection nine days later. In short order he then earned a bachelor's degree in law at Leipzig in 1665, on the topic of conditional judgements in law, and for his habilitation in 1666 submitted a thesis, *Dissertation on the Combinatorial Art*, which was in many ways definitive for Leibniz's whole subsequent vision of how to do philosophy, as we will see in chapter 2. (Indeed, it was well enough regarded that it was republished in 1690 without his permission.) To complete his qualifications for a position in the faculty of law at Leipzig, he now needed a licence and a doctorate in law, so he duly applied for admission to the law faculty.

Given all he had achieved before he was even twenty years old, Leibniz was entitled to expect an offer of admission, especially as the son of one of the university's most distinguished professors. But approval of the early graduation of younger colleagues was not in the interest of the older students competing for positions in the law faculty, and they succeeded in persuading the faculty not to approve his candidacy. Whether this setback put Leibniz off an academic career is not clear. What is clear, though, is that he decided to leave Leipzig immediately, and to leave it for good. Having packed his bags for the University of Altdorf in the free city of Nuremberg in October 1666, Leibniz only ever returned to his hometown for brief visits on his way somewhere else. He may already have had a good part of a thesis in hand when he set off, because six weeks after enrolling in the faculty of law at Altdorf, he had defended and earned a doctorate and licence in law.

The defence Leibniz presented to the law faculty at the University of Altdorf went down exceedingly well. First he gave a presentation in Latin prose, and then one in Latin verse. It was only when he began to read the latter, squinting myopically at the papers he held in front of his nose, that it was realized that he had not in fact read or memorized the preceding eloquent prose defence, but had delivered it unscripted in fluent Latin. The thesis, *Disputatio inauguralis de casibus perplexis in jure*, concerned *casus perplexi*, cases in which there were legal grounds for the judgment to go either way. Leibniz offered an original interpretation, to which we will return in chapter 8 below. He graduated with highest honours, and was almost immediately offered a professorship by the University of Altdorf, but he chose to turn it down, opting instead for wider horizons: 'to earn more glory in the sciences and to get to know the world', as he put it later (Antognazza 2009: 65).

Supporting himself by loans from the family estate, as well as by acting for some months of 1667 as paid secretary to an alchemical society in Nuremberg, Leibniz ended up in Frankfurt and then in Mainz. In Frankfurt he made the acquaintance of Baron Johann Christian von Boineburg (1622–72), who had served as first minister in the lively and tolerant court of the Catholic Elector and Archbishop of Mainz, Johann Philipp von Schönborn (1605–73). The Archbishop was a very powerful man, being the *primus* (first) of the electors of the Holy Roman Empire, and his express ambition to use this power to mend the rift between Catholics and Protestants would have been music to Leibniz's ears. Boineburg encouraged Leibniz to angle for a position in the Mainz court, and at his suggestion Leibniz took up his pen and (despite not having his books with him in Frankfurt) published a 200-page treatise, the *New Method for Learning and Teaching Jurisprudence*, dedicated to Schönborn. The gesture succeeded, and the Archbishop set him to work with the court jurist and counsellor Hermann Lasser for a weekly wage on a project of juridical reform, the very topic of Leibniz's treatise.

But no less important to Leibniz than the patronage of Schönborn was that of Boineburg himself. In Mainz they began a productive collaboration on the reform of the judiciary there, out of which came Leibniz's *Confession of Nature against Atheists*, as well as sketches for a hugely ambitious project, called the *Catholic Demonstrations*. In addition, at Boineburg's behest, Leibniz prepared a new edition of *Antibarbarus* by the nominalist Mario Nizolio (1488–1576), for which he wrote an introduction and included a revised copy of his 1669 letter to Jakob Thomasius stating his philosophical views. Also, as we'll see in chapter 3 below, his study of the philosophy of Thomas Hobbes (1588–1670) and news of the collision laws that had just been published stimulated in him a profound interest in natural philosophy, which resulted in his publication of *A New Physical Hypothesis* and its companion monograph, *Theory of Abstract Motion*, dedicated to the Royal Society of London and the Académie Royale des Sciences in Paris, respectively, and sent to both.

Boineburg was a man of influence, who lost little time in introducing his young protégé to various important people. One of his enthusiastic letters of introduction was to his own teacher, Hermann Conring, with whom Leibniz subsequently kept up a correspondence for many years, as we saw above. Conring was a prominent Lutheran intellectual who had been educated in Helmstedt, the base for Calixt's conciliatory theology, so this goes some way toward explaining how Leibniz and Boineburg were able to hit it off so well. A second introduction was sent to Henry Oldenburg (*c.* 1619–77), a German émigré who had become the secretary of the Royal Society in London. This was of major importance for Leibniz in the coming years, in that it gave him a point of entry into the English intellectual establishment. Another connection forged in Frankfurt that would prove crucial to Leibniz's future career was to his future employer Duke Johann Friedrich of Hanover (1625–79), to whom he had been enthusiastically recommended by a Swedish resident there, Christian Habbeus von Lichtenstern.

Paris

The most immediate result of Boineburg's influence, however, was to get Leibniz passage to Paris, the intellectual capital of seventeenth-century Europe. The purpose of this diplomatic mission was to persuade Louis XIV of France, the 'Sun King', to adopt the *Egyptian plan* Boineburg and Leibniz had proposed. They had drafted several hundred pages of arguments to show how the French could wrest control of sea and commerce more easily from the Dutch by seizing Cairo and Constantinople than by attacking Holland (where French forces would be threatening the bordering German states). Boineburg engineered a mission to Paris, bringing Leibniz in tow. Unfortunately, by the time they arrived at the end of March 1672, England had already declared war on Holland and France was just about to do the same, making the plan redundant. Nevertheless, Leibniz was overjoyed with the French capital, and once he had arrived he strove strenuously to prolong his stay. A second diplomatic mission, to recover the French rent and pension owed to Schönborn, also eventually came to nought, but Leibniz got himself appointed tutor to Boineburg's son, Philipp Wilhelm, who arrived in November along with Schönborn's nephew Melchior on a peacekeeping mission with the French court, for which Leibniz's talent for writing political briefs was again put into play. In the meantime, he had applied himself to his philosophical writing as usual, reworking his *New Physical Hypothesis* into a substantial treatise, *Certain*

Physical Propositions, presumably intended for publication but which, like so many of Leibniz's writings, remained in manuscript form. He also composed a dialogue, *A Philosopher's Confession*, on issues he would later discuss in the *Theodicy* – the problems of evil, divine justice and human freedom – which met the same fate, although in 1673 he did manage to show it to Antoine Arnauld and Gilles Filleau des Billettes (1634–1720). Most importantly for his future development, Leibniz made the acquaintance of the brilliant Dutch natural philosopher and mathematician Christiaan Huygens (1629–95), who had been put in charge of organizing the Académie Royale des Sciences.

Within a month of the arrival of Boineburg's son and Melchior von Schönborn, however, Leibniz's cherished hope of permanently remaining in Paris received a massive blow with the unexpected death of his good friend and patron from a heart attack in December at the age of fifty. Thankfully, Boineburg's widow allowed him to remain as tutor to her son, and after Melchior's failure to persuade Louis XIV to convene a peace conference in Cologne, Leibniz accompanied the Archbishop's nephew on a diplomatic mission to England for a hearing in the court of Charles II. Leibniz was able to meet Henry Oldenburg in person, and hoped his compatriot would engineer his election into the Royal Society. He arrived with a letter of introduction from Huygens and cradling his new calculating machine, which he subsequently demonstrated to the Royal Society on 1 February 1673. The brilliant but cantankerous curator of the Society, Robert Hooke (1635–1703), belittled Leibniz's calculator, which, unlike his own, was designed to do multiplication and division, although it was not in working order owing to defects of craftsmanship. Hooke then produced a very similar one to the Society two weeks later. Leibniz also gained an audience with the great experimental philosopher Robert Boyle (1627–91), although this was also marred by embarrassment. Proudly reporting the success he had met with summing infinite series by difference series in the presence of the mathematician John Pell (1611–85), Leibniz was summarily reminded that such results had already been accomplished by François Regnaud and published by Mouton in Lyon in 1670, obliging him to dash off a letter of defence against the suspicion of plagiarism. Although the doyen of British mathematicians, John Wallis (1611–85), offered encouragement about his *Theory of Abstract Motion*, the jealous but underappreciated Hooke was not so generous in his evaluation. To cap it all, Leibniz and Melchior had to leave in great haste on learning that the latter's uncle and

Leibniz's employer Archbishop von Schönborn had taken seriously ill. By the time they reached Calais, they received news of his death. All in all, Leibniz's trip to England was not a great success, although his efforts did finally bear fruit in April 1673, when he was elected to the Royal Society.

Returning to Paris, Leibniz continued his efforts to be appointed to the Académie Royale des Sciences, and to find a new benefactor after Schönborn's successor declined to continue funding him. In the meantime he was joyfully sampling the currents of Parisian intellectual life, making the acquaintance of the philosophers Nicolas Malebranche (1638–1715), Antoine Arnauld, Gerauld de Cordemoy (1626–1684), Pierre-Daniel Huet (1630–1721) and Simon Foucher (1644–97), of the mathematicians Jean Gallois (1632–1707) and Jacques Ozanam (1640–1718), and of the natural philosophers Edme Mariotte (1620–84) and Claude Perrault (1613–88). He arranged a meeting with Claude Clerselier (1614–84), the custodian of Descartes's writings, and managed to gain access to them. Indeed, we only have some of Descartes's earlier writings thanks to copies Leibniz made of them on this visit. But regarding employment, all that came up was an invitation to return to Germany as a counsellor in the court of the Hanoverian Duke, Johann Friedrich. Leibniz hung on for the best part of three years before accepting the appointment, in the hope that something would materialize for him in Paris.

Near the end of Leibniz's time in the French capital, in October 1675, he met a young German nobleman, the mathematician Ehrenfried Walther von Tschirnhaus (1651–1708), who had just returned from England after an initiation in Leiden into Cartesian philosophy. Leibniz had been making extraordinary progress on geometry and the summing of infinite series under Huygens's prompting since first arriving in Paris. With Tschirnhaus he undertook a study of the mathematical manuscripts of Blaise Pascal (1623–62), and this gave him the crucial clues to the completion of his invention of the differential and integral calculus in 1675–6, to be discussed in chapter 4 below. But just as important to Leibniz was his younger compatriot's acceptance in Spinoza's circle of trusted acquaintances. As we'll see in chapter 5, Leibniz's immersion in and confrontation with Spinoza's views, insofar as he could glean them through Tschirnhaus's understanding and contacts, were extremely important in his philosophical development.

Finally Leibniz left to take up his post in Hanover, but by a circuitous route that took him back to England first, and then to

Hanover via the Netherlands. In England he dropped in on Oldenburg, but was unable to meet with Wallis or Newton as he had planned, having to make do instead with some manuscript papers from James Gregory (1638–75) and Newton (which were later used as evidence by Newton that Leibniz had plagiarized his methods, although by then Leibniz had already discovered and articulated his differential calculus). Leibniz's visit to Holland seems to have been motivated by intellectual considerations, primarily to meet Spinoza. In preparation for this he had written notes on Spinoza's proof of God, and, while awaiting clement weather aboard Prince Rupert of the Rhine's yacht in the Thames estuary, he had also written a substantial dialogue on the continuity of motion. His first stop in Holland was in Amsterdam, where he made contact with members of Spinoza's inner circle, Georg Hermann Schuller (1651–79), Lodewijk Meyer (1629–81) and Jarig Jelles (*c.* 1620–83), and also visited the mathematician Jan Hudde (1628–1704) and the microscopist Jan Swammerdam (1637–80). In Delft he paid his respects to Anton van Leeuwenhoek (1632–1723), 'the first microbiologist', whose observations of the tiny creatures in water and house dust made lasting impressions on him. Then in The Hague he met 'several times and at great length' with Spinoza – actually a somewhat dangerous move for a court counsellor, which he would do his best to downplay later, whenever it appeared that admitting the liaison might compromise his position.

Hanover

On arrival in Hanover, Leibniz was chastened to realize that he was low in the pecking order of court counsellors, and that rather than being a senior officer of state at the court, he would have to be content with the role of librarian. Undeterred, he set to work with his prodigious energy on various projects. It was in these early years in Hanover that he first conceived the leading ideas of his dynamics, including the formulation of the law of conservation of force (what we call energy), an algebraic logic anticipating Boole's by a century and a half, the beginnings of his generalized geometry or Analysis Situs, and his reform of metaphysics built around a refurbished conception of substantial form. Amazing though these intellectual achievements are, they came about almost as by-products of Leibniz's grander projects at this time. The grandest of these was his project for a universal characteristic. As we will see in chapter 2, this had by now evolved from its beginnings in the combinatorics of Lull and the Herborn school into an ambitious project for the creation of an encyclopaedia of all knowledge, one that would require an entire academy to work on. Financing this would be beyond the means of Leibniz's employer, the portly and immobile Duke Johann Friedrich, so Leibniz busied himself with trying to raise funds, while at the same time enhancing the library.

The glorious period of innovation in Leibniz's first years in Hanover was brought to an end by the death in December 1679 of his patron, Johann Friedrich, while Leibniz was away. The Duke was succeeded by his brother, Ernst August (1629–98), who was not at all interested in Leibniz's intellectual pursuits except insofar as they directly served his own political ambitions. He reluctantly allowed Leibniz to pursue his project to pump water from the mines of the Harz mountains (see below), but ordered him to abandon it in 1685. Johann Friedrich's death was a bitter blow to Leibniz's ambitions, aggravated by the fact that his attempts to consolidate his connections elsewhere in Europe had also come unstuck. His hopes for a position in the Académie Royale des Sciences in Paris had withered on the vine, and the manuscript on the calculus that was supposed to secure his invitation there was somehow mislaid. Meanwhile in England, his friend and supporter Henry Oldenburg had died suddenly on his farm in Kent in September 1677, and any sympathetic reception to Leibniz inside the Royal Society had by and large died with him. Spinoza, too, had died in 1677, followed by his and Leibniz's mutual friend Georg Hermann Schuller in 1679, thus depriving Leibniz of any further direct connection with the radical Dutch enlightenment.

One scheme for raising money that Leibniz had hatched in those early years in Hanover was a project involving the production of phosphorus from urine. The alchemist Hennig Brand had accidentally discovered this remarkable chemical while trying to convert silver into gold, and Johann Daniel Crafft, a friend from Leibniz's days in Mainz, had brought it to his attention. Leibniz published a paper on the discovery in the *Journal des sçavans*, but the ambition of the two friends was to turn phosphorus production into a viable commercial enterprise (this is one of the many Leibnizian themes improvised on by Neal Stephenson in his historical novel trilogy *The Baroque Cycle* [2003–4], where he has his protagonists producing explosives from urine in the deserts of seventeenth-century India!)

But the wealth of the duchy had been built on the silver mines in the Harz mountains, which were now hardly productive because of flooding. Here Leibniz saw a more viable enterprise, marrying theory with practice by applying his new ideas about force (i.e. energy, the ability to do work) to the problem of storing it in the reservoirs of rainwater that had been constructed half-way up the mountains. He therefore sank some of his own money along with Duke Johann Friedrich's into the project for improving the pumping of water from the mines by new windmill technology of his own devising, hoping to be able to raise sufficient funds from royalties accruing from his inventions to finance the planned academy. With much persistence, he finally persuaded the Duke to let him try his new designs for wind-driven pumps, over the objections of the miners and others involved in the operation. Between getting Johann Friedrich's permission for the work in 1679 and belatedly obeying his brother's order to cease the project in 1686, it is estimated that Leibniz spent 165 weeks in the Harz. He continued to return to the Harz area afterwards, especially in connection with his geological and palaeontological researches, and tried again with his efforts to drain the mines in 1693–6, but with no greater success than before. It is not that his designs were unimplementable – his idea for a continuous cable, for example, was later realized, and is still in use today. It is more likely, as his biographer writes, that he 'underestimated the amount of practical expertise needed by the machine builders and operators themselves' to get his ideas to work (Antognazza 2009: 335).

Returning from his labours in the Harz, however, Leibniz again entered into an extremely fecund period of philosophical writing. In 1686 alone he composed not only the above-mentioned *Discourse on Metaphysics*, but a major work in logic, the *General Investigations*, an important work in theology, the *Examination of the Christian Religion*, an attack on Cartesian physics published in France, the *Brief Demonstration*, and his second publication on the calculus. Also never far from Leibniz's mind were his plans for church reunification. Initially he had had the support of Duke Johann Friedrich, himself a tolerant convert from Lutheranism to Catholicism (like Leibniz's earlier benefactors Boineburg and Schönborn), and also of Gerhard Molanus (1633–1722), a graduate of the conciliatory school of Calixt who was in the Duke's court when Leibniz arrived. In 1683 he helped Molanus in his negotiations with the Catholic Bishop Cristobal Rojas y Spinola (*c*. 1626–95), and tried again with Rojas later. In 1700 he was summoned to Vienna by Emperor Leopold for further talks on reunification, but all these attempts met with insuperable obstacles. Leibniz's skills as a political theorist and pamphleteer were also put to use by his employers. One of these was a stinging political attack on the Sun King's insatiable appetite for war, *Mars Christianissimus*, published anonymously in 1684.

Despite Ernst August's lack of appreciation for Leibniz's intellectual endeavours, however, there was one project Leibniz had conceived for Johann Friedrich that did appeal to his brother's desire for aggrandizement. This was Leibniz's idea to prove a connection between the origins of his own house of Brunswick-Lüneburg (the Guelphs) and the Italian noble house of Este. The Duke seized on this, and made the preparation of the history of the Guelphs one of Leibniz's main duties.

Italian Sojourn

Ernst August's main interest in the genealogy was the inheritance to which he might be entitled if Leibniz could indeed establish legal claims to a connection between the houses of Guelph and Este. Leibniz's interest was much more scholarly. In the years 1687–90 he set off on a grand fact-finding tour of Germany, Austria and Italy to explore archives for clues. After visiting Frankfurt and Munich, he spent nine months in Vienna, where he declined an offer to become the historiographer of the Emperor because of the lack of status of the position. It was here that Leibniz first came across Newton's *Principia* (*Mathematical Principles of Natural Philosophy*). He dashed off a series of articles to learned journals, expanding on his own work on motion in a resisting medium, and refashioning Newton's physics into a cosmology consistent with the mechanical philosophy, giving in the process the very first application of his own newly invented differential equations to a problem in physics. The fact that he dissimulated, pretending to have merely read a review of Newton's work before fashioning his own mathematical cosmology, was a grave mistake. This only served to feed Newton's suspicions that Leibniz had plagiarized his calculus, an accusation made in the 1690s which flared into controversy during the last years of Leibniz's life. For by the early 1700s Leibniz's publication of his rules for differentiation and various other papers on the application of the calculus had caught the imagination of some of the best mathematical physicists in Europe.

Meanwhile, on his trip to Italy, Leibniz had been well received in Rome, and when he finally received permission to visit the principal location of the family records of the Este family near Modena, he was able to corroborate the connection between the two houses that he had already triumphantly uncovered in Augsburg in April 1688. The epitaphs on the tombs in the monastery of Vangadizza revealed that Azzo II of Este had married Countess Kunigunde von Altdorf, and that their son, Welf IV, was the founder of the Guelph dynasty.

Back in Hanover

On his return to Hanover in 1690, Leibniz accepted an additional appointment as librarian in nearby Wolfenbüttel in order to augment his salary. He continued to work for the Duke on his history of the Guelphs, but having established the desired connection with the Estes, his interests in the history steadily diverged from his employer's. He had begun with Otto the Child (768), but by the time he died he had got only as far as the year 1005. What drove his interest was setting this local political history in its total context. To this, everything was relevant, from cosmology to geology. In 1692–4, as a kind of preface, Leibniz wrote his *Protogaea* (first published in 1749), a history of the Earth from the point of view of Saxony. His immersion in ancient texts also stimulated his interest in etymology, on which he wrote a treatise in German in 1696–7. Some idea of his manic energy and application can be gleaned from what he wrote to his friend Vincent Placcius in 1695:

> I cannot tell you how extraordinarily distracted I am. I dig up various things in the Archives, I inspect old maps and search for unpublished manuscripts, from which I am trying to throw light on the Brunswick History. I receive and send a huge number of letters. Indeed, I have so many new things in mathematics, so many philosophical thoughts, so many other literary observations that I do not wish to disappear, that I often don't know where to start, and feel close to Ovid's 'my wealth has made me poor' [Ovid, *Narcissus*, Met 3. 466]. It is already more than twenty years since the French and English saw my Arithmetical Instrument. . . . Finally, by engaging a craftsman and stinting neither costs nor time until it was brought to completion, a machine has been constructed with which one can do multiplications up to twelve decimal places. A year has gone by, but I still have the craftsman with me to make more machines of this type, since they are in constant demand. (A II iii 80)

A vital compensation for Leibniz in Hanover was the friendship and intellectual companionship provided by Ernst August's wife

Sophie (1630–1714), and her daughter Sophie Charlotte (1668–1705), who later became Queen of Prussia, based in Berlin. Although he never married, Leibniz was clearly comfortable in the company of intelligent women. Sophie regarded him as an 'oasis in the intellectual desert of Hanover', and he in turn corresponded with her as an intellectual peer, opining that she always wished 'to know the reason why behind the reason why' (Rescher 2003: 212–13). He was particularly close to Sophie Charlotte, with whom he would discuss his ideas in the grounds of the palace when he was in Berlin. He was devastated by her death in 1705. On her deathbed she is reported to have said: 'Don't grieve for me, for I am about to satisfy my curiosity about things even Leibniz was never able to explain – space, the infinite, being and nothingness – and for my husband, the king, I am about to provide a funeral-spectacle that will give him a new opportunity to display his pomposity and splendour!' (Mates 1986: 26–7). Leibniz also had cordial relations with other women-savants of the time, such as Viscountess Anne Conway (1631–79) and Lady Damaris Masham (1658–1708), daughter of the Cambridge Platonist Ralph Cudworth (1617–88), at whose home the great English empiricist philosopher John Locke (1632–1704) was staying. Leibniz had hoped also to engage Locke in an amicable exchange of ideas, for which purpose he composed a substantial treatise responding point by point to Locke's *Essay Concerning Human Understanding*, his *Nouveaux essais* (*New Essays on Human Understanding*). But Locke responded coldly, and when he died in 1704, Leibniz declined to publish, although the work had a considerable impact on Enlightenment thought when it finally appeared in 1765.

Meanwhile Leibniz continued to advise the Duke on political and legal matters, and threw himself into his various duties with his usual vigour. Ernst August died in 1698, to be succeeded by his son, the boorish Georg Ludwig, later to become George I of England in the Hanoverian succession Leibniz had helped to arrange. Hardly tolerated by Georg Ludwig, but protected by his mother Sophie, Leibniz built an empire of correspondents around the known world, establishing himself as one of the pre-eminent figures in European thought. In 1700 he finally succeeded in establishing a scientific academy in Berlin, of which he became first president. He tried to intercede in the dispute among the Jesuits concerning the Chinese rites of ancestors, arguing that they were not idolatrous, and wrote a treatise on the natural theology of the Chinese to prove it.

Among Leibniz's major correspondences were that with the Swiss mathematician Johann Bernoulli (1667–1748), and through him with the Dutch natural philosopher Burchard de Volder (1643–1709). The latter was interested in finding out more about Leibniz's claim to have grounded the mechanical philosophy with his philosophy of active and passive forces. But De Volder had no appetite for Leibniz's claim that the 'derivative' forces operating among bodies needed metaphysical foundation in 'primitive force', conceived as an enduring substance whose states were essentially representations or perceptions, and the correspondence ended with a whimper in 1706. Similarly inconclusive was Leibniz's attempt in his correspondence with the Jesuit Batholomew des Bosses (1668–1738) to sketch a way in which his metaphysics could be augmented so that it would be acceptable to the Jesuits. Another major philosophical exchange was occasioned by the sympathetic treatment of his views by the Huguenot philosopher Pierre Bayle (1647–1706) in the latter's *Dictionnaire*, which issued in Leibniz's writing (and actually publishing!) a full-length treatment of the problem of evil in his *Theodicy* (1710). Finally, Leibniz precipitated a controversy with Newton and Clarke through the intermediation of his protégé Caroline, Princess of Wales, spouse of the future George II of England. By this time, however, his world had begun to unravel. The Hanoverian succession in 1714 had come hard on the heels of the death of Leibniz's only ally in court, the Duchess Sophie, while he was away engineering plans for a scientific academy with Tsar Peter the Great. By the time Leibniz returned, the court had moved to England without him. Although the views he expressed in the correspondence have since been highly influential, his hold over Caroline was insufficient to withstand Clarke's persuasive arguments in the future queen's presence.

Leibniz had a deep distrust of the medicine of his time. 'It is nature that cures us, rather than medicine,' he wrote (GP vi 110/T 131). Of the professors of medicine he said, 'they speak more to the ears than to the understanding'. In a treatise written when he was only twenty-four, *Directions Pertaining to the Institution of Medicine*, he suggests numerous improvements in the practice of medicine, well summarized by Mates: 'blood tests and transfusions, autopsies, experimentation with animals and even with human beings if not dangerous to them, study of the spread of disease, regular measurement of the patient's temperature, regular physical examinations, routine recording of data about the course of the patient's illness, establishment of more medical schools, and socialized medicine' (Mates 1986: 29; see also Smith 2011: 275–87). Little wonder, then, that he did not consult physicians about his gout, with which he was increasingly afflicted in the last two years of his life. This was probably exacerbated by his habit of working in his chair, sometimes for days at a time. He had some wooden clamps made, which he screwed onto his leg whenever the pain became too hard to bear. Eventually, however, the leg became infected, and he was confined to bed. He suffered the further indignity of an attack of kidney stones, and only on the day before he died (in November 1716) did he summon a physician, who gave him laudanum for relief of pain.

So much for Leibniz's life. Now let's proceed to his ideas.

2

Logic, Language and the Encyclopaedia Project

Studies of Leibniz often begin at the end, with his mature philosophy of monads. But we can get a better grasp of what he was about by beginning at the beginning, with his first original work, the *Dissertation on the Combinatorial Art* (1666), which he had written for his habilitation and finished by the age of twenty. For it is here that Leibniz first articulates his vision of a thoroughgoing reform of language, and thereby of thought, a vision which was to determine his whole approach to philosophy.

What Leibniz envisaged was the creation of a universal language by means of which thoughts could be expressed more clearly and explicitly than by natural languages. In itself this idea was by no means new. The Catalan monk Ramon Lull (1232–1315) had set things in motion with his proposal for a combinatorial art in his *Ars magna* of 1305. Lull wanted to bring about a reconciliation of Islam and Christianity by articulating the basic concepts that their belief systems held in common, and then inventing a device that would allow these concepts to be combined. In this way, he thought, all valid arguments could be generated, and the truth could be recognized on all sides. Others, such as Nicholas of Cusa (1401–64) and Guillaume Postel (1510–81), had been inspired by him to elaborate proposals for a language that could be understood by all, and Lull's proposal that true propositions could be delivered by combinatorial means had been taken up by the Herborn scholar Johann Heinrich Alsted (1588–1638), who, along with his students Johann Heinrich Bisterfeld (*c.* 1605–55) and Jan Amos Comenius (1592–1670), was Leibniz's immediate source of inspiration. The idea that a universal language would serve an irenic purpose was not original with Leibniz either: all its proponents, from Lull and Cusa to Postel, Comenius and others, had stressed this as a major motivation for creating one. For if everyone used the same language and all inferences were generated from shared basic concepts, this would make for easier communication, fewer misunderstandings and controversies, and the furthering of a knowledge that would be shared by everyone and thus contribute to world peace.

The basic idea of the combinatorial art is to resolve complex ideas into their component simple concepts, then to combine them, through some mechanism, to generate complex concepts or propositions – possibly even ones that had not previously been thought of, as Leibniz suggested. By choosing an appropriate mechanism, moreover, one could combine concepts into valid arguments, thus generating all propositions that express true and certain knowledge. But Lull's combinatorial art had depended on Aristotle's category logic to provide valid arguments, and this logic was held in low esteem by those at the forefront of the new philosophy. Descartes himself, after an initial enthusiasm for Lull's combinatorial art, had become disillusioned with it as a means for generating new knowledge, and the desire to create a better art of discovery was a major motivation for his own (unpublished) *Rules for the Direction of the Mind*, and later for his *Discourse on the Method* (1637). Leibniz's studies of the Scholastics, however, had convinced him that logic was one of their strengths, not a weakness. Here his studies of the moderns factored in, for his bold stroke was to assimilate the Lullian idea of a combinatorial approach to creating a language with Hobbes's idea of reasoning as a kind of mathematical calculation. This enabled him to conceive of logic as a branch of mathematics, and consequently to make striking discoveries of many of the ideas subsequently rediscovered by nineteenth-century logicians like Boole, De Morgan and Frege. He also followed Hobbes in regarding the attribution of a sign to a concept as arbitrary or conventional, but insisted that what is important is not the character itself, but the way it is connected with other such characters. As a result he was led to his prescient notion of 'blind thought', reasoning by a manipulation of characters without being able to recognize what each character stands for. Essentially, Leibniz had the idea of a computer language, and effectively foresaw the massive increase in the power of reasoning that would follow from the invention of computers.

A second respect in which Leibniz threw in his lot with the moderns was in conceiving the universal language as a new artificial language, not as the rediscovery of the lost language of Adam, as so many of his contemporaries conceived it. According to the biblical account of the origins of language, God had 'formed every beast of the field, and every fowl of the air; and brought them to Adam to see what he would call them' (Genesis 2:19ff.). The German mystic Jacob Böhme (1575–1624) had conceived Adam as using a *Natursprache*, a kind of 'sensual speech', which the apostles also used later when speaking in tongues. Athanasius Kircher (1601/2–80) conceived Adam as creating language by a kind of Cabbalistic combination of these basic sounds, and then described in detail how this Adamic language evolved into modern languages. In his *Turris Babel* (*The Tower of Babel*), published in 1679 – a year before his death, and thirteen years after Leibniz's dissertation – 'the immortal Kircher' (as Leibniz calls him there) proposed that this Adamic language would subsequently have been lost in the confusion of Babel, when God, angered at humankind for its sinful pride in constructing the Tower of Babel, destroyed the tower and 'did there confound the language of all the Earth' (Genesis 11:1). Kircher was an extremely wide-ranging Jesuit scholar with an international reputation, whose work in geology, sinology, microbiology and medicine inspired many of Leibniz's reflections on the same subjects. He had a mastery of languages that was unparalleled – apart from modern European languages, Greek and Latin, he taught Hebrew and Syriac, and for his pioneering studies in Egyptology he had learned and published the first grammar of Coptic in 1636. So in his *Turris* he used this vast linguistic knowledge to describe how after Babel the Hebrew language of Adam's descendants had split into five main dialects: Chaldean, Samaritan (the ancestor of Phoenician), Syriac, Arabic and Ethiopic (Eco 1995: 85). Then, employing various fanciful etymologies, he described the emergence of the modern European tongues, explaining the evolution of the alphabet in the process.

Leibniz, by contrast, insisted that 'languages have a natural origin'; the Adamic language, if such a language had indeed ever existed, 'is either irretrievably lost, or survives at best in a few relics in modern tongues, where it is difficult to detect' (A VI iv 59). It is not that he was uninterested in etymology and the evolution of language – indeed, he was as fascinated by it as was Kircher, as we shall see. The point is that in the idea of a universal language he saw the potential for future discoveries rather than a reconstruction of the past. In this he was aligned with George Dalgarno (1626–87) and John Wilkins (1614–72) in England, who saw the project of creating a new universal language as that of devising an artificial language that would be of use for furthering knowledge. Instead of trying to discover the lost language of humanity – as had the Cabbalists, Kircher and various linguistic nationalists whom we will come to later – Dalgarno and Wilkins sought to create a new 'philosophical' language, one in which the meaning of the words could be directly read off from their components. Like Leibniz, they were influenced by the Herborn-trained Jan Amos Comenius, who had advocated the construction of a language that was strictly logical, and in which the rhetorical and figurative use of words would be precluded by the way it was constructed.

Nevertheless, Leibniz's conception of what a universal language should be was different from that promoted by Dalgarno and Wilkins. He saw them as conflating two distinct projects: that of producing a language that could be understood by all people, whatever their native tongue, and that of producing a logical or philosophical language, one that could act as a logic of discovery. He had already formulated this criticism by the time he first laid eyes on Wilkins' *Essay towards a Real Character and a Philosophical Language* (1668), sent him by Oldenburg in early 1673. 'These excellent men', he wrote of Dalgarno and Wilkins,

> seem not to have completely understood the magnitude or the true use of the project. For their language or writing only accomplishes what people who can speak different languages can easily communicate; but the true Real Characteristic, as I conceive it, must be reckoned among the most effective instruments of the human mind, as it will have the greatest power of invention, retention and judgement. For it will achieve in every subject matter what arithmetical and algebraic characters do in mathematics. (A VI iii 170)

Leibniz would in fact pursue the first project, that of reforming existing languages for easier communication, as we'll see below. But first let's examine his logic of discovery.

Combinatorics and the Alphabet of Human Thoughts

As we noted in chapter 1, even as a schoolboy, Leibniz had been fascinated by the project of reforming Aristotle's 'predicaments', and had drawn up long lists of basic categories. This earlier immersion in 'semi-Ramist' methods of learning would have made him particularly receptive to the approach of Alsted and his Herborn school. Where the Ramists had rejected Aristotelian first principles, maintaining that the 'scientific' way of proceeding was to identify the various divisions among categories that systematize any given subject matter, the Herborn semi-Ramists had adopted a compromise, where one could use the method of division to arrive at revised lists of the basic metaphysical categories. According to this method of division, a *genus* would be divided into different *species* by introducing some *difference*. Thus if the genus is *animal* and the difference is *rational*, this divides all animals into those that are rational and those that are non-rational. The paradigm was the so-called Tree of Porphyry (named after a third-century Aristotelian commentator), where things are divided into the material and the immaterial, the material (bodies) into animate (living) and inanimate, animate bodies into those that have sensation (animals) and those that do not (vegetables), and animals into rational and non-rational. Rational beings would then be divided into those that are mortal, and those that are immortal, and so forth. Accordingly, a human being would be classified as as *a mortal, rational animal*. Such a method of division is still used in taxonomy, where, for example, the family *Canidae* of dog-like animals is divided into the genus dog (*Canis*) and the genus fox (*Vulpes*), and *Canis* is further divided into two species, wolf (*Canis lupus*) and domestic dog (*Canis familiaris*). This kind of classification thus presupposes categories, such as 'dog', 'animal', 'rational', and so forth. But since these will generally not be simple, but will be further divided, the process could go on in principle until some simplest concepts are reached.

In practice, however, not all such differences are conceptual differences: not all divisions are made according to the defining properties of things. In Wilkins' scheme, for example, *dog* (*Zita*) and *wolf* (*Zitas*) appear as the first opposing pair *a* in the fifth difference *t* of the genus *beasts*, denoted *Zi*, where the final letter *s* denotes opposition (Eco 1995: 254). This nomenclature tells us where to find dogs in his classification, but tells us nothing about the properties that discriminate them from wolves, or indeed any other beasts. To find this out we have to consult Wilkins' tables, where he informs us that *Canis* is divided into 'either that which is noted for tameness and docility; or for wildness and enmity to sheep' (Eco 1995: 254). Thus while the method of division gives us a classification according to certain categories, it is no more than 'a catalogue of truths known from other sources . . . useful for reducing things already known into a synopsis,' as Leibniz wrote in 1708. As such, 'it does not preserve the order in which some truths are born from others; it is this order which produces science' (quoted from Rutherford 1995: 127). What Leibniz wanted was an ordering of concepts which would also yield an ordering of truths about them.

There was promise of such an ordering of concepts by derivation in Lull's combinatorics, which Leibniz probably met for the first time in Alsted's writings. But when he turned to the original, Lull's *Ars magna*, he found himself disappointed. Lull had taken the highest categories (the *'summa genera'*) to be divine attributes (as would Leibniz), but had restricted himself to only nine such 'absolute principles': goodness, greatness, eternity, power, wisdom, will, virtue, truth and glory. Using the nine letters B, C, D, E, F, G, H, I and K to stand for them, Lull had adopted the Cabbalists' idea of generating various combinations of them, but in such a way that each of the letters could also be interpreted in other ways: for instance, as a relative principle (such as difference or agreement), as a question (such as whether? what? or how much?), as a subject (such as God or angel) or as a sin (such as greed). In this way, various combinations could be produced, such as BC, BEF, and so on, which could then be interpreted in different ways: 'Angels are good', 'Whether the world is eternal?' (answered in the negative), and so forth.

For his part, Leibniz could see no reason for assuming so few primitive concepts, and imagined that they were vastly more numerous, and probably infinite in number. In his *Dissertation* he therefore set about systematizing Lull's combinatory art. There are, he argued, two different ways in which pluralities of things can be put together, depending on whether or not we take into account the order in which they are placed. If we do, then we have what is now called a permutation; if not, we have a combination. On this basis he derived some correct theorems for permutations and combinations, so that his treatise can be seen as a founding work in the science of combinatorics, now a flourishing modern discipline. Unfortunately, however, Blaise Pascal had already gone further, as Leibniz would see for himself when he gained access to Pascal's works seven years later in Paris.

But Leibniz regarded combinatorics not just as an exercise in mathematics, but also as 'sowing new seeds of the art of thinking or the logic of discovery' (GP iv 27), and in this respect Lull's combinatory art was lacking. For example, in his third figure the same pairing of letters produces both 'Goodness is great' and 'Greatness is good': goodness and greatness would be 'convertible', in the terminology of Aristotelian logic. But not all such pairs are convertible, and this is something one simply has to know. For instance, from 'To be an angel is good', it does not follow that 'To be good is to be an angel': 'being an angel' is not convertible with 'being good'. Likewise, you could not prove that 'God is different from goodness' by asserting the two premises 'Greed is different from goodness' and 'God is greedy' – a valid syllogism according to Aristotle's logic – since the second premise is known to be false (Eco 1995: 62). In these and countless other instances, Lull's method relies on existing knowledge to exclude unsound inferences from the combinatory art.

Leibniz, by contrast, was interested in devising a language in which the valid syllogisms would be generated by the method of combination itself, without appeal to external constraints or criteria. It seemed to him that this should be possible 'if we first possessed the true categories for simple terms'. This would be a catalogue of *summa genera* or highest categories, 'a kind of alphabet of human thoughts . . . out of whose combination inferior concepts might be formed' (A VI iv 538). If this could be achieved, the species would reveal the highest categories in their combination, as well as all the propositions that were true of them.

This is the gist of Leibniz's idea for *characteristica universalis* (universal characteristic), based on the art of combinations. Assuming we have a list of all such primitive concepts, which we may denote by the letters a, b, c, d, e, f, and so forth, from these we could build up further more complex concepts combinatorially. These Leibniz calls 'complexions'. All those complexions formed from the simple ones taken two at a time he called 'com2nations' (where the 2 stands for the Latin 'bi'), those consisting of primitives taken three at a time 'con3nations', and so on. Thus the genera immediately below the highest categories would be the com2nations ab, ac, bd, bf, and so forth, below them the con3nations abc, bdf, and so forth. In this way one could generate not only all known concepts, but even those no one had thought of before.

Moreover, one could then work out which concepts implied which, and thus produce a logical order of derived truths. Thus 'if some particular species is proposed, the propositions which are demonstrable about it could be enumerated in order, i.e. all its predicates could be listed, whether broader than it or convertible with it, and from these the more meaningful could then be selected' (A VI iv 539). For instance, Leibniz explains, if there is a species y

whose concept is *abcd*, then predicates such as *a*, *cd* and *bcd* will all be demonstrable about it. To take a specific example, suppose that *a* is 'is an *angel*', and *b*, *c* and *d* are predicates sufficient to identify the angel Satan, perhaps that he is *evil*, *fallen* and a *leader*. Then from Satan's concept *abcd*, we could, for example, deduce the propositions 'Satan is an angel', and 'Satan is a fallen leader'. Moreover, since *abcd* and *bcda* would be convertible, from 'Some angels are evil fallen leaders' we could infer the proposition 'Some evil fallen leaders are angels'.

Nominalism, Abstraction and Real Definition

An original feature of Leibniz's approach to combinatorics is in his conception of individuals as 'lowest species'. On the traditional view, as found in Porphyry's *Isagoge*, *man* would be a lowest species, since there is no difference by which that category can be further subdivided. Under *man* there are only individual people, such as Socrates and Cleopatra. These constitute the roots of Porphyry's Tree. But for Leibniz the particular individuals in which the hierarchy must terminate correspond to the most complex combinations of concepts, so that the lowest species would simply be the individual substances in all their differentiated glory, each corresponding to a complex of infinitely many concepts. For him, *man* is an abstract term which we arrive at by noting what individual people have in common while ignoring their differences. His philosophy is therefore *nominalist*, in that it denies that the universals denoted by abstract terms like *man* and *dog* are existents; what exist are the individuals possessing the properties that make them men and dogs. A *realist* about such terms, by contrast, holds universals such as *man* and *dog* to be real, and individuals to be mere instantiations of these realities. Leibniz explicitly subscribed to nominalism: 'there is nothing truer than this opinion,' he writes in his work on Nizolio in 1670, 'and nothing worthier of a philosopher of our time' (A VI ii 428).

There is a more extreme form of nominalism, however, that Leibniz rejects, namely that advocated by Hobbes. For Hobbes not only denied that abstract terms denote existing entities, but also claimed that since truth depends on the definition of terms, and definitions on human decisions, truth is a characteristic of thought, not of things. Leibniz responded that the very fact that characters can be applied to reasoning showed that there must be something in the way that they are situated that corresponds to the way things are. 'The basis of truth', he wrote in a short 'Dialogue' of 1677, 'lies always in the very connection of the characters and the way they are put together.'

> For though the characters are arbitrary, their use and connection has something which is not arbitrary, namely a certain proportion between the characters and the things, with the relations to one another of different characters expressing the same things. And this proportion or relation is the ground of truth. It brings it about that whether we use these characters or others, the same thing always produces either an equivalent thing, or one corresponding in proportion. (A VI iv 24)

In this notion that the relations between characters express the relations between things 'in proportion', Leibniz owes a profound debt to the ideas of the Herborn philosopher Johann Bisterfeld, who had maintained that 'to perceive is to have within oneself, efficaciously, an intrinsic similitude or disposition proportional to the disposition of things'. This is an aspect of what Bisterfeld called *immeation* – a kind of universal connection among things, 'the similarity and dissimilarity of all things with one another', as Leibniz explains in his *Dissertation*, 'whose principle is: Relations' (A VI i 199/GP iv 70). Here Leibniz explicitly acknowledges his debt to 'the most solid Bisterfeld', and indeed the *Dissertation* is permeated by the latter's notion of the *panharmonia* or universal harmony of all things. Furthermore, all the following theses propounded by Bisterfeld are also evident in Leibniz's mature philosophy:

1 the advocacy of *universal harmony* 'among spiritual beings, among corporeal beings, and finally of spiritual things and corporeal things' (Bisterfeld 1657: 25–6);
2 the assertion, as a consequence of this harmony, of *the connection of all things*, 'whose principle is relations' – 'nothing in all of nature is so absolute that it does not have some intrinsic rapport with another' (Bisterfeld 1661: vol. 1, 17–18);
3 the contention that 'in every single body there is at least some shade of *perception and appetite*, in virtue of which it perceives what is congruent to it, and what is not' (Bisterfeld 1661: vol. 1, 141); and
4 the conviction that *every being is intrinsically active*: 'no being is so insignificant or so abject that it does not also have its proportional operation' (Bisterfeld 1657: 65) – without which, as Leibniz

approvingly comments, 'it would be a useless member of the republic of beings' (A VI i 155).

These Bisterfeldian theses are not just echoed in Leibniz's philosophy, though; they are developed into some of his most distinctive, famous and idiosyncratic doctrines: his doctrine of pre-established harmony, his doctrine of the connection of all things, his relational theories of space and time, his insistence that everything that exists is not only active but has at least an analogue to perception and appetite, and his oft-repeated claims that 'there is nothing sterile or fallow' in the nature of things. Bisterfeld is, as it were, his first intellectual love, and Leibniz remains true to him to the last, as we will see in detail in the remainder of this book.

But to come back to the subject of truth, Bisterfeld's idea that the immeation or connection among things is reflected proportionately in a connection of concepts in thought is what for Leibniz accounts for the fact that we can know things about reality at all. Hobbes's 'ultra-nominalism' would lead to the untenable view that truth is dependent on our decisions. If, for instance, it is true that a penguin is a bird and not a mammal, Leibniz would insist that this is not simply because of some arbitrary definition. It is because of the actual properties the penguin possesses in common with other birds. This will then be reflected in the fact that the concept of birds is included in the concept of penguins, because the species penguin 'is composed of genus and differentia' (*Elements of Calculus*: C 52). This is to express the matter *intensionally*, in terms of concept inclusion: the concept *bird* is included in the concept *penguin*. We can also express the same fact *extensionally*, in terms of 'instances that are brought under general concepts' (C 53), in which case we would say that every instance of penguin is also an instance of bird. In Leibniz's words,

> when I say *Every man is an animal* I mean that all the men are included among all the animals; but at the same time I mean that the idea of animal is included in the idea of man. 'Animal' comprises more individuals than 'man' does, but 'man' comprises more ideas or more attributes; . . . one has the greater extension, the other the greater intension. (NE 486)

Leibniz preferred the intensional approach, however, 'because concepts do not depend on the existence of individuals' (C 53). On this view, the complete concept of any individual penguin will include all the properties contributing to the definition of *penguin*, and this will include all the properties involved in defining a bird. Thus the proposition 'every penguin is a bird' is true because the predicate 'is a bird' will be included in the notion 'penguin'. This is the origin of Leibniz's famous 'predicate-in-notion' principle: 'in every affirmative proposition, the predicate is said to be in the subject' (*A Calculus of Consequents*: C 85), i.e. its concept is included in the concept or notion of the subject.

A second important respect in which Leibniz's view differs from the orthodox nominalist one is in the status of the concepts themselves, which some nominalists regarded as existing only when they were thought of by individual humans. But in that case there would be no prospect of the kind of objective order of relations among concepts that Bisterfeld and Leibniz had supposed. Consequently Leibniz understood concepts as corresponding to eternal possibilities, with both concepts and their ordering having their foundation in the divine mind. The *summa genera* or simplest concepts are pure possibilities, and so are their various combinations. These all pre-exist in the divine mind, so that when God chooses to create the world, He selects those things represented by the most harmonious set of possible combinations of concepts. This distinctive philosophical position is thus a kind of compromise between realism and nominalism. Universals do not exist, but abstract entities such as numbers and relations may still represent objective truths. Although the concepts we possess are generally confused reflections of the eternal possibilities existing in the divine mind, when we are confronted with individual things we can then abstract from the concepts we have of those things the properties they have in common and so recognize the various genera or natural kinds. As Leibniz wrote in his *Dissertation* of 1666,

> 53. Our mind is so fertile in abstracting that it can discover the genus of any given number of things, that is, the concept that is common to them all and to none besides them. And if our mind does not discover it, God will know, and the angels will discover it. Therefore the foundation of all abstractions of this kind pre-exist. (A VI i 192)

Of course, not all combinations of concepts correspond to possible individuals. If Alexander was strong, he could not also have been weak; if a penguin is a bird, it cannot also be a fish. But Leibniz had in mind less obvious examples of impossible combinations, too. One of his favourites was the idea of a fastest motion, which implied a contradiction.[1] To avoid combining such incompatible concepts in the definition of something, Leibniz stressed, we must take recourse whenever we can to *real definitions*, as opposed to purely *nominal* ones. A real definition is one that establishes the possibility of combining the concepts involved, for instance, by giving the means of generation of the object concerned. For example, we could define a certain curve as 'a line in a plane any segment of which has the same (non-zero) curvature'. This might be sufficient to identify a circle and to differentiate it from other curves; but it does not establish the possibility of such a line. By contrast, Euclid's definition of the circle as 'a figure described by the motion of a straight line in a plane around one fixed end' provides what Leibniz regards as a successful real definition, since from this definition 'it is clear that such a figure is possible' (A VI iv 541/MP 12–13). Leibniz criticizes the Cartesians' version of the ontological argument on this basis: you cannot prove that God exists from the definition of Him as containing all perfections (including existence) if you have not first established that the concept of such a being is possible. This, then, is Leibniz's answer to Hobbes's scepticism: 'concepts cannot be conjoined arbitrarily, but a possible concept must be formed from them, so that one has a real definition' (542/13). Thus not all possible individuals exist: an Adam who does not sin is possible (if we accept that Adam really existed, and freely chose to disobey God; for if he freely chose to sin, then the opposite course of action must have been possible). But existing things are certainly possible. So any existing thing, such as a flying bird, must have a corresponding concept that is a combination of simple concepts that are all compatible.

There are, however, certain propositions whose truth we cannot readily establish by examining their concepts. Compare, for example, the proposition 'Some officials are corrupt' with 'Some penguins are birds'. The latter can be derived from 'All penguins are birds', since if all penguins are birds, certainly some of them are (deriving 'some' from 'all' is the traditional logical operation called 'subalternation'). But we cannot derive the first proposition in this way, since it is not a timeless truth that all officials are corrupt: *corrupt* cannot be derived from the concept *official*. The truth of 'Some officials are corrupt' is contingent on certain facts. In the *Dissertation* Leibniz excludes propositions of this kind, contingent propositions, from the purview of his logic, which 'is directed toward theorems, or to propositions which are eternal truths' (A VI i 199). Contingent propositions, in contrast, such as 'Augustus was

Emperor of the Romans', are true 'as if by chance, or by the judgement of God' (199). This is an early version of Leibniz's mature division of truths into 'necessary or eternal truths, and truths of fact or contingent truths' (A VI iv 1616/LoC 305). But at this point he lacks a clear criterion for distinguishing between them. As we shall see in chapter 4, it is not until the 1680s that Leibniz discovers such a criterion; and this occurs only after he has come to realize that the complete concept of an individual would have to embrace not only simple concepts but also all the predicates that are true of it at one time and not another.

Universal Language and the Encyclopaedia Project

From the idea of propositions being built up by combining concepts it is just a short step to the idea of a universal language. For, provided everyone is equipped with the same primitive concepts – as Leibniz assumed in 1666 – then once these have been determined, the only other thing required to make a universal language would be an accepted set of characters to stand for them. This had already been recognized by Dalgarno and Wilkins, and it will be worth exploring further how Leibniz's conception differed from theirs.

In his *Art of Signs* (1661) Dalgarno proposes a language in which the letters or syllables stand for some existing properties, in such a way that every word would have a unique and unambiguous meaning that could be read off from how the word was spelt. Thus N stands for concrete, corporeal entities. Those that are animate are animals, and these are divided into those that are aquatic (t), aerial (p) or terrestrial (k). These are further divided into those with cleft hoofs (e), those with uncleft hoofs (η), and others. Among those with uncleft hoofs, the horse is designated η and the elephant is designated *a*, so that Nηkη is *horse* and Nηk*a* is *elephant*. Recognizing that this is a classification rather than a definition, Dalgarno proposes that horse could be defined as sensitive (P), and as possessing one of the nine principal passions (o), namely courage (t). Thus a *horse* is classified as NηkPot, 'animal with uncleft hoof that is courageous'.

But classifying according to such definitions seems arbitrary and tendentious. As Eco objects to Dalgarno's definition of *horse*, 'why could we not say the same of the elephant?' (Eco 1995: 235). We saw a similar problem with Wilkins' scheme above: in order to learn how to distinguish *dog* from *wolf*, we had to consult his tables, where the additional information was expressed in natural language. But this defeats the purpose of his characteristic language, according to which 'we should, by learning the *Characters* and the *Names* of things, be instructed likewise in their *Natures*' (Wilkins 1668: 21; cited in Eco 1995: 250). This flaw is wittily lampooned by Jorge Luis Borges in his essay 'The Analytical Language of John Wilkins':

> These ambiguities, redundancies and deficiencies recall those attributed by Dr Franz Kuhn to a certain Chinese encyclopaedia entitled *Celestial Empire of Benevolent Knowledge*. On those remote pages it is written that the animals are divided into (a) those that belong to the Emperor, (b) embalmed ones, (c) those that are trained, (d) suckling pigs, (e) mermaids, (f) fabulous ones, (g) stray dogs, (h) those that are included in this classification, (i) those that tremble as if they were mad, (j) innumerable ones, (k) those drawn with a very fine camel's hair brush, (l) others, (m) those that have just broken a flower vase, (n) those that resemble flies from a distance. (Borges 1964b: 103)

Borges comments: 'obviously there is no classification of the universe that is not arbitrary and conjectural. The reason is very simple: we do not know what the universe is' (104).

Leibniz did not share this pessimism. He saw the arbitrariness of Wilkins' and Dalgarno's classification schemes as a defect of their systems, rather than as a defeasing objection to a universal language as such. Wilkins wished to proceed empirically by making an inventory of all the notions held in common by the whole of humanity. Leibniz had no objection to this in principle, and made copious notes on both Dalgarno's and Wilkins' classifications. What he recognized, though, was that this was no simple matter of experimental philosophy, of canvassing existing knowledge systems for commonalities – and this for the very reasons that Borges stresses: the words in existing natural languages classify the universe in a way that is 'arbitrary and full of conjectures'. Rather, a proper classification system required the latest scientific knowledge. Indeed, a successful basis for a universal language would go hand in hand with the establishment of the best scientific knowledge obtainable. It would, in short, require an *encyclopaedia*.

Leibniz would have been familiar with the idea of an encyclopaedia from his reading of Alsted. In fact, one of the schemes he had hatched in his collaboration with Boineburg was to prepare a revised version of Alsted's now dated work. This would be divided into two parts: a theoretical part, listing all truths of reason that have been discovered, perhaps including Hobbes's *De corpore* and Euclid's *Elements*, and an empirical part, listing all truths of fact. But by the late 1670s, Leibniz had come to see that such a joining together of the works of others would not be feasible, because of the polemical nature of philosophers' works. Instead, 'we must believe that it will only be little by little, in various stages or by the labour of many, that we will arrive at the demonstrative elements of all human sciences' (GP vii 158). From this collaborative labour there could then emerge a 'demonstrative encyclopaedia'. The creation of such a work became a priority for Leibniz, and he would keep returning to it throughout the rest of his life.

For the theoretical part, the aim was to order each science from its first principles down to all the theorems derivable from them. This would be achieved by identifying the 'principles of invention' of each science, and then combining these with the general art of invention, or universal characteristic, 'to deduce all the rest from them, or at least all the most useful truths' (GP vii 168). For the empirical part, Leibniz followed Dalgarno and Wilkins in conceiving the classification as including not only natural genera and species, but also artefacts and accidents – something quite alien to the Aristotelian tradition. Consequently, Leibniz insisted that the encyclopaedia should include knowledge gleaned from artisans and the world of manual labour – prefiguring the design of the *Encyclopédie* of Denis Diderot (1713–84) and Jean le Rond d'Alembert (1717–83), whose encyclopaedia project that was at the heart of the French Enlightenment some eighty years later.

Leibniz's initial conception of how the encyclopaedia could be achieved, in fact, sounds a lot like the *Encyclopédie*. In a draft for a proposal to Duke Johann Friedrich in early 1679, he wrote: 'it will be good to establish a kind of society of some able people in Germany, who work each at his own cost and at his pleasure following the method I will propose to them' (March or April 1679: A VI iv 161). Later, though, his efforts crystallized around the plan for the establishment of an Academy of Science. Numerous petitions to various princes finally succeeded with the establishment of the Berlin Academy of Sciences in 1700, of which Leibniz himself was the first president.

Where does this, then, leave the project for a universal language? By 1679, Leibniz had realized that his original project to discover all the primitive concepts was rather utopian. As he wrote in *An Introduction to a Secret Encyclopedia*, 'it may be doubted whether any concept of this kind would appear distinctly to people, namely, in such a way that they would know that they have it' (A VI iv 528/ MP 7). On the one hand, he believed, there must be such concepts, because 'we can have no derivative concepts except by the aid of a primitive concept' (529/7). But on the other, 'an analysis of concepts through which we can arrive at primitive concepts, i.e. those which are conceived through themselves, does not seem to be within the power of humans to bring about' (530–1/8). Leibniz's response to this human predicament, as we have seen, is the encyclopaedia project. But complementing this a posteriori approach, he also pursues an a priori approach. Even if primitive concepts are out of reach, 'the analysis of truths is more within our power' (531/8), and we may still arrive at concepts that are 'if not absolutely primitive, then at least primitive for us' (C 176). So the project of achieving an ultimate analysis is replaced by the less utopian one of analysing concepts into simpler ones from which they follow, which Leibniz attempts by a constant reshuffling of schemes of categories arranged according to such divisions. Paper after paper through the 1680s, and late into his career, consists of such divisions. Using '<' to denote division into two concepts separated by '|', a typical categorial division would be: term < impossible | possible < nonbeing | being < abstract | concrete < adjective | substantive < attribute | ultimate subject < individual substance | real phenomenon (Rutherford 1995: 105–11).

Complementing these two approaches to identifying basic categories, moreover, are reforms and rationalizations of the principles of the sciences. Here again Leibniz was extremely ambitious. One of Wilkins' more fecund ideas was that of 'real characters' for his universal language: characters of a new script he had invented to represent primitive concepts directly. Leibniz took this idea, and adapted it to the special sciences. Real characters, in his vision, would not be characters of some arbitrary script, but would be adapted to the 'principles of invention' of each special science. A particularly good example of what Leibniz had in mind here would be his invention of the notation for differentiation and integration in the calculus, as we'll see in chapter 4.

Leibniz's optimism here can usefully be contrasted with Descartes's pessimism. Considering the possibility of deriving a kind of mathematics of thought from the assigning of numbers to clear and distinct ideas, Descartes opined that such a project could be realized only 'if the world were turned into an earthly paradise, which is too much to suggest outside of fairyland' (to Mersenne, 1629: AT i 82/CSMK 13). In a note penned around 1680, Leibniz responded that 'this language can still be established even if philosophy itself is still imperfect: and to the extent that human knowledge increases, so will this language as well.' For combining the principles of the special sciences, even metaphysics, with the universal characteristic 'will serve to end controversies in matters which depend on reasoning. For then reasoning and calculating will be the same thing' (A VI iv 1030). Let's look at that idea more closely.

From Combinatorics to Blind Thought

In his *Baroque Cycle* trilogy, Neal Stephenson portrays Leibniz as a kind of Charles Babbage figure, who is intent on producing a 'Knowledge Engine' in the library at Wolfenbüttel, while his protégé (the fictional Daniel Waterhouse) is in Massachusetts constructing an 'Arithmetickal Engine' with pulleys and gears (Stephenson 2003–4). Allowing some poetic licence, the gist of this portrait seems accurate, for there is a suggestive connection between Leibniz's design for a universal characteristic as a mathematics of thought and his practical invention of superior calculating machines that could perform ever more sophisticated operations. As mentioned above, he essentially foresees the utility of a computer program, an anticipation that appears all the greater in hindsight because of his invention of binary arithmetic, and his attempt to design calculating machines that operate on such an arithmetic.

The connection between Leibniz's machines and his characteristic is, in a word, *multiplication*. The idea of a machine to mimic reasoning was perhaps suggested to him by Lull's device for generating triples of letters that would correspond to valid arguments. For Lull's fourth 'figure' was in fact a plan for a practical mechanism, a disc split into three turnable concentric circular segments one inside the other, each bearing the nine letters, and held together by a knotted cord. By turning the circular segments, one could generate all possible triples of Lull's nine letters, such as BFH, BCD, CEH, and so on. Further, from Hobbes Leibniz had taken the idea of reasoning as calculating. But although he had initially interpreted this in terms of the addition and subtraction of concepts, following Hobbes, he came to see multiplication as a better model for the composition of concepts (since after all they were decomposed by the method of *division*, not subtraction). Thus even though the calculating machines Leibniz invented in 1672 and later had obvious utility for the plain purpose of aiding in calculation, it may be no accident that one of their main advantages over their competitors was that they could perform multiplication and division.

We can get a good idea of how the modelling of reasoning on multiplication is supposed to work by reference to the manuscripts on logic Leibniz wrote in 1679 after returning to Hanover. In one written in April, *Elements of a Universal Characteristic* (A VI iv 181–94), Leibniz begins with the traditional definition of 'man' as 'a rational animal', so that the concept *man* is composed of the two concepts *rational* and *animal*. He then assigns numbers to the concepts, modelling composition of concepts by multiplication. Thus if we assign the number 6 to *man* and the number 2 to *animal* and 3 to *rational*, then the concept *man* is represented equivalently by 6 or by 2×3. Now in order for a proposition to be true, its predicate must be contained in the subject. This is represented numerically by the number of the predicate being exactly divisible into the number of the subject. Thus the number 2 for *animal* is exactly divisible into the number 6 for *man*. Since $6/2 = 3$, which is an integer, the proposition 'Every man is an animal' is true. On the other hand, if *monkey* is expressed by the number 10, say, then 'Every monkey is an animal' is true because 10 is exactly divisible by 2, but 'the concept of monkey does not contain the concept of man, nor, conversely, does the idea of the latter contain that of the former, because 6 is not exactly divisible by 10, nor 10 by 6' (C 54–5). A concept that is primitive is one that cannot be further resolved, so this will be represented by a prime number, since this has cannot be exactly divided by any other number. A compound term, on the other hand, will always be expressible as a product of prime numbers.

So far, though, this logic still concerns only affirmative propositions. In another essay of April 1679, *A Calculus of Consequents*, Leibniz elaborates a scheme which is able also to accommodate negative predicates. Here a categorical proposition is composed of both positive and negative parts: 'It is necessary to bear in mind, above all, that every compound concept consists in a plurality of other concepts, as many positive as negative' (A VI iv 226). In this scheme the subject S and the predicate P of a universal affirmative categorical statement will be represented by the number couples $\langle +s, -t \rangle$ and $\langle +p, -r \rangle$, respectively. Here in order for the predicate to be included in the subject, $+s$ must be exactly divisible by $+p$, and $-t$ exactly divisible by $-r$, where a positive number represents a term that applies to the individual, while a negative one represents a term that does not apply. If, on the other hand, s and r (or t and p) have common divisors, then some concept and its negation will both be true of the individual, which is a contradiction. In that case, the proposition will be false. If, for example, we take the proposition 'All toads are amphibians', and represent *toad* by the couple <+49, −12> and *amphibian* by <+7, −4>, then the proposition comes out true. If, on the other hand, the term *oyster* is represented by <+10, −3> and *having lungs* by <+14, −5> (Leibniz's examples are *pious* and *wretched*), we see that +10 and −5 have the common divisor 5, so that 'All oysters have lungs' comes out not only false, but contradictory. Leibniz comments: 'It is clear that the terms +10 (that is, twice 5) and −5 are incompatible, for they signify contradictory things; and it is consequently immediately apparent from their characteristic numbers that the proposition to which these numbers apply is *false* in terms, while its contradictory is *true* in terms' (A VI iv 226).

Clearly, we do not generally know the characteristic numbers of terms, which would require their resolution into primitive concepts – the 'ultimate analysis' that Leibniz has by 1679 already conceded to be unattainable. Nevertheless, he maintains, despite the 'extreme difficulty' of discovering the characteristic numbers of concepts, he has thought up an 'elegant device, if I am not mistaken, by which reasonings can be shown to be provable by means of numbers' (*On Characteristic Numbers for Establishing a Universal Language*, spring–summer 1679?: A VI iv 269–70). This is to 'pretend that the characteristic numbers are already given, and then, having observed a certain general property to hold for them, [to] assume numbers of such a kind as to be congruent with this property'. By using such numbers, he claims, we can work out what other true propositions follow from them, and in this way 'demonstrate all the rules of logic with wonderful reason through numbers, and show how to recognize whether certain arguments are in valid form' (270).

Indeed, through the use of his 'elegant device' of dummy characteristic numbers, Leibniz is able to elaborate a criterion for the *formal validity* of arguments that is identical to the modern notion. He contends that for any given syllogism of traditional logic, it will be possible to see whether numbers can be found which at the same time satisfy the premises and the contradictory of the conclusion of the figure under consideration. If that can be done, that argument will be invalid, while if they cannot be found, 'the argument will conclude *in virtue of form alone.*' Here Leibniz is applying what we now call the Method of Counterexample to determine invalidity; correlatively, he is assuming that if there is no attribution of numbers that can make the premises come out true and the conclusion false, the argument is valid in virtue of its form.

For Leibniz this idea of being able to reason correctly without knowing the primitive concepts is an instance of how we reason generally. Because it is impracticable to keep in mind a complicated concept when we are reasoning about it, we use a sign to stand for it instead. In his *Meditations on Knowledge, Truth and Ideas* of 1684, Leibniz gives the example of a 'chiliagon', a figure with a thousand equal sides. When reasoning about such a figure,

> I do not always consider the nature of a side, equality or being a multiple of a thousand (that is, of the cube of ten), but I use these words – whose sense the mind is aware of obscurely and imperfectly at best – in place of the idea I have of them, since I remember that I know the meaning of these words, but judge that it is not now necessary to make it explicit. (A VI iv 587/AG 25)

This is what Leibniz calls *blind thought*: thinking with signs or symbols in place of the ideas or concepts that they stand for. As he observes, this is not only what is standardly done in an algebraic or arithmetical calculation, but occurs 'almost everywhere': when we think of a complex concept, 'we cannot think of all the concepts which compose it at the same time' (587/25). One upshot of using such composite concepts in our reasoning is that we may think we have an idea of something when in fact the concept we are using involves a contradiction – hence the necessity of real definitions, as explained above. All this is consistent with Leibniz's analysis of concepts as combinations of simpler concepts. We do not need to reach the simplest, irreducible concepts in order to see which concepts follow from which: we use characters to stand for them, and 'provided we observe a certain order and rule in their use, they give us results which always agree with one another' (A VI iv 24). If we could resolve a given concept into its primitive notions, then we would achieve *intuitive knowledge*. In the normal run of things, however, 'having learned the reality of certain concepts by experience, we then compose other concepts from them following the example of nature' (A VI iv 590/AG 26).

Leibniz's Philosophy of Natural Language

According to a current view in contemporary philosophy of language popularized by Jerry Fodor and Steven Pinker, there is a 'language of thought' occurring below the level of expression. When we are trying to articulate something, trying 'to find the right words', we are already thinking in this language of thought, or 'mentalese': we are thinking without words. At first sight, it seems that this is the opposite of Leibniz's view, since he holds that 'if characters were lacking, we would never distinctly know or reason about anything' (A VI iv 24). But the opposition is merely apparent. Leibniz cedes that 'there can be thought without words', but 'not without some other signs' (24). Every actual human thought must be expressed in words or signs of some other kind. This leaves open the possibility that there is a subliminal level on which we think, and that natural languages are an imperfect expression of the way symbolic thought is structured on this deeper level.

Here one might be tempted to identify Leibniz's universal characteristic as an attempt to discover such a language of thought, and to purge natural language of all vagueness. Russell suggests some such role for logic in the 1920s when he quips about his own mathematical logic being unsuited for public occasions: 'I shall therefore, though regretfully, address you in English, and whatever vagueness is to be found in my words must be attributed to our ancestors for not having been predominantly interested in logic' (Russell 1923: 84). But, as mentioned above, this is where Leibniz parted company with Wilkins and the proponents of a philosophical language. He did not confuse the project of the universal characteristic, which for him was perfecting the logic of discovery, with that of perfecting natural languages as a means of communication.

At the very deepest level, of course, the structure of symbolic thought would consist in the true connections among all the primitive concepts – in God's own intuitive knowledge of the created world. But Leibniz acknowledges that (with the possible exception of some perfected mathematical knowledge) 'for the most part we have only symbolic knowledge of composites', obtained through experience. The fact that all human languages are adapted to much the same experiences, however, suggests that the language of thought might also be approached through an empirical investigation. This explains Leibniz's attempt to uncover a *universal* or *rational grammar* by an analysis of natural languages. His point of departure was the study of the grammatical structure of Latin, this being the language of international communication used by learned people in the seventeenth century. By comparing its structure and grammar with modern European languages, he hoped to lay bare the structure common to them all. This was to be achieved by certain simplifications, with a view to determining the smallest set of grammatical rules common to all existing languages. Giuseppe Peano built on this with his proposal in the early twentieth century for an international auxiliary language, *Latino sine flexione*, which he explicitly based on Leibniz's ideas. Rather than simply aiding in communication, however, Leibniz hoped his studies would enable him to discover the basic grammatical trunk from which the various historical languages had branched. In this respect he anticipates Noam Chomsky and the modern science of linguistics, as Chomsky is happy to acknowledge.

In his empirical studies of language, however, Leibniz did not remain content with such conceptual and comparative analysis of natural languages. The origins of natural language, he was convinced, made it entirely different in kind from artificial languages 'such as Dalgarno and Wilkins and others have devised':

> Languages have a certain natural origin, deriving from the agreement of sounds with the affects which the images excite in the mind. And I would maintain that such origins occurred not only in the primordial language, but also in the languages that developed as a result, partly from the primordial language, and partly from the practices of peoples scattered throughout the Earth. (A VI iv 59)

Thus Leibniz was deeply interested in the evolution of natural languages, which he sought to uncover with detailed historical (including archival) research into the oldest European writings available. His researches led him to believe that the Germanic and Nordic languages as well as Britannic and Gaelic 'can be regarded as variants of a single language which could be called "Celtic"' (NE 280). He went on to conjecture that the explanation for the many roots common to Latin, Greek and Celtic languages lies in 'the common origin of all the peoples descended from the Scythians who came from the Black Sea and crossed over the Danube' – a hypothesis later scholars built on to establish the existence of Proto-Indo-European. In the *New Essays* Leibniz provides several pages of such etymological studies, but cautions that one must always be careful to try to find confirming evidence of supposed derivations, 'especially evidence provided by intervening peoples' – otherwise one will 'goropize', that is, produce fanciful and ridiculous etymologies like those of Jan van Gorp (Goropius), who 'proved' that the Antwerpian dialect of Dutch was the Adamic language (NE 285).

For Leibniz, in the primordial language (or languages) the connection between words and things is founded on an emotional reaction (*affect*) of people confronted with a thing or an event. They respond to it by imitating the sound, so that the most primitive words and word-stems are *onomatopoeic*, 'as when we attribute a *croak* to a frog, when we say "sh!" to admonish someone to be silent or quiet, when we use "*r*" to signify running, "*hahaha*" to signify laughter, and "*alas!*" to signify sadness' (A VI iv 59). A croak is a reproduction of the frog's characteristic sound, and similarly words such as 'rumble', 'buzz', 'roar', 'whisper', and so on, simply reproduce the sounds heard. Moreover, Leibniz explains in the *New Essays*,

> as the letter *R* naturally signifies a violent motion, so the letter *L* signifies a more gentle one. Thus we see children and others who find *R* too harsh and difficult to pronounce replace it with the letter *L* – and ask their palish pliest to play for them. This gentle motion appears in *leben* (to live); *laben* (to comfort or give life to); . . . *lentus* (slow); *lieben* (to love); *lauffen* (to glide swiftly, like water flowing); *labi* (to glide) . . . . I could mention any number of similar terms which prove that there is something natural in the origin of words – something which reveals a relationship between things and the sounds and motions of the vocal organs. (NE 278)

Leibniz goes on to explain how abstract terms get built up from such concrete ones through the use of *metaphor*, *metonymy* and *analogy*, giving the example of how the Hottentots, when they had to translate 'Holy Spirit', used a word which for them signified 'a benign and gentle puff of wind'. In his discursive comments on Locke's views about general terms, he writes:

> I will add that *proper names*, such as Brutus, Caesar, Augustus, Capitone, Bucephalus, . . . have usually originated as *appellatives*, i.e. general terms. . . . In fact we know that the original Brutus got this name on account of his apparent stupidity; that Caesar was the name of a baby delivered by an incision in its mother's abdomen; that Augustus was a name expressing veneration; that Capitone means bighead, as does Bucephalus. . . . It can therefore be said that the names of individuals were the names of species of things that were given to the individuals as prime examples of the species or for some other reason, as the name *Grosseteste* might be given to the person who had the biggest head in the city or to the most eminent bighead one knew. . . . Similarly, the names of genera are given to species that are contained in them, that is to say, it suffices to use a more general or vaguer term to designate a more particular species, if the differences are of no interest. (NE 288–9)

This account tallies with Leibniz's views on individuation. A proper name only designates an individual by association with the incomplete concepts we have of that individual; but there will be a complete concept that God has of that individual from which all the particular predicates characterizing that individual could be derived. It is just that such a complete concept is inaccessible to us. 'Paradoxical as it may seem,' Leibniz tells Locke's representative Philalethes,

> it is impossible for us to know individuals or to find any way of precisely determining the individuality of any thing except by keeping hold of the thing itself. For any set of circumstances could recur, with tiny differences which we would not take in; and place and time, far from being determining factors in themselves, must themselves be determined by the things they contain. The most important point in this is that individuality involves infinity, and only someone who is capable of grasping the infinite could know the principle of individuation of a given thing. (NE 289–90)

But this doctrine about general terms not being derived from individuals also tells us a lot about what it means to think about things, since all we ever have are incomplete concepts. This is not a disadvantage, however, but a necessity. As Massimo Mugnai writes: 'If a child that was just beginning to speak attributed a name to each object that claimed its attention, it would never be able to *think*. A distinctive characteristic of thought is that it refers to further things simultaneously, by abstracting from their individual traits and acquiring a degree of generality that situates them above examples and singular cases' (Mugnai 2001: 244).

Jorge Luis Borges improvises brilliantly on these Leibnizian themes in some of his 'impossible fictions'. In one, 'Pierre Menard, Author of the *Quixote*', he recounts how his friend Pierre Menard had developed 'the admirable intention . . . to produce a few pages which would coincide – word for word and line for line – with those of Miguel de Cervantes'. The first method his friend devises is 'relatively simple': 'Know Spanish well, recover the Catholic faith, fight against the Moors or the Turk, forget the history of Europe between the years 1602 and 1918, *be* Miguel de Cervantes' (Borges 1964a: 66). That is, if Pierre Menard could imaginatively don 'every particular of time and place' that is specific to Cervantes, his individual concept would be identical with Cervantes'. He would be indistinguishable from Cervantes, even in the eyes of a divinity surveying all possible worlds; thus in creating that individual corresponding to that concept, God would in fact be creating not Pierre Menard, but Cervantes himself. (Menard rejects this method as 'too simple'!) In another fiction, 'Funes the Memorious', Borges describes the curious case of a Uruguayan from Fray Bentos, Ireneo Funes, who, after falling from a bronco, has been left hopelessly paralysed. But, as a fortuitous compensation, he has miraculously come by a prodigious and extraordinary photographic memory, leading him to develop languages that he thought would be adequate to the task of reproducing every distinct perception he has experienced. Writes Borges,

> Locke, in the seventeenth century, postulated (and rejected) an impossible language in which each individual thing, each stone, each bird and each branch, would have its own name; Funes once projected an analogous language, but discarded it because it seemed too general to him, too ambiguous. In fact, Funes remembered not only every leaf of every tree of every wood, but also every one of the times he had perceived or imagined it. (Borges 1964a: 93)

The narrator describes how Funes had invented a bizarre number system in which every number had its own individual name. 'I told him that saying 365 meant saying three hundreds, six tens, and five units, an analysis which is not to be found in the numerals *The negro Timoteo* or *meat blanket*. Funes either did not understand me, or refused to do so' (Borges 1964a: 93) He continues: 'I suspect, however, that he was not very capable of thought. To think is to forget differences, to generalize, to make abstractions. In the teeming world of Funes, there were only details, almost immediate in their presence' (Borges 1964a: 94). Borges shows himself again to be one of Leibniz's most faithful interpreters: thought requires the making of abstractions, without which language and communication are rendered impossible.

Leibniz would have made quite a name for himself if these powerful insights about the nature of language and its relation to logic were his only contributions to philosophy. As we shall see, however, that is far from the case. Although his vision of a universal characteristic remained a driving force behind his whole philosophical enterprise, he made original contributions in almost every field, including the natural sciences, as we shall explore next.

3

Natural Philosophy and the Science of Life

There are still chairs in natural philosophy in many university departments of physics around the world. These are simply chairs in physics. But in the seventeenth century the term had a much broader meaning, involving not only the burgeoning sciences of chemistry, geology, palaeontology, biology and psychology, which had not yet become independent disciplines, but also metaphysics and natural theology. Today a physicist who believed that there are no substances in the traditional sense, but only chemical substances composed of elementary particles, might still (if she were a practising Catholic) refer to Christ as 'being of one substance with the Father' without giving it a second thought. Nor would it occur to a contemporary biologist dealing with issues concerning the generation and propagation of living things that he should be taking into account the Church's condemnation of *traducianism*, the doctrine according to which the immaterial soul is passed on to offspring along with the organized matter of the seed at conception. These, though, were very much live issues in the seventeenth century, leading to a heady mix of ideas about animal generation, atoms, the nature of substance, cosmogony and the history of the Earth, the mathematical physics of force, and the difference between living and dead matter.

Worlds within Worlds

The importance Leibniz accorded to natural philosophy can be judged by his extraordinary efforts to become accepted as a natural philosopher in his early twenties. From his first acquaintance with the new laws of impact published by Wallis, Christopher Wren (1632–1723), Huygens and Mariotte in 1669, he worked diligently on the foundations of the new physics. Within two years he had composed the treatise on natural philosophy mentioned above in chapter 1, *A New Physical Hypothesis* (*Hypothesis physica nova*, hereafter *HPN*), together with the exposition of its mathematico-philosophical foundations in the *Theory of Abstract Motion* (*Theoria motus abstracti*, hereafter *TMA*), and sent both to the Royal Society in London and the *TMA* to the Académie Royale des Sciences in Paris.

Although this first contribution to natural philosophy is often dismissed as naïve (even by Leibniz himself in later years), the *HPN* in fact gives evidence of an impressive mastery of the field, drawing on atomism and chymistry – encompassing both alchemy and chemistry, which had not yet become distinct – as well as the physics of Hobbes; while the *TMA* is an ingenious attempt to found mathematical physics on a reinterpretation of Cavalieri's method of indivisibles (an important precursor of the calculus). The connecting link between the two treatises is Hobbes's notion of *conatus* or endeavour, a cardinally important notion for Leibniz, just as it had been for Hobbes, and also Spinoza. An endeavour is a 'beginning of motion', that is, a motion through a point of space in an instant of time (Hobbes 1668: 178). But in a human subject, according to Hobbes, such an incipient motion or tendency towards something is experienced as a desire, and a tendency away from an object is experienced as an aversion to that object. Endeavour thus forms a bridge between physics and psychology. It will perform the same role for Leibniz. But where for the materialist Hobbes it allowed the reduction of mental states to physical qualities, for Leibniz (following Bisterfeld) it showed that there is something analogous to perception and appetition within the deadest particle of matter, even when such tendencies are not accompanied by any awareness. We will come back to this later. For now we should just note that it did not make Leibniz's physics any less physicalistic than Hobbes's.

The eponymous 'new physical hypothesis' of Leibniz's treatise was a hypothesis both about the constitution of matter and about its genesis. Assuming that the Earth and Sun were originally homogeneous clouds of matter which gained their cohesion from a rotation around their own centres, Leibniz hypothesized that the action of light rays falling perpendicularly onto the spinning matter of the Earth would produce little spinning bubbles (*bullae*) of matter: just as in the workshops of glassmakers, 'a circular motion of fire and a straight one of spirit produces glasses', so 'by a circular motion of the Earth and a straight one of light, bubbles are produced' (A VI ii 226). Here the bubbles are Leibniz's 'atoms', consisting in a hard crust enclosing fluid matter within. By their agglomeration the Earth and other heavenly bodies are subsequently composed – much as, according to today's cosmologists, planets are thought to have been generated by an accretion of the 'planetesimals' that are formed by turbulent motions in a protoplanetary disc.

The idea that the solar system originated by the formation of whirls or vortices in an otherwise homogeneous matter is very ancient, going all the way back to Anaxagoras and Democritus (both active in Athens in the fifth century BC), and revived in Leibniz's own century by Kepler and Descartes. The attraction of the vortex theory – then, as now – is that two empirical phenomena are immediately explained, at least by analogy: (i) that the orbiting bodies are rotating in the same plane; and (ii) that the farther a body is from the centre of rotation, the more slowly it rotates. But more important to Leibniz and his contemporaries was the fact that a vortex theory provides a cause of the planetary motions in keeping with the insistence of the mechanical philosophy that all action must be by direct contact: it is the swirling matter of the vortex that carries the planets around its centre, just as leaves are carried round by eddies in a stream. As we shall see in chapter 6, this is what motivates Leibniz, when he learns of Newton's theory of gravitation as a force acting at a distance, to recast that theory as a vortex theory, and to re-derive the inverse square law by assuming that the planets are carried by the harmonic motion of the vortex, with gravity understood as resulting from a kind of differential pressure exerted by the surrounding fluid.

But there is much more to Leibniz's new hypothesis of 1671 than a vortex theory. At its heart it is an attempt to explain one of the most difficult problems in physics: the origin of the cohesion of matter. In one respect, Leibniz's contemporaries thought they understood this. Huygens and Boyle, for example, understood the union of a body to be the result of the ambient pressure of the atmosphere, a notion they tested by showing how two polished marble slabs that could not be prised apart in air were easy to separate in a vacuum chamber. (If it seems far-fetched to hold that our bodies are held together by atmospheric pressure, it is salutary to imagine what would happen to an astronaut in deep space who jumped out of a spacecraft without a pressurized spacesuit.) Leibniz considered this an adequate explanation of secondary cohesion, but objected that this only drove the problem of the cause of cohesion down further: 'in order to explain the fact that bodies cohere by pressure, one must first establish firmness in the parts' (A VI iv 1629). Without such an explanation one would have an unacceptable infinite regress, for what explains the original cohesion of the bodies that are forced together? What explains the cohesion of atoms?

As part of his *Catholic Demonstrations* written for Boineburg in 1668, Leibniz had seized on this lack of an explanation of original cohesion as providing an opportunity for proving the existence of God 'which I am surprised that neither Gassendi nor anyone else among the very acute philosophers of our age has noticed' (A VI i 492). In a reasoning analogous to Aristotle's argument for a prime mover, Leibniz had argued that unless one had recourse to a cause of firmness lying outside the regress, no account could be given for the 'ultimate corpuscles' composing matter. Leibniz was very taken by this form of argument involving the necessity for a reason lying outside the series, as we shall see further below. But he was soon to reject explanations involving the action of God as tantamount to bringing in a *deus ex machina*. (Theologians today are similarly wary of such 'God-of-the-gaps' proofs of God's existence.) Thus, in the *HPN* Leibniz declares: 'I agree entirely with the followers of those excellent gentlemen, *Descartes* and *Gassendi*, and with whomever else teaches that in the end all variety in bodies is to be explained in terms of *size, shape* and *motion*' (A VI ii 248). Here he might well have added the name of Hobbes, for it was from the English philosopher that he got the germ of a solution in keeping with the mechanical philosophy. This was to account for the firmness and longevity of atoms in terms of their spin.

It is one thing, though, to rely on the fact that spinning bodies (like eddies in a stream) are observed to remain intact for some time, and it is another to provide a theoretical explanation for this, as Leibniz claimed to do, based on Hobbes's notion of endeavour. According to Hobbes, an endeavour is proportional to the beginning of a line (point) covered in the beginning of an interval of time (instant). Leibniz's idea was that in that case points corresponding to different motions would be of different sizes in the same instant, and so two adjacent points would overlap. Crucially, though, where Hobbes had taken points and instants to be finite spaces and times – smaller than any quantity considered, but not indivisible – the young Leibniz took them to be infinitely small parts of space and time, actual indivisibles that are smaller than any assignable, but that still possess quantity. In the *HPN* Leibniz used this theory of indivisibles of different sizes to explain the cohesion of bodies in terms of the fusing together of their boundaries. When one body impinges on another, in the instant of collision the indivisible constituting the boundary of the impelling body is greater than that of the body with which it is colliding in proportion to the endeavours of their motions; their boundaries therefore overlap, so that the bodies are truly continuous and cohering, as opposed to being merely contiguous (touching). By this means, Leibniz sought to explain the original cohesion of the hollow atoms or *bullae* that he claimed in the *HPN* were formed shortly after Creation like the little globules of glass shooting off in a glassworks. The spinning motion imparted by the Sun's rays would result in concentric rings of matter made to cohere by the endeavours propagating around them. These atoms would have a spherical crust formed by the rotation of the matter at their surface, enclosing other matter within, analogous to little worlds or earthlets (*terrellae* in Leibniz's Latin). Thus they would contain their own matter in motion, smaller in proportion, and so on down (Leibniz asserted, in a vertiginous leap of faith) to infinity:

> For it should be recognized, as those celebrated Micrographers Kircher and Hooke have observed, that most of the qualities that we are sensible of in larger things the keen-eyed observer will detect in proportion in smaller things. And if this proceeds to infinity – which is certainly possible, since the continuum is divisible to infinity – any atom will be of infinite species, like a kind of world, and there will be *worlds within worlds to infinity*. (A VI ii 241/LoC 338)

This assertion, that there are 'worlds within worlds to infinity', will become a leitmotif of Leibniz's natural philosophy.

Leibniz also used the idea of *conatus* or endeavour to give a foundation for the laws of impact of Wallis, Wren, Huygens and Mariotte. Going to the heart of the mechanical philosophy, he reasoned that the Cartesian account of matter as pure extension left it with no foundation for a body to offer any resistance to motion. Natural philosophers of the time nevertheless followed Descartes in expressing their laws of impact in terms of the 'quantity of motion', conceived as the product of a body's speed and its bulk (*mola*). They realized, speaking somewhat loosely, that the 'more' of a body there is with a given speed, the more force of impact it will have on colliding with another body. Today we would say simply that the more (inertial) *mass* a moving body has, the more *momentum* it has, using the terms of Newtonian physics. In fact, even before Newton, Wallis, Huygens and company had already corrected Descartes's impact laws, arriving at the correct conclusion that it is the quantity of motion in a given direction that is conserved in collisions. But the Cartesians could not take mass as a primitive, since it is not derivable from extension and motion. Leibniz, aware that Descartes, Hobbes and Spinoza had tried to reduce force to endeavour or instantaneous tendency to move, decided to finesse this situation by constructing an abstract theory of collisions based solely on endeavour and eschewing the concept of bulk or mass altogether. 'The outcomes of all collisions would be determined by a simple composition of endeavours' (A II iii 99), with endeavours conceived as instantaneous velocities; a body, of itself, could offer no resistance to motion. Thus if two bodies moving with different velocities collide head-on, then, since neither offers resistance to the motion of the other, they will both proceed in the direction of the faster with a velocity that is the difference of their initial endeavours; if one body (no matter how small) collides with another at rest, it will impart all of its endeavour to the larger body, and they will move off together with the initial velocity of the smaller body (GP vii 280–2).

Of course, these rules of motion in the abstract are in conflict with what is experienced in practice, as Leibniz was well aware. He believed that this is because treating bodies as impenetrable or point particles is an unrealistic abstraction, since 'bodies are endowed with elasticity and are flexible, and often a part is impelled without the whole being impelled' (GP vii 283). But he did not want to take elastic force as a primitive, and tried instead (as he would throughout his career) to explain it consistently with the mechanical philosophy. So in the *HPN* he provided a subsidiary hypothesis designed to bring his abstract laws into agreement with experience. We have seen that he conceived body as an aggregate of little corpuscles, the *bullae*. Now imagine such a body A as a row of such corpuscles $a_1, a_2, a_3, \ldots a_n$, colliding with another body B moving with greater speed in the opposite direction. Then when B and a_1 collide, they will move in the direction of B with a velocity $v' = v_B - v_{a1}$; when these two together then collide with a_2, the three bodies will move in the same direction with a velocity that is further reduced, $v'' = v' - v_{a2}$, and so on down the line to a_n. Thus in colliding with A, the velocity of B will be reduced in a way that depends on the initial speeds of the two bodies and also on the quantity of matter (number of corpuscles) in the body A. Effectively, Leibniz is explaining inertial mass as an effect of collisions of constituent particles. Modern physicists might see a parallel with the Higgs mechanism, where the inertial mass of a particle is explained as an effect of its interactions with the Higgs field: the more interactions it has, the harder it is to change the particle's motion.

Leibniz abandoned this particular way of trying to found the laws of impact while he was in Paris. Apart from the difficulty of getting it to agree with experience, he was also obliged to change his views concerning the endeavour theory as his understanding of mathematics progressed, as we will see in chapter 4. But for him the lasting value of this failed attempt was heuristic, and in his mature work he recounts it again and again as an argument against Cartesian physics: if, like Descartes, you are committed to the identity of matter with movable extension, then (given the failure of the above attempt) there is nothing in body to offer any resistance to motion. It is therefore necessary to introduce some power in matter distinct from pure activity (here conceived as *conatus*) in order to account for the correct rules of collision. We will pick up this thread again in chapter 6, in connection with the development of Leibniz's mature dynamics.

Here it will be worthwhile to explore further Leibniz's theory of atoms, especially in connection with the tradition of seventeenth-century atomism on which it draws. For these atomist ideas were forged in a context rife with biological and theological implications, a context that is particularly important for understanding his later philosophy.

Atoms, Souls and Animal Generation

One of the chief merits of his early theory, as Leibniz enthusiastically informed several of his correspondents in 1671, was that it gave an explanation for the immortality of the soul. His idea, inspired by Hobbes's identification of endeavours with desires, was to equate thoughts with endeavours, and construe mind as an enduring entity sustaining these thoughts. As we have seen, in an instant of time an endeavour or instantaneous velocity would occupy a point of space, these points being conceived by Leibniz as mathematical indivisibles having sizes proportional to their differing endeavours. Since each endeavour occupies a point, mind too would be contained in an indivisible, and would therefore be indestructible. Whereas body, as an extended aggregate of indivisibles, can be 'obliterated, and dispersed to all corners of the Earth', he explained to his future employer Duke Johann Friedrich in May 1671, 'mind endures forever, safe and sound in its point. For who can obliterate a point?' (A II i 113).

All of this was to be explained in more detail in a treatise Leibniz was writing in 1671, the *Elements of Mind*. As he explained to the Duke, the crucial distinction between body and mind is that body exists only instantaneously, since it is formed by a different composition of momentaneous endeavours at each different moment. Indeed, Leibniz tells the Duke, 'if two contrary endeavours could persevere in the same body for longer than a moment, every body would be a true mind' (A II i 90). But this is exactly what does happen with a mind, which is able to 'retain all endeavours, or rather their arrangements or states' (A VI ii 285), these being thoughts or emotions that can be compared and contrasted. Just as in Hobbes's account, deliberation consists in the mind's weighing of alternatives, construed as endeavours for differing motions, and the resulting endeavour (desire or aversion) is the will. But while the mind or soul is constituted in a mathematical point, it is implanted in an extended physical point, 'the proximate instrument and as it were vehicle of the soul' (A II i 109), namely the indestructible atomic core or *bulla* described above. Moreover, each mind is associated with its own vortex of matter, which extends beyond the impenetrable spherical shell of the atomic core in which it is implanted. It constitutes a 'kernel of substance' that is 'diffused throughout the body' by means of the subtle matter in its vortex.

This theory, the young Leibniz maintained, could be of great use for solving some outstanding theological controversies. One of these was, intriguingly, the problem of cannibalism. If a cannibal eats the entire body of another human being, so that all the atoms constituting the victim's body become part of the cannibal's body, it is unclear to whom the body will belong when these people are resurrected come Judgement Day. In a little treatise appended to his letter to the Duke, *On the Use and Necessity for Demonstrations of the Immortality of the Soul*, Leibniz explains how his new conception can avoid such problems. At the moment of death the 'kernel of substance' is able to 'retract itself back into its source and fountain', namely the indivisible atomic core, where 'neither fire nor water not any visible force is able to harm it' (A II i 108–9). This 'flower of substance', analogous to the little bone that the Rabbis call the *Luz*, survives the death and apparent destruction of the gross body intact. 'Therefore when one man is eaten by another, the kernel of each remains what and how it was' (109). Upon resurrection, the kernel can expand its sphere of influence again to occupy the whole of the resurrected body.

Thus we see that Leibniz conceives the mind or kernel of substance as being what determines the identity of an individual, its principle of individuation, and that the atom containing one such kernel can be a constituent atom of the body of another substance (in this case, the cannibal). The same account also enables him, he believes, to offer a far superior account of the Eucharist than is possible on the philosophy of the Cartesians. According to the orthodox Catholic doctrine of the Eucharist, when the bread and wine are consecrated by the priest, they change substance (are 'transubstantiated') into the body and blood of Christ, despite their continued appearances as bread and wine. Now if the essence of body is extension, as the Cartesians maintain, it is impossible to say why it is called the body of Christ rather than the body of the bread (A II i 170). But if, as Leibniz maintains, the essence of body consists rather in motion, and its substance consists in its being the principle of motion of that body, the substance of a body lacks extension (A II i 175). Consequently it is possible for the substance of the same body – here, Christ's – to be in many different things simultaneously, so that Christ may be said to be substantially present in the bread and wine.

Here Leibniz is drawing on the tradition of Latin pluralism that would have been familiar to him from his studies of the Scholastics. The pluralists (including scholars such as William of Ockham [*c.* 1285–1349], John Baconthorpe [*c.* 1290–1347], Julius Caesar Scaliger and Jacopo Zabarella) are so called because they conceived it possible for the same matter to have more than one form, a plurality of forms. This contrasted with the more orthodox Thomist doctrine deriving from St Thomas Aquinas, where matter was conceived as a mere potentiality except insofar as it was made actual by a form: one actual piece of matter would be made actual by one form. Critics of Thomism found this to be especially problematic concerning what happens to the human body at death. During life, the form of the body is its soul; at death, the soul separates from the body. But since the lifeless body could not contain matter that is not actual, it would have to have its own form, the form of the cadaver. But then this would have to be specially created at the very moment of death. It was far more reasonable, the pluralists maintained, to suppose that the matter of the body already had forms within it making it actual, which would then remain after death. Indeed, this is empirically supported by the fact that dead bodies manifestly teem with living beings, as can be seen in the process of their decay. These the pluralists called *subordinate forms*; the soul of the living being would be the *dominant form*.

Similar considerations now apply to animal generation. On the orthodox account, when an animal is born, its soul is produced at the moment of conception. But how could a soul or form be produced? As Leibniz later explains in his *Theodicy*, it was commonly assumed that forms were 'derived from the potency of matter', a process going by the name of *eduction* (GP vi 150/T 170). This was usually explained by analogy with shapes being produced from matter. But, Leibniz objects (in agreement with Robert Boyle), if matter is merely passive, this is meaningless. Eduction, he grants, could in principle explain accidental forms, the evanescent qualities produced in things moment by moment. But this would require there to be an enduring substance of which these accidental forms could be modifications, just as shapes are modifications of extended things. Leibniz had proposed such a reinterpretation of accidental forms on that basis to his teacher Thomasius in the letter published with his edition of Nizolio in 1670. How eduction could produce substantial forms, though, was as incomprehensible to him as it was to Boyle.

One alternative to eduction was to have new forms derive from pre-existing active forms in matter, as Julius Caesar Scaliger suggested in his *De subtilitate* of 1557. As Leibniz remarks in the *Theodicy*, this set the stage for a return to Augustine's thesis of *traduction*, the idea that in biological generation the soul of the offspring is not created *de novo* by God, but instead results from a kind of budding of the parents' souls together with the genetic matter, by analogy with the grafting of trees: 'Daniel Sennert, a famous doctor and physicist at Wittenberg, cultivated this opinion, above all in relation to animate bodies, which are multiplied through seeds' (151/171). Actually, Leibniz is being rather coy here, for the ability to explain traduction was another of the vaunted merits of his own early theory of mind. We have seen that he conceived the mind as occupying a mathematical point; now if this point were the vertex of a pointed body, he argued, a division of the body along a line through the point could produce a multiplication of minds. Writing to the Dutch natural philosopher Lambert van Velthuysen in May 1671, he boasted that in this way he could explain 'with as much clarity as sunshine' how 'mind can multiply itself, without new creation, by traduction, with no mention of incorporeality' (A II i 97–8). By this rather condensed formulation, Leibniz meant that he could account for the production of a new soul without having to appeal to its being incorporeal, since soul and body would be divided together.

In fact, Leibniz's early theory had some other intriguing similarities to the ideas of Daniel Sennert (1572–1637),[1] for the Wittenberg professor of medicine had preceded him in advocating not only traduction, but also atoms containing souls. Now, Sennert was indeed heavily influenced by Scaliger, as Leibniz suggests. He had endorsed atomism in 1619, after many years of teaching chymistry on orthodox Aristotelian principles, but the atoms he adopted were the *natural minima* of Scaliger.[2] Where for Aristotle a natural minimum signified a lower limit of division of a natural kind of thing, Scaliger had reinterpreted such minima as actually existing indivisibles, the least particles of individual natural kinds. Moreover, he had given a theory of how these indivisibles combined to form a 'mixt' (chemical compound): such 'mixtion' occurs by a 'motion of minimal bodies toward mutual contact so that a union is made' (Scaliger 1557: 143). In this way the minima do not lose their individual natures, but form a union 'by a making continuous of the boundaries' on contact, as opposed to being merely juxtaposed, like Epicurean atoms.

Sennert (like Boyle after him) adopted this theory of mixtion with enthusiasm, for it opened the way for his acceptance of atoms in his chymical research. He found that after dissolving electrum (an alloy of gold and silver) in *aqua fortis* (nitric acid), he could precipitate out a *calx* (silver carbonate), and then, by heating and fusing this, reconstitute the silver. Following Scaliger, he concluded that gold and silver atoms must have been present throughout, retaining their own natures even when nothing metallic was apparent in the solution (Sennert 1619: 362). The silver atoms would lose their boundaries when they were dissolved, and while their natures or forms would become subordinate to the form of the mixt, they would not lose their identity and blend into that form. Sennert attributed form-containing atoms not only to chemicals – gold and silver, the chymical principles (sulphur, salt, mercury) and minerals – but also to 'certain animate bodies too, in which minimal bodies the soul itself can remain whole and conserve itself' (Sennert 1651: 21). In this he was persuaded by Fortunio Liceti's theory of spontaneous generation. Like Liceti (1577–1657), Sennert found it unintelligible that forms could suddenly come into existence in rotting matter; rather, there would have to be seeds (*semina*) latent in it, each of which is animated by a soul, which would account for the creature's future growth and development. He then argued that the same account of animal generation from a pre-existing seed should apply generally, even in humans: 'scarcely any solid reason can be brought against the propagation of the human soul through the seed', that is, by traduction (54).

One can see much the same kinds of influences and ideas at work in the young Leibniz. His theory of cohesion appears to be a reworking of Scaliger's theory of mixtion in terms amenable to the mechanical philosophy, where the 'motion towards contact' of Scaliger's natural minima is interpreted as the indivisibles' endeavour to penetrate – 'as if fornicating', as Leibniz joked to Pierre de Carcavy in June 1671 – that results in a continuity of boundaries. His mind-containing atoms, like Sennert's, contain principles of activity that are responsible for the 'generation of plants from seeds', the development and growth of seeds in animals' wombs, and even 'the essence of chemicals' (A II i 117). Similar conceptions had, in fact, also been advanced by Gassendi, who had so impressed Leibniz in his youth. Gassendi proposed that seeds were composite particles – it is to him that we owe the term 'molecule' – and, accepting the idea of 'seminal principles' advocated by the Danish chymist Severinus (aka Peder Sørensen, 1542–1602), he endowed each seed with its own form or principle of activity. He insisted on the propagation of souls from pre-existing souls in the organized matter of the seed at conception. (Gassendi, however, conceived all such forms and souls, save for the rational soul in man, to be material.)

Along with these scientific motivations, a major attraction of traduction in Lutheran circles and beyond was its consistency with the account of Creation in the Bible. There God is said to have created the originals of all the forms that now exist on the third day, commanding his creatures to 'Increase and multiply!' (Genesis I: 11–12). As Sennert reasoned, God's command would be empty if souls had to be created anew at each generation, as eduction required. Many thinkers – including Gassendi, a Catholic *abbé* – made the same argument. Eduction, it was thought, flew in the face of Divine Providence, of God's providing creatures with the means to breed and propagate themselves.

Now, as we shall see below, Leibniz's attachment to traduction does not survive the collapse of his theory of indivisibles – at least, if it is understood as a splitting or multiplying of souls. Yet he was as firmly convinced as Gassendi and Sennert that everywhere in living or dead matter where generation occurs there must be souls or forms, and therefore matter that is already organized: 'the formation of animate organic bodies does not appear explicable in the order of nature unless one assumes a *preformation* already organic' (GP vi 152/T 172). His solution was to infer that 'what we call generation of an animal is only a transformation and augmentation', and, by symmetry, that what we call death 'is only an envelopment' (152/172). That is, he solves the 'vexatious question' of the origin of substantial forms by cutting the Gordian knot: they have no natural origin. All existing souls and forms have been in existence since Creation, each has always had some body that it informs, and each embodied soul or form will continue in existence till the end of the world.

This was certainly a bold hypothesis. Leibniz was aware that Sennert had been denounced for advocating the immortality of animals and plants. In fact, the charge was unjust: on Sennert's theory the souls of plants and animals (though not rational souls) would cease to exist when their atoms were divided below the natural minimum for that kind. But to Leibniz the destruction of a substantial form appeared just as problematic as its creation, so they had to be indestructible, raising the spectre of immortality of animals and plants. His solution was to distinguish immortality from mere indestructibility. To be immortal is for one's personal identity to be conserved. This requires the conservation of '*consciousness,* or reflective inward feeling, of what is', for only then will a soul be 'rendered susceptible to chastisement or reward' (151/171). As he writes in the summer of 1676 in one of his myriad encyclopaedia drafts: 'On souls: all things are animate, but only the immortal soul remembers itself' (A VI iii 527/DSR 89). Beasts and plants lack this ability to reflect and be aware of their own identity, and so even if their forms are not destroyed when their gross body is, they cannot be classed as immortal. Leibniz describes his mature theory as a correction to traduction: 'it does not derive the soul from a soul, but only an animate thing from an animate thing, and avoids the frequent miracles of a new creation, which would cause a new and pure soul to enter a body that must corrupt it' (GP vi 352/T 361).

Thus Leibniz was motivated to reintroduce substantial forms for various reasons. They were necessary in order to account for the end-directed behaviour and self-identity of individuals through time, as well as to account for the actuality of matter; without them, there were no viable candidates for the individual substances of which the accidental forms (like shape, size and extendedness) could be the modifications. Sennert had argued much the same against the atomist theory of his contemporary Sébastien Basson in his *Physical Memoirs* of 1636, fifty years prior to Leibniz's *Discourse on Metaphysics*, insisting that if forms were regarded as merely mechanical combinations of atoms, it was impossible to account for the replication of forms of chemicals, minerals and plants, and the evident purposefulness of living creatures. But he was unable to explain how such forms acted on individual bodies, or how their range of influence could grow along with their bodies. Pointing up such difficulties, Robert Boyle had written a scathing rejection of Sennert's appeal to substantial forms in physical and chymical explanations in 1666. Leibniz was persuaded by this, as we saw from his letter to Conring of 1678 (see chapter 1), where he insisted that all particular phenomena had to be explained mechanically. But he was equally persuaded by the arguments of Sennert and others that a rejection of teleology in nature would make it impossible to account for Divine Providence without requiring God to act directly on matter in the natural course of things, like a *deus ex machina*. What was required, then, for a successful rehabilitation of substantial forms was a satisfactory account of their relation to bodies, and, as we shall see in chapters 5 and 6, Leibniz does not achieve this until after his engagement with Spinoza's philosophy in the late 1670s, when he works out a new theory of how substances act that is entirely compatible with the mechanical philosophy. But when he does so, he falls back on the 'pluralist' framework outlined above: there is no actual matter that does not contain forms or entelechies, so that the body of any given substance will itself contain further entelechies with their own bodies.

Machines of Nature

The breakdown of Leibniz's early metaphysics is conditioned in part by developments in his understanding of the infinite, as we'll see in chapters 4 and 5. Once he had developed the main ideas of his infinitesimal calculus by 1676, it was no longer possible for him to conceive of the continuum as composed of points, or of locating minds in them. Also, by then he had come to the conclusion that minds are inherently naturally indestructible, and this obviated the need for any bubble-atoms to house them. Third, he had been led to abandon the idea that force could be construed solely in terms of endeavour, as mentioned above. Thus his early metaphysics lay in ruins, and in the late 1670s Leibniz began to search for new principles to ground mechanics.

A good specimen of this interregnum in his metaphysics is provided by the dialogue *Pacidius to Philalethes*, which Leibniz wrote on board Prince Rupert of the Rhine's yacht in November 1676, while awaiting clement weather in the Thames estuary for the trip to Holland. In the setting of a letter to Philalethes (literally, 'lover of truth'), the dialogue is a fictional report by Pacidius ('peace of God', representing Leibniz) of a conversation he had about the continuity of motion with characters modelled on his younger friend Tschirnhaus and their German hosts in Paris. Regarding motion, he concludes that no action is to be found in motion as it is manifested geometrically. Endeavour is nowhere mentioned in the dialogue. Instead, Leibniz argues, any given motion is divided into stretches of uniform motion with no state of change between them. But each of these is itself further divided, so that, no matter how far one divides, one never comes across a motion that is perfectly uniform, or a state of action in bodies. Similarly, matter is also actually infinitely divided without this issuing in points or indivisibles. Thus the division of the continuum should not be conceived 'to be like the division of sand into grains, but like that of a sheet of paper or tunic into folds'. These will be 'multiplied to infinity in such a way that there is no fold so small that it is not subdivided by a new fold'. Yet 'the tunic cannot be resolved all the way down into points; rather, although some folds are smaller than others to infinity, bodies are always extended, and points never become parts, but always remain mere extrema' (A VI iii 555/LoC 185–7).

On this conception of matter as divided into pleats or folds, 'body is everywhere flexible', and its parts have various degrees of elasticity or resistance to being folded: there is no such thing as an absolutely hard atom, or a perfect fluid. Leibniz may owe the idea of matter's pleats to Francis Bacon, and that of its inherent elasticity to Hooke, Mariotte and Boyle as well, but many of his contemporaries appealed to immaterial or semi-material natures in matter responsible for its unfoldings and orderly development. Severinus' notion of a *seminal force* directing the development of plants, animals and minerals was widely influential, and Sennert, for example, had posited such a force in his atoms. By contrast, Leibniz insisted that elastic force was to be understood wholly mechanically, in terms of the motions of a fluid (consisting of micro-particles) within the elastic body. Since these particles will also be elastic, moreover, their elasticity will require them to contain a still subtler fluid, and so on all the way down. Thus there are no atoms in the sense of 'bodies so firm that they do not suffer any subdivision or bending' (A VI iii 561/LoC 199).

The notion of matter as inherently elastic is not new for Leibniz in 1676: even in 1671 when he was advocating his indestructible *bullae*, he rejected the idea of unyielding atoms. But now that he no longer thinks immaterial minds need atomic casings for their continuance in existence, the way is open for him to reject atoms completely. This must have seemed especially prudent, given that the type of atoms advocated by most of his contemporaries (e.g. Huygens, Cordemoy, Hartsoeker) were the perfectly hard atoms that he regarded as incompatible with the elasticity of matter. So from 1676 on, the rejection of (absolutely hard) atoms and the argument from the mechanical explanation of elasticity to the infinite division of bodies both become bedrocks of Leibniz's mature natural philosophy. As he writes later in the *Specimen of Dynamics* of 1695,

> There is no body so very small that it does not have elasticity, and so is not permeated by a fluid even more subtle. And therefore *there are no elements of bodies*, no perfectly fluid matter, and no supposed solid globules of the second element, of fixed and unchanging shape; rather the analysis proceeds to infinity. (GM vi 249/WFT 171)

In the *Pacidius*, Leibniz does not mention his *bullae*, although he allows that there could be relatively hard parts of matter that retain their shape for a while and are then transformed, moving in a fluid that itself has parts that are similarly 'opened up and folded together in various ways' (A VI iii 555/LoC 185). Nevertheless he still upholds his thesis of worlds within worlds to infinity, which he takes to be supported by the infinite enfoldment of matter: 'in any grain of sand whatever there is not just a world, but an infinity of worlds' (566/211).

On arriving in Holland a couple of weeks after penning the *Pacidius*, Leibniz was delighted to find his 'worlds within worlds' thesis visually confirmed in the microscopes of the Dutch virtuosi Swammerdam and Leeuwenhoek. He took the organisms[3] they showed him at previously unimagined realms of minuteness to confirm what he had earlier gleaned from his reading of Robert Hooke, Pierre Borel (*c.* 1620–71) and Marcello Malpighi (1628–94): the existence of matter imbued with life and form at all scales. Thus he assimilated the infinite foldings of matter to the envelopment of other organisms within the body of any living organism, and saw this as further evidence for the preformation of matter in form-containing seeds not visible to the naked eye. Moreover, he acknowledges his debt to Swammerdam for showing how 'the parts of the butterfly are already enveloped in the caterpillar', convincing him that that the unfoldings of organic matter correspond to the generation of new bodies, and their compactification to the appearance of death. Living organisms, he came to see in the late 1670s, and not mind-containing atoms, are the true temporal continuants. As he later explained to the Dutch atomist Nicolaas Hartsoeker (1656–1725) in 1710,

> Messieurs Swammerdam, Malpighi and Leeuwenhoek, who are among the greatest observers of our time, have come to my aid and enabled me to admit more easily that the animal or any other organized substance does not have its beginning when we think it does, and that its apparent generation is only a development and a sort of augmentation. (GP iii 507–8)

Not every fold of matter, of course, corresponds to a living organism. Like the atomists Basson and Sennert, Leibniz distinguished *beings per se* from *beings by aggregation*. Where they depicted atoms as indestructible beings per se and the bodies aggregated from them as subject to generation and dissolution, he contended that what are indestructible are the substantial forms informing organic bodies, and that all inorganic bodies are dissoluble aggregates of organic ones. Thus for him matter is basically organic: 'all organic bodies are animate, and all bodies are either organic or collections of organic bodies' (A VI iv 1798/LoC 277), he wrote around 1685 in criticism of Cordemoy's atomism; and in another draft from that time, 'bodies that lack a substantial form are merely aggregates, like a woodpile or a heap of stones, and consequently do not possess cognition or appetite' (1508/287). In bodies possessing such substantial forms, on the other hand, as we shall see in chapter 5, there is cognition or perception – 'that is, a representation of external things in a certain individual thing', together with 'a kind of appetite or endeavour, according to this cognition of its acting' (1508/287).

In the *Monadology*, Leibniz famously argues for the impossibility of an explanation of perception on mechanical principles, that is, solely in terms of shapes and motions. He asks us to 'imagine a machine which by its structure produced thought, feeling, perception' (§ 17; GP vi 609/WFT 270), and to suppose it enlarged proportionally to the dimensions of a mill, which we could go inside. But on entering all we would see would be pieces pushing against one another, and nothing corresponding to perception. He concludes that perception cannot be found in a composite body like a machine, but must be sought instead in a substance containing no parts, a 'simple substance' – another term for a monad, or entelechy.

It is tempting to conclude from this that Leibniz holds that life is not explicable without supplementing mechanism with some kind of vital force as the cause of the behaviours of living things – like the *plastic force* of the Cambridge Platonist Ralph Cudworth (1617–88), or the *élan vital* of Henri Bergson (1911). This would be a mistake. Although Leibniz believes that there is some perception and appetition in all living beings, he consistently opposes the idea of a vital force as a causal agent. 'I attribute to mechanism everything that happens in the bodies of plants and animals,' he writes in the *New Essays*, 'except for their initial formation . . . and I do not approve of recourse to the soul when it is a matter of explaining the details of the phenomena of plants and animals' (NE 139). Thus while he can agree with Cudworth that 'matter arranged by divine wisdom must be essentially organized throughout', for him this means that 'there are machines in the parts of a natural machine to infinity, so many envelopes and organic bodies enveloped one within another, that one can never produce any organic body entirely anew and without any preformation' (*Considerations on Vital Principles and Plastic Natures*, 1705: GP vi 544/L 589). He therefore dismisses Cudworth's 'immaterial plastic natures', along with Scaliger's notion that 'the soul fashions its body', with the comment: '*Non mi bisogna, e non mi basta* [For me it is neither needed nor enough], for the very reason that this infinitely complex organism provides me with material plastic natures sufficient for the need' (544/589).

How, then, does Leibniz account for the difference between organic and inorganic matter? In a text from 1680–6 whose full title is *The Human Body, Like That of any Animal, Is a Sort of Machine* (Smith 2011: 290–6), he argues that 'any machine . . . is best defined in terms of its final cause, so that in the description of the parts it is therefore apparent in what way each of them is coordinated with the others for the intended use' (290). The best way to describe a clock, for example, is as a machine made to tell the time, so that 'the function of a clock hand lies in its uniform motion for some period of time' (290). Such an artificial machine cannot move itself, however, or sustain itself in existence; it requires as external agent to set it in motion, and once it has used up its stored energy, it stops. The body of an animal is a superior kind of machine in that it has organs for nutrition and excretion which enable it to nourish itself, importing through its interaction with its environment the energy necessary to sustain itself. Also, even though it may cease or die when it is no longer able to sustain itself as a body of that kind, it has reproductive organs: machines of this kind 'are able to produce other machines of a nature similar to themselves' (292). Thus, Leibniz concludes,

> [T]he Bodies of Animals are Machines of perpetual motion, or, to put it more clearly, they are machines comparable to a certain fixed and singular species of perpetual organic motion that is always maintained in the world. Thus for as long as there are spiders there will be weaving machines, for as long as there are bees there will be honey-producing machines, and for as long as there are squirrels there will be dancing machines. (290–1)

Therefore organic bodies are self-moving and self-sustaining machines, able to replicate other machines of the same kind. As Leibniz tells the vitalist Georg Stahl (1659–1734) in their controversy on the nature of life in 1709–10, organism is really a mechanism, although 'a more exquisite one' (Stahl and Leibniz 1720: 6–7/Smith 2011: 326). And the organs these machines must possess to perform functions such as digestion and reproduction are themselves very complex mechanisms. Each of these machines has its own function, yet also contributes to the functioning of the larger organic body of which it is a constituent part. And the same applies, as Leibniz explains in the *New System* of 1695, to its own constituent parts:

> It must be recognized that the machines of nature have an infinity of organs, and are so well apportioned and resistant to all accidents that it is impossible to destroy them. A natural machine remains a machine in its least parts, and what is more, it remains the same machine that it always was, being merely transformed by the different folds it receives, now extended, now contracted, and as it were concentrated when we think it has been destroyed. (GP iv 482/AG 142)

Thus, as the philosopher Gilles Deleuze has observed, Leibniz does not fault mechanism 'for being too artificial to account for living matter, but for not being mechanical enough, for not being adequately machined' (Deleuze 1993: 8). We can make an artificial machine like a clock, building it up out of inorganic bodies like its metal cogs, pendulum and hands; but these parts are not themselves machines contributing to its function by their own self-directed actions, as is the case with an organic body. To make an organic body we would have to be able to make machines within machines to infinity, with all their actions coordinating to produce the actions of that body. Thus, as Leibniz remarked in his notes on Cordemoy in 1685, not even an angel could 'form a man or any true animal except from a seed, where it already pre-exists in some way' (A VI iv 1801/LoC 283). However organized any artificial machine might be, its unity will never be more than accidental and prone to dissolution.

Life, Programs and Final Causes

For Leibniz, what makes a natural machine the *same* machine in its least parts is its possession of a substantial form or monad. It does not have to have the same parts from one instant to another, so long as the parts it does have contribute to its own functions and end. For this it needs to be the source of its own actions, and also to have a law or 'program' for the development and unfolding of these actions. Each of these two aspects of Leibnizian forms is crucial. The need for a substance to have its own force in order to bring about its own actions explains why Leibniz is not finally ready to 'rehabilitate' substantial forms until he has fashioned a viable conception of force and its conservation in the late 1670s, as we'll see in chapter 6. And on the other hand, it is the internal law governing the unfolding of the states of a substance that accounts for it having a genuine unity, as opposed to the accidental unity of an artificial machine: the latter has only the end or purpose for which it is designed by humans, whereas a natural machine has one that is inbuilt, together with the active force necessary to bring it about.

Every substance, according to Leibniz, is alive. Natural machines are the bodies of living creatures, and every substance has such an organic body: 'each monad, with its particular body, makes a living substance' (GP vi 599/AG 208). Leibniz has therefore given a second condition for creatures to be counted as alive: not only will their bodies be natural machines, but in order for these bodies to be self-moving and self-sustaining machines, able to reproduce, they must also contain within themselves an internal law or 'program' according to which their development and changes unfold. Their being self-moving and self-sustaining sounds very modern; but the second condition also has an echo in contemporary biology, as Ohad Nachtomy has observed. He quotes the molecular biologist François Jacob: 'For the biologist, life begins only with what could constitute a genetic program' (Nachtomy 2009: 13). Such a program, written in the code of DNA, contains instructions for the production of the sixty-four different proteins necessary for life, and 'variations in the DNA sequence constitute the genetic information necessary (but of course not sufficient) for the development of the set of unique properties of all biological individuals as well as the genetic material they transmit to future generations' (17). There is an obvious resonance here with Leibniz's idea of the complete concept of an individual substance containing all the information necessary for the development of that individual, and with his earlier idea that this could be captured in infinite combinations and permutations of basic concepts: in modern genetics, information is carried in combinations and permutations of four organic bases, A, G, C and T.

The very idea of an internal law or program, moreover, implies end-directed action, as Jacob has argued. Leibniz explicitly recognized this, arguing that Descartes and Spinoza were wrong to think mechanism precludes teleology. On the contrary, teleology is intrinsic to what a machine is, since it must be identified by its function: as we saw, 'any machine is best defined in terms of its final cause'. Although we may in certain circumstances be able to explain the workings or effects of a machine in terms of efficient causes, this will often not be the case, especially in biology. In such cases, Leibniz tells Stahl, 'since the internal parts are unknown to us, it may be easier to understand [the effects] from the final causes rather than the efficient ones' (Stahl and Leibniz 1720: 6–7/Smith 2011: 92). So, teleological explanation complements explanations in terms of cause and effect, the actions of bodies on one another through their motions. It relates to the function or purpose of the machine, and thus to the soul or form. Considered in itself, the form or soul 'tends through final causes to the goal that the corporeal machine, considered in itself, attains through efficient causes' (176/91).

Of course, there are many salient differences between Leibniz's views and modern biology. While the notion of a program regulating the development and structure of an organism, and even the idea of sub-programs regulating structures and developments of organisms within the body of the original organism, are common to both, Leibniz's natural machines are characterized by a nested structure that is both structurally and functionally infinite, in contrast to the finite nestedness of bodies assumed by modern biology, and indeed the finiteness of the information encoded in them. Again, for Leibniz, living creatures are all created by God in Creation, and remain self-identical through all their changes of outward form until the end of the world, in obvious contrast to the finitude of life assumed in modern evolutionary biology. Finally, the internal laws containing the genetic information of Leibnizian individuals evidently do not evolve by natural selection, but simply unfold this information on the occasion of changes in their environments. Nevertheless, all Leibniz's natural machines are interconnected, despite their lack of substantial interaction, and in this way can be said to constitute one interwoven machine, the created universe. Proposing this all-encompassing mechanism is deliberate on Leibniz's part, since it supports Divine Providence: the machines of nature – 'divine machines' – are designed by God to contribute to the overall perfection of the universe, which they do individually, yet in complete harmony, without needing to be 'steered' by a soul acting on them.

Leibniz's uncompromising mechanism, as well as his commitment to providence, are also both evident in his 1694 work on geology, the *Protogaea*. Here, though, we get to see another side of Leibniz, where he fills out his bookish learning with first-hand observations. Thus he notes that the entrances and tunnels of the silver mines in Rammelsberg in the Harz mountains are narrowing because of the forming of mineral deposits. But where Severinus and the alchemists had understood such deposits as metals growing from seeds, Leibniz insisted that 'the waters there, which carry along copper vitriol and material mixed with metal, are depositing sediment; they are merely transporting the copper or lead, not generating them' (Leibniz 2008: 29). Similarly, having earlier believed Kircher's theory that fossils were sports (games of nature) that grew in the earth, he had learned from Nicolas Steno (1638–86) (whom he met in Hanover in 1677) that glossopetrae ('snake's tongues') were in fact fossilized shark's teeth, formed by the successive replacement of the material of the teeth by minerals (Steno [1669] 1916). This Leibniz was able to verify with his own observations of glossopetrae and numerous other fish fossils from Lüneburg, far from any sea. He explains how fossil sea shells 'did not arise in the rock', since they contain fossils smaller than their openings, which could thus 'only have come in from the outside' (Leibniz 2008: 61) before fossilization. Vividly describing his spelunking in the caves of Scharzfeld and Baumann (105–15), he gives accurate descriptions of the fossils that could be found in them, as well as their situations in the various earths and rocks. He reports seeing 'something like part of [an elephant's] shinbone' dug out of these caves, as well as 'entire bones of sea monsters and other animals from an unknown world' (99, 97), and speculates about what cataclysms

might have led to creatures being deposited so far from their pre-
sumed origins.

Of course, this implies that the Earth has had a violent history,
which Leibniz proceeds to reconstruct. Following Steno, he realized
that the principle underlying the formation of fossils by successive
layering could be generalized, so that a chronological sequencing
of ages in the history of the Earth could be read off the spatial dis-
tribution of layers of different earths and minerals. He supposed
that the planet had begun in a molten state and then cooled, forming
a double vaulted crust separated by water and air, which then col-
lapsed to form the great mountain ranges, like bones of the Earth.
This process would have taken very much longer than the six mil-
lennia supposed by many of his contemporaries (including Newton).
But on this heterodoxy Leibniz maintains a discreet silence (Leibniz
2008: xxviii), preferring to emphasize how God's providential plans
are embodied in the successive enfoldings and eruptions of the
planet's surface.

Leibniz's natural philosophy, with its supposition of infinitely
nested individuals and the fundamentally organic nature of matter,
is apt to seem arcane and far-fetched. But it is perhaps less so than
it appears. Where his contemporaries regarded parasites as viola-
tions of the natural order, we now know that the human body, for
instance, contains some ten times as many bacterial cells as human
cells, and cannot function at all without the actions within it of life-
forms with their own DNA. The lifecycle of our stomach bacteria
depends on their being in our stomach, and equally, we cannot
digest properly without these bacteria. Such symbiosis – biological
individuals contained within the body of another individual, each
necessary for the other's functioning as a dynamic, kinetically stable
system – is now recognized to be far more the norm than the exception. Moreover, it has been proposed that the continual transformation of 'regular' matter into replicative matter by drawing energy
from the outside, in just the way Leibniz proposed in defining his
'machines of nature', suggests 'that in some fundamental manner
replicative matter is the more "stable" form' (Pross 2011: 12, 14). As
our understanding of the cosmos progresses in astrobiology, we
may come to see that Leibniz's vision of matter as fundamentally
made up of self-sustaining replicating machines is not so very far
from the truth.

4

Mathematical Philosophy

Leibniz's contributions to mathematics were very profound. In terms of orthodox mathematical talent, he probably ranks below mathematicians like Gauss or Riemann, or even his rival Newton – perhaps in part because of his having come late to the subject. Even so, the originality and utility of his contributions rank alongside the very best in history. He is famous, of course, for his discovery of the calculus and for the protracted priority dispute with Newton that dragged on for almost two centuries before scholars established that each had discovered the Fundamental Theorem of the Calculus independently. But Leibniz made numerous other original contributions to mathematics. He is known for his work on infinite series, in particular his discovery of the series named after him and the expression for $\pi/4$ derivable from it. He defined the osculating circle and showed its importance in the study of curves, distinguished transcendental from algebraic numbers, and anticipated Legendre's conjecture that π is a transcendental number (i.e. one not expressible as the root of an algebraic equation) by 118 years. He framed the concepts of matrix determinant and Gaussian elimination, inventing the so-called Leibniz formula for determinants, anticipated some of the main concepts of fractal geometry and information theory, and inaugurated the idea of a generalized geometry or Analysis Situs, which was later developed by by Hermann Grassmann (1809–77) into his vector algebra and by Henri Poincaré (1854–1912), L. E. J. Brouwer (1881–1966) and others into combinatorial topology (see chapter 7).

This is not the place to set about explaining all this technical work. Rather, what I want to do in this chapter is to explain how

Leibniz's work in mathematics grew with and informed his philosophy. Although he himself tended to avoid explaining the mathematics behind his inspirations for fear of taxing the patience of his readers, it is not clear that this strategy worked very well. Reactions ranged from the incomprehension of some of his non-mathematically inclined correspondents to the scathing remarks of mathematically astute critics like Euler and Russell, who lauded his mathematics but not his application of it to his metaphysics. So here I shall try instead to give enough explanation of Leibniz's mathematical philosophy for the reader to understand at least how his mathematics informed his characteristic doctrines.

For Leibniz was above all a mathematical philosopher. We have already gained a sense of this in chapter 2, where we noted how his articulation of some of the basic ideas and theorems of combinatorics, as well as his formulation of mathematical logic, were embroiled in his project for a universal characteristic. But other aspects of his mathematical work were also implicated in and grew out of this project. One of these was his insistence on designing appropriate notation, the 'real characters' that would facilitate discoveries in different fields. This recognition of the importance of notation was an insight very much underestimated by his contemporaries. Huygens, for example, was slow to appreciate the power of Leibniz's invention of differentials and integrals. Although he himself could handle infinitesimals with great facility, he initially regarded algebraic methods involving them as merely heuristic measures, to be replaced by geometric constructions in rigorous proofs. Newton's reaction was even more severe. At the height of their priority dispute, Newton contemptuously dismissed Leibniz as someone who liked to take others' discoveries, invent fancy new terminology for them, and then pass them off as his own. Newton was in fact sceptical of the algebraic methods he himself had helped to pioneer, which he came to regard as lacking in rigour, rejecting the idea that method should depend on the forms of symbols. Here Leibniz was more perceptive: where Newton had a battery of powerful methods he could deploy to solve a huge range of mathematical problems, but no one algorithm he identified as the calculus, Leibniz gave the world a novel algorithm with its own notation designed to facilitate discoveries and easy demonstration. And it did. Continental mathematicians took up Leibniz's differential calculus with enthusiasm and applied it productively to a wide range of new problems, while their counterparts in Britain were held back by their loyalty to Newton's geometrical methods. It was, moreover, a wonderful illustration of Leibniz's idea of blind thought: one could do complex calculations using differentials without having first resolved the problem of the composition of the continuum, that is, without needing to know exactly what differentials denoted, so long as one had a way of interpreting both the problem and the results in terms of them.

Leibniz's main interest in mathematics, however, was fuelled by his fascination with the infinite. It is not an exaggeration to say that his whole philosophy was framed by his passion for the infinite and the indivisible, from his earliest theory of indivisibles of motion to his mature depiction of monads as infinite series of states produced according to the law of the series. And many of his other characteristic doctrines were also inspired by his mathematical work related to the infinite and the continuum. His analysis of body as an infinite aggregate lacking unity, his solution to the problem of contingency in terms of an analogy with incommensurable proportions, his conception of derivative forces as instantaneous modifications, and his sophisticated understanding of teleological behaviour in terms of the optimization of paths, all owe a substantial debt to his mathematical understanding. So let us begin with Leibniz's philosophy of the infinite.

From Indivisibles to Fictions

One of Leibniz's most distinctive doctrines is his advocacy of the *actual infinite*. Although this had precedents in the views of Nicholas of Cusa (1401–64), Giordano Bruno (1548–1600) and Galileo Galilei (1564–1642), the great majority of mathematicians and philosophers had sided with Aristotle, who denied that an infinity of things could exist. Aristotle had formulated his views largely in response to the famous paradoxes of Zeno, a fifth-century BC philosopher from the Greek colony of Elea. With his paradoxes Zeno purported to show the impossibility of motion and also of plurality – thus establishing indirectly the teaching of his mentor, Parmenides, that all that exists is One, changeless and indivisible. Zeno contended that if there are Many, there must be an assignable number of them. Now, anything that is divisible can always be further divided. Each part could itself be divided into parts, these parts into further parts, and so on without limit. But then there would be no assignable number of parts – a contradiction. Likewise, nothing finite could consist in an infinity of finite parts, since an infinity of finite parts added together would make something infinite in size. In his Dichotomy Paradox, Zeno made similar claims about motion. In order for a body to move through a given interval, it would first have to move through a half of that interval, and before that, a half of that half, and so on without limit. Therefore the motion would never get started.

Aristotle responded by insisting that the parts of a continuous thing are nothing but potential parts: they are parts into which it *could be divided*. There is thus a *potential infinity* of parts, but not an actual one: nothing can be actually infinitely divided. Thus a continuous line, for example, is infinitely divisible: one can mark each such potential division by a point. But this is not an actual point; an actual division would result in two discrete, touching line segments, each with its own endpoints, and one would no longer have a continuous line. Likewise with Zeno's Dichotomy: the interval is indeed divisible into a half, then a quarter, then an eighth, and so on, and there is an infinity of such potential parts. But since the interval is not actually divided, the body does not have to cover an actual infinity of sub-intervals. Moreover, Aristotle reasoned, if half of the interval is covered in half the time, and a quarter of the interval in a quarter of the time, and so on, this is entirely compatible with the whole interval being covered in the whole time (*Physics* 233a).

Now, by Leibniz's time it had been demonstrated by Gregory of St Vincent (1584–1667) that one of Zeno's assumptions was fallacious: an infinity of finite parts does not necessarily add up to an infinite whole. It will if there is a least finite part, but not if the parts themselves decrease geometrically, as in the Dichotomy. There the semi-intervals add to 1, even though there are an infinity of them, all finite, with no least sub-interval. Gregory demonstrated this geometrically, but it can be shown non-rigorously as follows. Denote their sum, $\frac{1}{2} + \frac{1}{4} + \frac{1}{8} + \frac{1}{16} + \ldots$, by S. Now $\frac{1}{2}S = \frac{1}{4} + \frac{1}{8} + \frac{1}{16} + \ldots$. But then $S - \frac{1}{2}S = \frac{1}{2}$, so that $S = 1$. Also, Galileo had argued that there is nothing to prevent a finite continuum from having an actual infinity of parts if these parts are not themselves finite, but are rather infinitely small points, lacking any quantity. For then an infinity of them would not yield an infinite quantity. (Indeed, there was a significant faction among the Jesuits, known as the Zenonists, who thought that this is just what the historical Zeno had intended: the continuum is composed from an infinity of points.) Against this proposal, however, were ranged some weighty mathematical arguments against composing a continuum from points. It could be shown, for example, that there would be as many points in the side of a square as in its diagonal, by setting them in one-to-one correspondence. But then a line that is the difference between the two should have no points at all! Also there were Aristotle's arguments (in *Physics* 231b) that indivisibles or partless points could not be set next to each other to make a continuous line, as they had no extreme points that could coincide.

Leibniz seems to have been convinced of the actual infinitude of the world from the outset. As we have seen, the proposal that the world is actually divided to infinity, 'worlds within worlds to infinity', occurs already in some of his earliest writings. But his interpretation of how such an infinite division is to be understood undergoes some profound changes as his knowledge of mathematics deepens. To begin with he conceives it in terms of a division into infinitely small points. However, by the time he had finished laying the groundwork for the calculus in 1676, he already had an interpretation of the mathematical infinite and infinitely small as *fictions* – as a means of abbreviating statements about an arbitrarily large number of things of arbitrary smallness. Just as the infinite is not an actually existing whole made up of finite parts, so infinitesimals are not actually existing parts which can be composed into a finite whole. Borrowing a term from the Scholastics, Leibniz called the infinite and the infinitely small *syncategorematic terms*: like 'it' or 'some' in a meaningful sentence, they do not in themselves refer to determinate things, but can be used perfectly meaningfully in a specified context.

Again, we can throw light on how Leibniz came to these conclusions by following the genesis of his thought, beginning with his theory of indivisible points in the *Theoria motus abstracti (TMA)*. There he begins by asserting the actual infinity of parts of the continuum, appealing to an argument Descartes had given in his *Principles of Philosophy* for the indefinite division of matter into actual parts. Descartes had reasoned that each part of matter is individuated by having a motion in common: everything in the same part moves together. But if one now imagines a liquid swirling as if in a vat that has a cylinder placed in it off-centre, then in order for the liquid to move round the vat through the narrower space without a vacuum forming, it must move progressively faster through that space. Consequently, matter there will be actually divided into parts with slightly differing motions to infinity. Descartes had described this as an 'indefinite' division into ever smaller actual parts, where 'indefinite' connotes 'something that our mind perceives to be true, even though it does not comprehend how it occurs' (AT viii A 59/

CSM ii 239). But Leibniz will have none of that, dismissing Descartes's 'indefinite' as 'not in the thing, but the thinker' (A VI ii 264/ LoC 339). He contends that the same argument should apply to all matter everywhere in the plenum at any instant. Moreover, it is not motion that divides the matter, since there is no motion in an instant, but only a tendency to move or endeavour. Thus the actual parts of matter will be individuated by differing endeavours to infinity.

Leibniz then proceeds to assimilate Descartes's indefinitely small actual parts to Galileo's points, but with a subtle reinterpretation: his points, unlike Galileo's, have quantity. For he cedes the force of Aristotle's argument against composing a line from partless points (minima), but thinks he can circumvent it by defining a point, not as 'that which has no part', as had Euclid, but as 'that which *has no extension*, i.e. whose parts are indistant' (264–5/339–40). On the one hand, since these indivisibles contain parts, Leibniz has avoided Aristotle's objection to points composing a continuum, and on the other, since he defines magnitude as 'the multiplicity of its parts', his points (unlike Galileo's) could have a magnitude. Thus whereas a partless point or minimum would have a ratio to a finite line of 0 to 1 (i.e. no definable ratio, since however many 0s one takes, they will not add up to 1), a Leibnizian point or indivisible is defined to have a ratio to a line of 1 to ∞: each is precisely an infinitieth part of the line.

But Leibniz's main argument for these extensionless indivisibles is an ingenious inversion of Zeno's Dichotomy. If motion is to occur, he agrees, then it must have a beginning. But whatever is moving in a given interval must already have been moving in the first half of that interval, so the beginning of the motion must be contained in that half-interval. But what is moving in the first half must already have been moving in the first half of this half, and so on to infinity. Again Leibniz agrees, but where Zeno concluded that motion could never begin, Leibniz draws a different conclusion. Taking for granted the reality of motion, he reasons that since the beginning of any motion cannot consist in an extended stretch of motion, this beginning must be unextended. Indeed, since this argument is applicable to any sub-interval of the motion – or likewise to any sub-intervals of lines, bodies or times – it entails the stronger conclusion that any sub-interval whatever must contain an unextended beginning.

As we saw in chapter 3, Leibniz identified these beginnings of motion as endeavours, conceived as proportional to the beginning of a line (point) covered in the beginning of an interval of time (instant). It follows that if we take two points p and q that are the beginnings of two different lines described in time T by the unequal uniform motions whose speeds are M and N, they will be proportional to the endeavours that are the beginnings of these motions, M/∞ and N/∞, respectively. Therefore, even though these points are infinitely small, they will be in the ratio $M:N$, that is, in the same ratio as their generating motions. An infinity of points of length MT/∞ will compose a line of length MT, just as an infinity of endeavours M/∞ will compose the motion M.

Using this Hobbesian concept of endeavour, Leibniz was able to answer another of Zeno's famous arguments against motion, the Arrow Paradox. Zeno had argued that an arrow at any instant of its motion would occupy a place equal to itself; but anything occupying a place equal to itself was by definition at rest. So the arrow must in fact be at rest, since it does not differ from one at rest at any instant of its motion. But according to Leibniz it does differ, since at every instant it will have an endeavour that is proportional to the motion of which it is a beginning. As he will later argue in a controversy with Johann Christoph Sturm (1635–1703), 'at any moment of its motion, not only is a body in a specific place, but it also has a tendency or endeavours to change that place'; moreover, if this were not so, 'there would be no way at all to distinguish between bodies, since in a plenum of masses that are uniform in themselves there is no way of distinguishing except by motion' (GP iv 513/ WFT 218–19). Leibniz also infers from this that '*there is never any true rest in bodies*' (GM vi 252/WFT 174). A body always has some endeavour: even if this is infinitely small compared to a body in motion relative to it (in a ratio of 1 to ∞), it is never in the ratio 0 to 1, as it would be if it were perfectly at rest.

This first theory of the infinitely small, however, depends crucially on Leibniz's distinction of his indivisibles from minima, or partless points. Minima cannot compose a continuum, since then there would be as many points in the side of a square as in its diagonal, as we saw above: 'a minimum cannot be supposed without it following that the whole has as many minima as the part, which implies a contradiction' (A VI ii 264/LoC 339). But by late 1671, Leibniz has realized that the same argument can be applied to indivisibles: if they can be taken as the endpoints of lines, then they cannot compose a continuum without violating the part–whole axiom. So he is forced to abandon indivisibles.

To begin with, Leibniz does not see this as obliging him to abandon infinitely small actual parts in the continuum. His inversion of Zeno's Dichotomy can be saved if the infinitely small actuals are reinterpreted as extended and therefore divisible, and defined in terms of their proportionality to the endeavours in a motion. This, at any rate, is how Leibniz interprets Cavalieri's indivisibles in his mathematics, following Hobbes's lead. By 1676, however, as we'll see below, his position has changed. His increasing proficiency in mathematics, especially his work on decreasing infinite series like the dichotomy series, has led him to conclude that infinite series cannot be regarded as true wholes. To say that there are infinitely many terms in the series is to say that no matter how many terms are taken, there are more; but they do not form an infinite collection, and there is no infinite number of them. Likewise, there is no infinitieth term, $1/\infty$; we can calculate as if there is an infinitieth term, but strictly speaking this is to be interpreted as a finite term that can be made as small as desired by taking sufficiently many terms in the series.

Correspondingly, the infinite division of matter need not issue in minimal points: 'if we suppose that any body whatever is resolved into still smaller bodies, that is, that there are always some worlds within others,' Leibniz asks himself in April 1676, 'would the body thereby be divided into minimal parts?' If not, 'being divided without end is different from being divided into minima, in that there will be no last part, just as in an unbounded line there is no last point' (A VI iii 513/LoC 119). By November he is asserting that exactly this is the case. As we saw in the previous chapter, he likens the actual infinite division of body to 'a tunic that is scored with folds multiplied to infinity in such a way that there is no fold so small that it is not subdivided by a new fold' (555/185). 'The parts take shape for some time, and are transformed, and yet there is no dissolution all the way down into points. . . . Instead, although some folds are smaller than others to infinity, bodies are always extended, and points never become parts, but remain mere extrema.' Points, he would hold from now on, are of dimension 0, and thus not homogeneous with a line of dimension 1. A point is therefore to be distinguished from an infinitely small line segment, which must be homogeneous with the whole of which it is (fictional) part; it would therefore have extension, be further divisible, and would itself be bounded by endpoints.

On this conception of actual division, Leibniz will argue, bodies cannot be unities. They are pluralities, aggregates of the parts into which they are divided, but always further divided. They are thus infinite aggregates in the syncategorematic sense: no matter how many parts are taken, there are always more. Each part corresponds to an endeavour, but it always has within it other parts corresponding to their own endeavours. All the parts are actual, but there is no part so small that it does not contain another smaller part. But if there is no such thing as *one* body, 'it follows that there are no bodies either, these being nothing but one body after another. Hence, it follows that either bodies are mere phenomena, and not real entities, or that there is something other than extension in bodies' (A VI iv 1464/LoC 259). Bodies, if they are not to reduce to mere appearances, *presuppose* unities. This becomes one of Leibniz's favourite arguments for his monads: 'I hold that where there are only entities by aggregation, there will not be any real entities. For every entity by aggregation presupposes entities endowed with a true unity' (to Arnauld, 30 April 1687: GP ii 96/WFT 123). A body, that is, cannot be an aggregate of aggregates to infinity, since we would never arrive at anything it is aggregated from. What it is aggregated from cannot be extended, otherwise it would be divided, and therefore itself an aggregate. There must, therefore, be unextended unities everywhere in matter. As can be seen, this is a development of the argument Leibniz originally gave in response to Zeno's Paradox of the Dichotomy in the *TMA*. But one finds it even in the *Monadology*: in order for there to be composites – bodies that are aggregates – there must be unities. Since every actual part of a body presupposes such unities, and is infinitely divided into further such parts, there must be monads everywhere in matter.

To summarize, Leibniz's solution to the continuum problem falls into two parts. On the one hand, a body is a plurality – indeed, an infinite plurality: it is just all the unities or simples presupposed in all its actual parts. 'In actual things, the simples are prior to the aggregates' (GP ii 379/LDB 141). The reality of any phenomenal body is constituted by an infinity of these unities or monads; since such a unity is presupposed in any actual part of the body, their multiplicity 'is greater than any number whatever' (GP ii 282/LDV 333). To perceive or understand something as continuous, on the other hand, is to abstract from all the particularities of existence, to perceive it as an ideal thing, and 'in ideal things the whole is prior to the part' (GP ii 379/LDB 141). 'There are no divisions in it except those made by a mind' (GP ii 278/LDV 327). Its parts are indeterminate, and can be assigned as needed. Thus a continuous whole can be treated as if it consists in an infinity of infinitesimals; but although by such means one can represent truths, there are not such things in reality as infinite wholes or infinitely small parts.

Infinite Series, the Differential Calculus
and the Law of Continuity

This brings us to Leibniz's work on infinite series and the calculus. On his arrival in Paris in 1672, Leibniz devoted himself to a serious study of mathematics. At Huygens' suggestion he read the mathematical work of Pascal, where he found confirmation of his construal of infinitely small parts as dimensionally homogeneous with the whole they compose. On this conception, the area under a curve could be calculated by regarding it as made up of an infinity of infinitely small rectangular areas, each with the height of an ordinate and with an infinitesimal width. Thus the area could be expressed as a sum of an infinite series of terms.

This was serendipitous, since (with Huygens' encouragement) Leibniz had made swift progress in his studies of infinite series, discovering a simple relationship between a series of terms and a second series whose terms are the differences of the first, his 'Difference Principle'. If, from a given series A, one forms a difference series B whose terms are the differences of the successive terms of A, the sum of the terms in the B series is simply the difference between the last and first terms of the original series: 'the sum of the differences is the difference between the first term and the last' (A VII iii 9). As an example, suppose one wants to find the sum of the first five terms of the series of reciprocal triangular numbers, $T = \frac{1}{1} + \frac{1}{3} + \frac{1}{6} + \frac{1}{10} + \frac{1}{15} + \ldots$. Comparing T with the series of reciprocal natural numbers, $R = \frac{1}{1} + \frac{1}{2} + \frac{1}{3} + \frac{1}{4} + \frac{1}{5} + \ldots$, we see that each term of the T series is twice the difference between successive terms of the R series: $\frac{1}{1} = 2(\frac{1}{1} - \frac{1}{2})$, $\frac{1}{3} = 2(\frac{1}{2} - \frac{1}{3})$, $\frac{1}{6} = 2(\frac{1}{3} - \frac{1}{4})$, $\frac{1}{10} = 2(\frac{1}{4} - \frac{1}{5})$, and so on. So $\frac{1}{2}T$ is the difference series for the reciprocal numbers, R. Applying the Difference Principle, $\frac{1}{2}(T_1 + \ldots + T_5) = R_1 - R_6 = 1 - \frac{1}{6} = \frac{5}{6}$, so $(T_1 + \ldots + T_5) = \frac{5}{3}$. Extending this to infinite series, $\frac{1}{2}(T_1 + \ldots + T_\infty) = R_1 - R_\infty = 1 - \frac{1}{\infty} = 1$, so the sum of the infinite series $T = \frac{1}{1} + \frac{1}{3} + \frac{1}{6} + \frac{1}{10} + \frac{1}{15} + \ldots = 2$. This is to treat the infinite series *as if* it has a last, infinitieth term. But Leibniz is sensitive to the need for rigour, and, by replacing the infinitieth term by a yth term that can be made sufficiently small by taking y sufficiently large, demonstrates that the same result 'can come out in the infinite' (A VII iii 362).

With his characteristic genius for generalization, Leibniz extended the Difference Principle to continuous quantities, introducing the notation $\int$ to stand for the sum of a series of terms (whether discrete or continuously varying) and dx to stand for the difference of two consecutive values of x. In his own words, 'differences and sums are the inverses of each other, that is, the sum of the differences of a series is a term of the series, and the difference of the sums of a series is a term of the series; the former of which I express as $\int dx = x$, the latter as $d \int x = x'$ (Leibniz 1846: 36). In this way, by 1675 Leibniz had formulated what we now call the Fundamental Theorem of the Calculus, relating the area under a given curve to an expression for the slope of the tangent to a related curve at an arbitrary point x. Thus for a given curve y the area under the curve between $x = a$ and $x = b$ (its quadrature, Q) can be represented as an infinite sum of infinitesimal rectangles whose width is dx and whose height is $y(x)$, so that $Q = \int y(x)dx$. Now if one has an expression for the general term of another series $z(x)$ for which the difference between its successive terms is $dz = y(x)dx$, one may apply the Difference Principle: the sum of the differences equals the difference between the last term and the first – what we would now call the definite integral evaluated between first and last terms, $\int_a^b y(x)dx = [z(b) - z(a)]$. But as Leibniz had learned from Pascal, the slope of the tangent to a curve $z(x)$ at an arbitrary point x can be expressed as dz/dx, the quotient of the two sides of an infinitesimal right triangle, the 'characteristic triangle'. But by the definition of z, $dz = y(x)dx$, so that $dz/dx = y(x)$. This gives us the fundamental connection between the problems of finding the tangent to a curve, and determining quadratures, the areas under curves. Later, Leibniz will generalize this into an algorithm of extremely general application. Conceiving the taking of differences of a continuously varying quantity as the operation of 'differentiation', and that of taking the infinite sum as 'integration' (Bernoulli's term), the above reasoning shows (albeit non-rigorously) that the operations d/dx and $\int dx$ are inverses of one another.

In a paper of October 1674 that is particularly germane to the interpretation of the calculus, Leibniz uses his emerging techniques to calculate two areas under a hyperbola. The first is an area A under the curve between the lines $x = 0$ and $x = 1$, which he calculates as $A = 1 + \frac{1}{2} + \frac{1}{3} + \frac{1}{4} + \frac{1}{5} + \ldots$, a sum which is infinite. The second is an area B under the curve which can be seen to be a finite part of the infinite area A. Leibniz calculates B as $1 - \frac{1}{2} + \frac{1}{3} - \frac{1}{4} + \frac{1}{5} - \ldots$. Therefore $A - B = (1-1) + (\frac{1}{2} + \frac{1}{2}) + (\frac{1}{3} - \frac{1}{3}) + (\frac{1}{4} + \frac{1}{4}) + (\frac{1}{5} - \frac{1}{5}) + \ldots = 1 + \frac{1}{2} + \frac{1}{3} + \frac{1}{4} + \frac{1}{5} + \ldots$. But this equals A! As Leibniz notes, 'the area of the space [A] remains the same even when the finite space [B] is subtracted from it'. From this he concludes that 'the infinite is not a whole, but only a fiction; for otherwise the part would be equal to the whole' (A VII iii 468).

The area under the hyperbola is a wonderfully visualizable example of an infinite whole which violates the part–whole axiom. But Leibniz is aware of other examples, such as the set S of all square numbers as part of the set N of all natural numbers. Every natural number has a square, so there are as many numbers as squares, and $S = N$. But some of the natural numbers are non-squares, so S is only a part of N: the part equals the whole. Since he takes the part–whole axiom to be constitutive of quantity, Leibniz concludes that such examples establish the impossibility of infinite wholes and infinite quantities and collections generally. Having reached this conclusion in 1676, he holds it from then on: 'there is no infinite number, nor infinite line or other infinite quantity, if these are taken to be genuine wholes' (NE 157). There is an actual infinite, but it must be understood *syncategorematically*: to say that a series has infinitely many terms means not that it has N terms where N is greater than any finite number, but that for any finite N it has more terms than that, 'more terms than one can specify'. Thus, since there is no completion of an infinite series, there is no infinite collection of its terms, and therefore, strictly speaking, no sum.

Nevertheless, as Leibniz's work on infinite series and the calculus demonstrates, one can still treat such an infinite series as approaching arbitrarily close to a quantity which can therefore be regarded as its sum, under the fiction that it has a last, infinitieth term. The fictional infinitely small last term then stands for the fact that one can make the error in terminating the series after a finite number of terms smaller than any pre-assigned error.

By 1676 Leibniz has already developed these arguments for the fictional character of the infinite and the infinitesimal into a sophisticated foundation for the calculus. On this conception, an infinitesimal is a *compendium* (an abbreviated expression) for a variable finite quantity that can be made as small as desired. That any magnitude can be made as small as desired is guaranteed by the Archimedean axiom: 'Those magnitudes are said to have a ratio to one another which are capable, when multiplied, of exceeding one another' (Euclid's *Elements*, Book V, Def. 4). This implies that no matter how small a geometric quantity is given, a smaller can be found. The infinitesimal is treated *as if* it is an actual quantity in certain defined circumstances, although one that can be ignored by comparison with a finite quantity. For example, in a formula obtained by treating dx as a non-zero quantity, the neglect of resulting expressions involving dx in comparison with x is justified by reference to the Archimedean axiom. If $y = x + dx$, where dx is an arbitrarily small variable quantity, and D is any pre-assigned difference between y and x, no matter how small, then dx may always be taken so small that $dx < D$. Therefore, since dx, the difference between y and x, is smaller than any assignable, it is unassignable, and effectively null.

Building on these ideas, Leibniz formulated his influential Law of Continuity. In its first version, in *On a General Principle . . .* of 1687, it runs: 'when the difference between two instances in a given series (or in what is supposed) can be diminished below any given magnitude whatever, the corresponding difference in the things sought (or in what results) must also become diminished below any given magnitude' (GP iii 51/L 351). This is a generalization of the approach to the calculus based on the Archimedean Axiom, where the neglecting of 'unassignable quantities' is justified by the claim that any quantity that can be made smaller than any given quantity can be set equal to zero. Thus a difference that can be made smaller than any given (finite) difference is effectively null. More informally, 'Nature never makes leaps.'

Leibniz was very proud of his Law of Continuity, which he regarded as an architectonic principle that could be used as a touchstone for the consistency of theories, as well as a fruitful principle of discovery. In his 1687 paper he applied it to show how Descartes's Rules of Collision (still adhered to by Malebranche) could not be upheld: by allowing the difference in magnitude of two unequal bodies (rule 2) to diminish to nothing, he found the result incompatible with what was predicted for rule 1. Similar incongruities could be derived from applying the law to the differences in the other cases covered in Descartes's rules.

The close connection among Leibniz's various principles can also be illustrated by applying this law to qualitative differences, and interpreting 'assignable' as 'discernible'. Then any difference that is smaller than any difference that can be discerned is null. That is, indiscernible things are identical. This is Leibniz's famous *Principle of the Identity of Indiscernibles*.

Contingent Existents and Possible Worlds

Leibniz's mathematical ideas about the nature of the actual infinite were to play a crucial role in helping him to resolve a severe difficulty about contingent existence. To see how, we need first to return to a consideration of his theory of truth and the three great principles it is based on: Contradiction, Sufficient Reason and Perfection.

Leibniz's early combinatoric approach to truth depended heavily on what he would later call the *Principle of Contradiction*, 'by virtue of which we judge to be false that which involves a contradiction' (*Monadology* § 31: GP vi 612/WFT 272). If, when we analyse a concept into its constituent terms, we find among them both A and not-A, we have established that this is an *impossible* concept. Similarly, when a proposition is such that its subject can be analysed to contain some term A while its predicate contains a term not-A (or vice versa), then the proposition is necessarily *false*. On the other hand, a proposition whose opposite involves a contradiction is necessarily *true*. Suppose now, given some proposition 'A is B', we have definitions of all the terms involved in the analysis of the proposition, such as A = CD, B = EFG, and so on. If by a process of substituting terms in the analysis of both subject and predicate by their definitions we can show that A is not not-A, we will have proved the proposition true; equivalently, we will have proved that the original proposition reduces to an identity, A is A. Thus, demonstrating the truth of a proposition is equivalent to reducing it to an identity, a view Leibniz has already articulated in *On the Secrets of Motion* of summer 1676: 'Every demonstration is made by a resolution into identical propositions by means of definitions' (Hess 1978: 203). Crucially, all such demonstrations must involve only a *finite* number of steps, for otherwise an identity would never have been reached.

All of this, however, concerns necessary or 'eternal truths', those which are logically true by virtue of the relations among combinations of concepts. In his *Dissertation*, as we saw, Leibniz regarded the truth of contingent propositions, such as 'Augustus was Emperor of the Romans', to depend on the divine will. Although there would be a reason known to God for establishing such contingent facts, this would be beyond our ken, and we would have to fall back on experience to establish their truth. That there would have to be a reason for every fact, including contingent ones, is of course an instance of Leibniz's second great principle, the *Principle of Sufficient Reason*: 'there can be no real or existing fact, no true proposition, without there being a sufficient reason why it should be so and not otherwise, though in most cases these reasons cannot be known to us' (*Monadology* § 31: GP vi 612/WFT 272). Leibniz had already stated this principle in a paper of 1671–2. But there he also offers a demonstration of it, derived from Hobbes, which is worth noting. He defines a 'sufficient reason' as 'that which, being given, the thing exists', and a 'requisite' as 'that which, not being given, the thing does not exist'. It follows that whatever exists has all its requisites, since if it lacked any of them it would not exist (by the definition of 'requisite'). Likewise, given all its requisites, the thing must exist, since if it lacked any of its requisites, it would not exist. Thus, by the definition of 'sufficient reason', all the requisites constitute a sufficient reason for the thing's existence. It follows that 'whatever exists has a sufficient reason' (A VI ii 483/DSR xxiii).

This theory of requisites, however, would seem to have some radical consequences, as Leibniz proceeded to discover on the eve of his visit to Spinoza in 1676. The 'ultimate reason of things', or God, would have to 'contain by itself the aggregate of all requisites of all things' (A VI iii 573/DSR 93). This ultimate reason of all things would then be unique. But then so would be their essence, 'given that an essence is the aggregate of all primary requisites'. Thus the essence of all things is the same, and 'things differ only modally, just as a town viewed from the highest point differs from the town seen from a plain' (573/95). But this is just Spinoza's view! And from it – as Leibniz seems to have discovered on meeting with him – the Dutch philosopher drew the following conclusion: 'there is absolutely nothing in things on account of which they can be called contingent' (Spinoza 1882: *Ethics* IP33S). We call things contingent when we are insufficiently knowledgeable about all the causes involved in their production. But if all the requisites for a thing's existence are in place, then that thing must occur. Therefore, Spinoza concludes, everything that happens happens out of strict necessity. People's freedom consists only in this, 'that they are conscious of their actions and ignorant of the causes by which they are determined' (IIP35S).

For reasons to be explored in chapter 8, Leibniz had initially accepted Spinoza's views about human freedom as compatible with his own. But after meeting with Spinoza in December 1676, he realized he was on the brink of falling into necessitarianism. What drew him back from this precipice, he tells us in *On Freedom and Contingency* of 1689, was 'a consideration of those possibles which do not exist, have not existed, and never will exist' (A VI iv 1653/AG 94). For, he explains, 'if there are possibles that never exist, then the things that exist cannot always be necessary'.

In a paper of 1677 entitled *That Not All Possibles Come into Existence*, we can see Leibniz arguing exactly this (A VI iv 1352). He gives the example of a world consisting only of spherical bodies. This in itself entails nothing contradictory, but it is incompatible (he argues) with other shapes of bodies coming into existence. So 'something possible in itself cannot exist because of other supposed things, that is, because of the state of the universe' (1352). That is, Leibniz realizes, the reason why certain things do not exist is not because they are impossible in themselves, or have concepts that contain a contradiction, but because they do not fit in with what exists in the actual world. Questions of existence are quite distinct from questions of possibility. As he writes in *On Freedom and Necessity* (*c.* 1680–4), 'the reason why some contingent thing exists rather than others should not be sought in its definition alone, but in a comparison with others' (A VI iv 1445/AG 19). Thus Leibniz was led to his idea of a *possible world*: a world of possible individuals (like the spherical bodies) whose states are compatible with one another throughout their existence, even if incompatible with the states of things that actually occur.

Thinking in terms of possible worlds has become so commonplace now that it is hard to appreciate that Leibniz was breaking new ground here. For according to the Aristotelian position embraced by Descartes, Hobbes and Spinoza, if a state of things is possible, it must occur at some time, whether past, present or future; if it occurs at all times, it is necessary; and if it never occurs, it is impossible.[1] By contrast, Leibniz has advanced a logical interpretation of possibility that makes no reference to time: an individual is possible if its concept contains no contradiction, and impossible if its concept does contain a contradiction. Existence is another matter. Whether a possible world will actually be brought into existence depends, Leibniz asserts, on the amount of perfection it contains. Since God is perfect, He will create the world containing the greatest degree of perfection. Earlier, Leibniz had called this principle 'the principle of the harmony of things': whatever is more perfect, or has more reason to exist than other things, will exist rather than them (A VI iii 472/LoC 45). Here he calls it the *Principle of Perfection*. Thus, whereas possibility and necessity are decided by the Principle of Contradiction, 'all truths concerning contingent things or the existence of things rest on the principle of perfection', where the perfection lies not in the thing taken in itself, but in its harmonious coexistence with other things (A VI iv 1445/AG 19).

In the same paper, Leibniz illustrates this distinction by reference to a perfect pentagon. 'The pentagon is not absolutely impossible, nor does it imply a contradiction, even if it follows from the harmony of things that a pentagon can find no place among real things' (1448/21). Actually, though, the example of the pentagon is potentially misleading, and it will be instructive to see why. For according to Leibniz's considered theory, it is not the kind of entity that *could* exist – it simply does not have the required complexity to qualify as an existing thing. There would be no possibility of it existing at a particular time and place, since its concept contains no spatial and temporal relations to other things, as would the complete concept of an individual. As Leibniz says of the similar example raised by Arnauld of a sphere, the concept of such an abstract kind or species is incomplete: it 'contains only eternal or necessary truths, whereas the concept of an individual contains, considered as possible, what in fact exists or what is related to the existence of things and to time' (GP ii 39/AG 70). The concept of a concrete individual sphere, like the one on Alexander's tomb, would include reference to 'the matter it is made from, the place, the time, and the other circumstances which by a continual sequence would finally envelop the whole succession of the universe, if one could pursue all that these notions entail' (39/70).

This illustrates an important feature of Leibniz's complete concept theory of truth and its connection with his criterion of contingency. This is that questions of existence and contingency (as opposed to possibility) necessarily involve a consideration of *time*. The complete concept of an individual must embrace not only simple concepts but also all the predicates that are true of it at any given time. Thus the complete concept of an individual substance is not simply a set of predicates, since the predicates true of the individual change from one instant to the next. It involves, rather, an *order* of states, with the predicates that are true of the subject at any given time corresponding to one of these states. Likewise, in order for two individuals to belong to the same possible world, any predicate ascribable to one at a given time must be compatible with every predicate ascribable to every other coexisting thing at the same time. For this, Leibniz coined a new word: *compossibility*. Any two possible things whose states are compatible with each other throughout their existences are *compossible*; a possible world is then an aggregate of compossible individuals. There is, moreover, a generating principle (the 'law of the series') which produces the ordering of these states, where simpler states contain the reason for more complex ones. The simpler ones are 'prior by nature' to the more complex ones; and, as we shall see in chapter 7, this order is the basis for their temporal ordering.

By itself, however, this inclusion of a temporal ordering in the complete concept does not solve the problem of contingency, but only exacerbates it. For according to his theory of truth, Leibniz explains in *On Freedom and Contingency*, 'in every true affirmative proposition, universal or particular, necessary or contingent, the concept of the predicate is involved somehow in the concept of the subject'. But then 'if at a given time the concept of the predicate is in the concept of the subject, how, without contradiction and impossibility, could the subject then lack the predicate while leaving its concept unchanged?' (A VI iv 1654/AG 95). Moreover, if a predicate truly applies to a subject at a given time, and this is derivable from its concept, then this cannot *not* be true. That is, it will be necessarily true that the predicate applies to it at that time. But in that case there would be no contingent truths.

Thus the supposition of uncreated possible worlds is merely a supposition: Leibniz needed to demonstrate its possibility.

Truth, Contingency and Incommensurables

Here, Leibniz informs us, 'a new and unexpected light dawned from where I least expected it, namely from mathematical considerations on the nature of the infinite' (1654/95). This illumination depends on an analogy with incommensurables in geometry which, he grants in *On Contingency* of 1689, 'is hard to understand if one does not have a smattering of mathematics' (A VI iv 1650 /AG 28). Perhaps for this reason he left it out of his account of contingency in the *Theodicy*. But he does explain the analogy elsewhere, and it is not that hard to understand. To see how infinity comes into it, though, we need to say a little more about requisites.

In April 1676 Leibniz had already realized that the divine attributes – which he had taken to be the *summa genera* from which all individual concepts must be combined – must be distinguished from requisites of existing things. For the divine attributes are affirmative and indefinable, and therefore necessarily compatible with one another. Requisites, on the other hand, involve connections among the modifications of attributes, modifications that vary in place and time. As a result, 'sensible things cannot be perfectly understood by us, since infinitely many things concur in their being constituted, because of the divisibility to infinity of time and place. Hence it happens that the perception of a sensible quality is not one perception, but an aggregate of infinitely many perceptions' (A VI iii 515/DSR 71). Thus requisites involve a connection among perceptions, and pertain not to essence, but to existence at a particular time. Now since a requisite 'can only be conceived through others' – and an actual infinity of others, given the infinite division of space and time – it follows that the sufficient reason for any existing thing involves an actual infinity of requisites.

Thus the complete concept of an individual thing is distinguished from that of an abstract entity like a sphere by its infinitude. Still, it is possible that this actual infinity of requisites for any of its states could be resolved into one sufficient reason. One would then have an infinite series of states each constituting the sufficient reason for the next, much as Spinoza had envisaged. Although the individual itself would be contingent, the sequence of its states would be necessary. What Leibniz needed to demonstrate was that although there is a reason for a contingent predicate's applying at a given time, this reason is not deducible from its concept or from any preceding state.

This is where the mathematical analogy with incommensurables comes into play. In geometry, two lines are said to be commensurable when a common measure for them can be found. For example, if one has a right triangle with sides 117, 156 and 195 metres long, one can find by inspection a common measure for any two of the sides, namely 39 metres. Thus 195 divided by 117 is 5×39 divided by 3×39, $= \frac{5}{3}$, and $156/117 = \frac{4}{3}$. But for other cases a common measure cannot be found. For example, it might be supposed that the area of a circle would have a determinable ratio to the area of a square erected on its diameter. Indeed, several of Leibniz's contemporaries – most notoriously, Hobbes – were confident that they could find a finite expression for this ratio of πr^2 to $(2r)^2$, or $\pi{:}4$, thus 'squaring the circle'. Now, it is possible to find an expression for $\pi/4$ involving only finite ratios. One of Leibniz's own notable discoveries in his work on infinite series was the so-called 'Leibniz series', expressing $\pi/4$ by an infinite series with alternating signs: $\pi/4 = 1 - 1/3 + 1/5 - 1/7 + 1/9 - 1/11 + \ldots$

Terminating this series after some very large finite number of terms gives us a good value for $\pi/4$, but then there will be 'a new remainder that results in a new quotient', which itself is explicable as a series of infinitely many further quotients. This, Leibniz held, is analogous to a contingent truth: a contingent truth 'involves infinitely many reasons, but in such a way that there is always something that remains for which we must again give some reason' (*On the Origin of Contingent Truths*: A VI iv 1662/AG 99). But given

Leibniz's doctrine explained above that all demonstrations must involve only a *finite* number of steps, this means it is impossible for there to be a demonstration of a contingent truth, since such a demonstration would require an infinite analysis.

> In necessary propositions, of course, one arrives at an equation of identity by means of an analysis continued to a certain point; and this is precisely what it means to demonstrate truth with geometrical rigour. In contingent propositions, however, the analysis proceeds to infinity, through reasons for reasons, so that there is never a full demonstration; nevertheless, the reason for the truth always subsists, although it can be perfectly understood only by God, who alone can go through the infinite series in a single mental thrust. (1650/28)

Although God has certain knowledge of each contingent truth, He knows the reason for it intuitively, not by resolving it into all its constituent reasons. By defining a contingent truth as one in which, although the predicate is in the concept of the subject, it is impossible for this to be demonstrated, Leibniz has proved its possibility, a possibility revealed to him by the analogy with incommensurables. It is true that Adam ate the apple, but his not having eaten it implies no contradiction. There is therefore another possible world in which Adam (or at least someone indistinguishable from him in all relevant respects) does not eat the apple.[2]

Applying the Calculus

Perhaps the most notable way in which Leibniz's mathematics informs his philosophy, however, is in his conception of a monad or simple substance by analogy with infinite series. He explains this to his correspondent Burchard de Volder in 1704 as follows:

> The succeeding substance is held to be the same when the same law of the series, or of continuous simple transition, persists; which is what produces our belief that the subject of change, or monad, is the same. That there should be such a persistent law, which involves the future states of that which we conceive to be the same, is exactly what I say constitutes it as the same substance. (GP ii 264 /LDV 291)

Thus, to take a simple example, if the first term of a geometric series is 3 and the law of the series is to multiply each term by $-1/3$ to get its successor, then from a particular term in the series, such as $1/3$, we can determine the next term in the series and all those following it: –1/9, 1/27, –1/81, and so on. Analogously, Leibniz reasoned, since God has perfect foreknowledge of everything that will happen to any individual substance, and creates each one to be autonomous and self-sufficient, there must be a 'law' by which each state of a substance 'tends toward or pre-involves its following state'. Accordingly, 'every present state of a simple substance is a natural consequence of its preceding state, so that the present is pregnant with the future' (*Monadology* § 22: GP vi 610/WFT 271). As we saw above, however, although each state involves a reason for the subsequent states of the same monad, the sufficient reason or sum of requisites for each state is infinite: between any two states, there is an infinite chain of intermediate states, unlike in the simple example of the geometric series. The law governing the series of states of each individual substance is known intuitively by God, but is completely unknowable by us.

In the same correspondence with De Volder (as well as in published writings), Leibniz applies the analogy with infinite series also to *force*: 'derivative force is the present state itself insofar as it tends towards a following state, i.e. it pre-involves the following state . . . primitive force is the law of the series, as it were, while derivative force is the determinate value which distinguishes some term in the series' (GP ii 262/LDV 287). As we'll see in chapter 6, Leibniz conceives primitive forces as enduring powers, and derivative forces as instantaneous modifications of primitive forces. In his physics, derivative forces are represented by differentials, denoting perhaps the differences between successive terms of a continuous series, rather than the terms themselves. Leibniz uses them to set up differential equations, as in his derivation of the inverse square law for gravity (chapter 6).

One of the main applications of differentials is in solving problems involving the optimization of paths. Here Leibniz pioneered the modern technique of determining a maximum or minimum of a quantity by setting its differential equal to 0. In this way he was able to solve such problems as determining the optimal path of a refracted light ray, or the shape of a hanging chain ('the catenary'), or the curve of shortest descent between two given points ('the brachistone'). The latter two are particularly interesting in that they illustrate how 'the optimum of these forms and figures is found not only in the whole but in the part' (GP vii 272). In the brachistone, for example, 'if we choose any two other points on this curve, the portion of the curve between them is again necessarily the curve of shortest descent with respect to them' (272). For Leibniz this is an example of how 'the least parts of the universe are ruled according to the order of greatest perfection; otherwise the whole would not be' (272–3). In other words, optimal behaviour in any part of the created world contributes to it being the best of all possible worlds.

We will return to the matter of the perfection of the universe in chapters 6 and 8 below. But first we need to give a detailed treatment of Leibniz's innovations in metaphysics, and how he came to make them.

5

The Reform of Metaphysics

Leibniz's mature philosophy is conventionally dated as beginning in 1686, the year in which he 'went public', after a fashion, announcing his reform of metaphysics in his *Discourse on Metaphysics* and consequent correspondence with Arnauld. The prominence in those works of his predicate-in-notion principle led Russell to take it as the founding premise of Leibniz's mature philosophy. In fact, though, Leibniz had formulated his predicate-in-notion principle in his logical studies of the late 1670s, and had by then already made most of the theoretical advances announced to Arnauld: by 1679 he had concluded that all bodies contained a kind of sensation and appetite, proposed that every mind perceives confusedly everything that happens in the universe, discovered the conservation of *vis viva*, identified substance with force, and announced the rehabilitation of substantial forms. What was novel in the 1680s was not the principle itself, but the way in which Leibniz had managed to integrate it with his new views on substance, body and motion, and to complete his theory of truth through his newly discovered account of contingency, treated above in chapter 4. So, as we shall see in this chapter, Leibniz's innovations in ontology were the result of his sustained reflections about metaphysics, not logic. And these date from ten years earlier, which is where we will begin.

Metaphysical Problems and Insights

From late 1675 through 1676, Leibniz applied himself in earnest to the study of metaphysics. This was prompted in part by the deepening of his understanding of the infinite and infinitely small, which (as we have seen) made his former conception of the relation of mind to matter extremely problematic. During the same time, however, he was much stimulated by what he could learn of Spinoza's philosophy through his friend and younger contemporary in Paris, Ehrenfried Walther von Tschirnhaus, who as a student at Leiden in *c.* 1673–5 had been admitted to the circle of Spinoza's confidants. The result was a series of draft manuscripts for which Leibniz had suggested the title *De Summa Rerum*, a phrase that may mean either 'on the totality of things' or 'on the Supreme Being' – an ambiguity, we may note, that evokes Spinoza's equating of God with the natural universe in his provocative formula *Deus sive natura*, 'God, or nature', even if Leibniz himself did not intend to equate them.

Let us sketch some of the difficulties in Leibniz's own views that were concerning him at this time. This will enable us to get a perspective on how his philosophy was both inspired by his engagement with Spinoza's, and yet conditioned by his desire to avoid those views of Spinoza he disagreed with. (He will later take strong exception to Spinoza's position on necessity and freedom of the will, but this disagreement was not obvious to him in 1676, as we'll see in chapter 8.) Such a comparison will give us some insight into just how Leibniz's reform of metaphysics came about, and how the various strands constituting his mature conception of substance come together into one coherent picture.

First of all, there was the problem of what is responsible for the *unity of bodies*. As we saw in chapter 3, Leibniz had originally adopted a kind of atomism, where his hollow mind-containing atoms or *bullae* were held together by the overlapping of the boundaries of the parts of their crust moving with differing endeavours. And, as we also saw there, he had strong motivations for wanting to retain these mind-containing atoms, especially in connection with issues such as preformation and the resurrection of soul and body. But as he developed his mathematics of the infinite and infinitely small, this explanation of their cohesion in terms of overlapping points had come to seem untenable. As a result, he was struggling to provide an account of how the atoms were held together. This was only accentuated by his conviction, arising from his mathematical studies, that an infinite aggregate of parts could not constitute a true whole or unity. Thus in the manuscripts of the *De Summa Rerum* we find him speculating that matter is actually infinitely divided all the way down into points, and that these material points are welded into a solid body or atom 'by motion or by a mind of some sort', and vacillating on whether he had proved this. In one manuscript, dated 18 March 1676, he reasons that if the minds of two mind-containing bodies were to coalesce when their bodies collided, then one of the minds would cease to exist, contrary to the indestructibility of minds that he argued for. So there must be a portion of the body that is 'solid and unbreakable'. Unless there were such unbreakable portions of matter 'informed by a mind of some kind', Leibniz argues, they would all have been dissipated long ago by the actions of the surrounding matter (A VI iii 393/LoC 59). He concludes: 'it follows that thought enters into the formation of this portion, and that, whatever its size, it becomes a body that is single and indissectible, i.e. an atom, whenever it has a single mind' (393/57).

So a second problem Leibniz is wrestling with in 1676 is the *mind–body problem*, in relation both to bodies in general and to human beings in particular. 'What I believe', he wrote on 15 April, 'is that the solidity or unity of body is due to the mind, that there are as many minds as vortices, and as many vortices as solid bodies' (509/117). Thus at this time Leibniz was still entertaining the idea that every atom contains a mind or soul, each associated with its own vortex. In February he had written that the human soul perceives 'by means of a certain liquid, or if you prefer, an ethereal substance, continuous, and diffused through the whole body . . . which inflates, contracts and dilates the nerves' (A VI iii 480/DSR 35). His speculations on the relation of mind and brain are decidedly physicalist. The soul is described as 'a kind of font of motion and dilation in the liquid' that is capable of acting on matter. 'Moreover, every kind of gyration seems to be performed in the cavities of the brain, as the soul observes its own vortex.' Appearances are 'nothing but undulations of the liquid impressed on it', each such undulation being 'conserved forever, even if, when compounded with others, it becomes imperceptible'. That 'the soul itself should agitate the vortex' Leibniz writes, is a 'wonder'. 'But it does so nonetheless, for we do not act through a simple mechanism (*machina*), but through reflections, i.e. actions, on ourselves' (480/37).

In the summer of 1676, however, Leibniz underwent a kind of conversion from the materialist trend of these speculations. This may have been induced by his reading of Plato's dialogues, two of which he was then translating, particularly the passage from Plato's *Phaedo* where Socrates criticizes his former teacher Anaxagoras for 'introducing mind but making no use of it' (Plato, *Phaedo* 97b–99c).

We know that Leibniz was particularly taken with this passage, since he mentions it in the *Discourse on Metaphysics* § 20, leaving a note to himself to insert a translation there of 'a memorable passage by Socrates in Plato's *Phaedo*, against over-materialistic philosophers' (GP iv 446; GP ii 13). In the passage in question the condemned Socrates chooses to remain in captivity even when it is made clear to him that he could escape. Plato suggests that Socrates' remaining on the bench in prison cannot be understood in terms of matter and motion, but can only be understood teleologically: that is, in terms of his mind acting according to its own end-directed laws, in step with his body acting according to the laws appropriate to matter. Any model of the mind such as Leibniz had previously been entertaining, where the mind acts on the matter of its own vortex, he would from now on reject out of hand as too naïve. Reinforcing him in this opinion would have been the occasionalist arguments familiar to him from his discussions with Malebranche and Cordemoy during his four years in Paris. Malebranche (in company with Cordemoy and La Forge) argued that the purely passive nature of body – conceived as mere extended substance – precludes it from having any power to 'transmit to another body the power transporting it' (Malebranche [1674–5] 1980: 660), a power which must therefore reside only in God. Although Leibniz wanted each body to contain its own principle of activity, and thus to be more than mere extended substance, he had to concede to Malebranche that there was no way to conceive how such a principle could act on anything outside of itself, even its own body. Thus, as Leibniz explains much later in an unsent note for his correspondent Des Bosses in 1709, he came to see that his earlier speculations about souls in points being multiplied by dividing their bodies involved a kind of 'category mistake'. 'Those things which pertain to extension', he writes, 'should not be attributed to souls, and their unity and multitude should not be taken from the category of quantity, but rather from the category of substance' (GP ii 372/LDB 129).

Another way in which Leibniz conceived the mind as serving as a principle of a body is as its *principle of individuation*, and this constitutes a third problem he was concerned with in 1676. As we saw in chapter 1, Leibniz had cut his teeth on this problem as a student, concluding that each individual substance is individuated by the intrinsic principles which constitute its whole being. Subsequently he had rejected such Scholastic accounts, concluding in his *Philosopher's Confession* of 1672 that souls or minds are individuated by considerations of place and time. Using the example of two perfectly similar eggs, Leibniz argues there that you could nevertheless identify which egg is which if you were able to 'continuously follow the motion of each, through each place, either with your eyes or hands or some other kind of contact'. Thus 'to ask why this soul rather than another is subjected from the beginning to these circumstances of time and place (and from which the entire series of life, death, salvation or damnation arises)', Leibniz writes, 'is to ask why this soul is this soul' (A VI iii 148).

Leibniz builds on this argument in his studies of 1676. In a piece entitled *Meditation on the Principle of Individuation*, dated 1 April, he assumes that if two perfectly similar things have been produced, then the only way they could be distinguished is through their different histories. He gives the example of two perfectly similar squares, one that has been produced by the coming together of two triangles, the other, by the coming together of two rectangles. If they are to be existing things, Leibniz argues, each square should somehow bear the mark of its individual history, and this will be its principle of individuation. But if their different histories are not 'discernible in the squares that have been produced', then it will follow that the principle of individuation will be 'outside the thing, in its cause', and then 'the one thing will not differ from the other in itself', contrary to the assumption. Here Leibniz appeals to the principle that 'the effect involves its cause – that is, in such a way that whoever perfectly understands some effect will also arrive at a knowledge of its cause' (A VI iii 490/DSR 51). But two squares that are perfectly similar 'cannot be distinguished from one another even by the wisest being'. Therefore 'it is impossible that two squares of this kind should be perfectly similar'. This marks the first (implicit) appearance of Leibniz's Principle of the Identity of Indiscernibles: 'two different things always differ in themselves in some respect as well' (491/51). Conversely, two things that are perfectly similar must be abstractions: they cannot be existing things.

From this line of reasoning, Leibniz derives some important consequences. First, 'matter is not homogeneous': two portions of Cartesian extended matter of the same shape and size, mutually at rest, could not be distinguished one from the other. This becomes one of Leibniz's main arguments against the atoms and corpuscles assumed by his contemporaries. Thus we find him deploying it in his reading notes on the atomist Cordemoy in 1685. Cordemoy had defined atoms as portions of Cartesian extended matter of a certain shape and size that were strictly indivisible. But, Leibniz argued, two perfectly similar atoms formed from the coalescing of differing shapes, being strictly homogeneous, could bear no marks of their histories, and thus would be indistinguishable (A VI iv 1799/LoC 279). Such atoms would therefore be mere abstractions, not anything that could exist in reality. Second, Leibniz concluded that since we cannot think of anything else by which existing matter would 'retain the effect of its former state' save a mind, any portion of existing matter (an existing body) will have a kind of mind as its principle of individuation. (Today, knowing about such things as metal fatigue in aircraft, we could go along with the idea of inhomogeneous matter bearing traces of its history without being persuaded by Leibniz's appeal to mind.) Implicit in this reasoning about the principle of individuation is also a further consequence that Leibniz will later draw out explicitly: in order to retain a memory of its 'circumstances of time and place', the mind (or an analogue thereof) will have to contain within it at any time some sense of the body's spatial relations to coexisting things, as well as traces of its own individual history.

Related to these problems concerning the relation of mind to body was a further problem about *action in bodies* that was troubling Leibniz, this one involving the continuity of motion that a principle of action was supposed to supply. Previously he had taken the principle of action to be an endeavour, conceived as an infinitely small element of motion, so that a continuous motion would consist in a string of infinitely many endeavours. By April 1676, however, he had come to reject the reality of infinitesimals, including infinitesimal elements of motion. 'I have demonstrated elsewhere very recently', he proclaimed in a manuscript written at the beginning of that month, 'that endeavours are true motions, not infinitely small ones' (*On Motion and Matter*: A VI iii 492/LoC 75). This would appear to be a reference to his syncategorematic interpretation of infinitesimals, discussed in chapter 4 above: they are not infinitely small actuals, but in fact stand for arbitrarily small but finite quantities. At any rate, Leibniz interprets this as implying that motion is not after all continuous, but instead consists in a succession of very small, finite motions along the tangents to a given curved trajectory. 'From this it will follow', he writes, 'that there is no really curvilinear motion in things which endeavour along tangents.' Otherwise, if instead a continuous motion were conceived as involving a different (infinitely small) endeavour at each instant, 'time would be actually divided into instants, which is not possible' (492/75). Thus Leibniz declares the impossibility of the perfectly parabolic motion envisaged by Galileo, where the motion at each instant is compounded from an inertial motion in a tangent and an acceleration due to gravity: 'So there will be no uniformly accelerated motion anywhere, and so the parabola will not be describable in this way' (492/75) (This criticism will resurface much later in Leibniz's reaction to Newton's proof of the inverse square law in his *Principia*.)

With continuous motion thus rejected, Leibniz concludes that the only alternative is for it to occur by leaps:

> I am forced to conclude that motion is not continuous, but happens by a leap: that is to say that a body, staying for some time in one place, may immediately afterwards be found to be in another place; i.e. that matter is extinguished here, and reproduced elsewhere. Yet a mind always remains intact that assists it. (494/79)

This assisting mind, Leibniz argues here, is not the individual mind contained in each body, but the 'universal mind', that is, God 'understanding a certain relation' (493/77). Leibniz coins a new term for this idea that motion is continued by the direct action of the divine mind in accordance with a certain relation: *transcreation* (or, equivalently, *transproduction*.) 'Even though everything is new,' he explains a little later, 'still, by the very fact that this transproduction happens by a certain law, continuous motion is imitated in a way, just as polygons imitate the circle' (*Infinite Numbers*: A VI iii 503/LoC 99). This is the main theme of *Pacidius to Philalethes*, the dialogue Leibniz wrote on his way to see Spinoza, discussed in chapter 3. There he concludes that 'action in a body cannot be conceived except through a kind of aversion. If you really cut to the quick and inspect every single moment, there is no action' (A VI iii 566/LoC 211). So, transcreation is necessary: 'the special operation of God is necessary for change among things' (569/211) – a position Leibniz will soon forcefully reject when he sees how to attribute action to creatures.

But Leibniz has another motivation for bringing God into play as the immediate cause of a continuing motion, and this concerns the laws of collision of bodies. A universal mind is needed to ensure that the bodies follow a law of collision in such a way that 'magnitude compensates for speed' (A VI iii 493/LoC 77). This is a reference to the fact that the 'quantity of motion' in a given direction (what we now know as momentum, the sum of the products of the bodies' masses and velocities) is conserved in every collision. Now if all motion is relative, and only relative motion is conserved, as Leibniz had learned from Huygens in Paris, this means that every collision must occur in such a way that the quantity of motion is conserved no matter which body is taken to be at rest. So motion does not appear to be a property of individual mind-containing bodies. As Leibniz explicitly concluded in early 1677, 'its subject will not be any one individual body, but the whole world' (A VI iv 1970/LoC 229). The absolute motion we imagine is 'nothing but an affection of our soul' which occurs when we consider ourselves or other things as being at rest, 'since we are able to understand everything more easily when these things are considered as immobile'.

We have considered five main problems that were concerning Leibniz in 1676: (1) that of the unity of bodies; (2) that of the relation of mind to matter; (3) that of individuation; (4) that of accounting for action in bodies; and (5) that of determining the subject of motion, given its relativity. Now we are in a position to evaluate his engagement with Spinoza's philosophy in this period.

Leibniz's Reaction to Spinoza's Philosophy

First, concerning the unity of bodies, Spinoza had also seen this as a major problem in Cartesianism. We already examined in chapter 4 the importance of the 'argument from the solid in a liquid' that Leibniz probably found in Spinoza's exposition of Descartes's *Principles*: the argument that a solid body immersed off-centre in a circulating fluid would actually divide the fluid to infinity, which Leibniz took as a proof that existing matter is actually infinitely divided, and thus infinitely complex. When in April 1676 he lays his hands on Spinoza's *Letter on the Infinite* – which he had received from Schuller, along with the definitions of God and substance from the unpublished *Ethics* – he finds the argument repeated again. There Spinoza is scathing about 'those who hold extended substance to be made up of parts or bodies really distinct from one another' (A VI iii 278/LoC 107). The point is that if bodies are conceived as divided, then they must be actually infinitely divided, as 'the argument from the solid in the fluid' shows. But this, Spinoza contends, leads to a contradiction: a divided piece of matter must have a determinate number of parts, but to say their number is infinite is to say that no number can be applied: 'the nature of the thing cannot admit a number without manifest contradiction' (280/111). So, he concludes, substance in itself is not divisible and has no parts. If we divide quantity in our imagination, Spinoza declares, 'we find it to be finite, divisible, and composed of parts';

but 'if we attend to it as it is in the intellect alone, . . . we find it to be infinite, indivisible, and unique' (211/107). That is, there is only one extended substance, and even though it can be imagined to have parts, in reality it is both infinite and indivisible.

Spinoza does not deny that there are many individuals in the world, but he thinks that they are only modally distinct from one another, not really distinct: they are different modes or ways of existing of the one true substance. Each body in the world is a mode with its own distinctive relations to other bodies. It is held together by its endeavour (*conatus*) to conserve itself in being, which it achieves so long as it can preserve the same characteristic ratio of 'motion-and-rest' among its constituent parts. But Leibniz is not persuaded by Spinoza's arguments that these parts are not really distinct because not susceptible to number. He agrees that the parts of an infinitely divided liquid exceed any finite number, but cannot see why Spinoza thinks that mathematicians do not infer this from the multiplicity of the parts of the liquid. He has Tschirnhaus write to Spinoza for a clarification. Although this may seem a very technical point, what is at stake is the status of bodies as infinite aggregates of their parts. Leibniz wishes to insist that bodies really are divided into infinitely many parts, but interprets this in terms of the syncategorematic actual infinite (see chapter 4 above), thus avoiding the Eleatic conclusion Spinoza wishes to draw, that what is One has no really distinct extended parts. Nevertheless, he agrees with Spinoza (and the Scholastics) that substance cannot be divided. So where Spinoza concludes that the parts and their number are merely facets of our imagination, Leibniz is forced to conclude instead that body is infinitely divided, and *therefore* it is not a substance.

In manuscripts written in his early years in Hanover, Leibniz makes this argument explicit. In one he argues that 'bodies are actually infinite, i.e. more bodies can be found than there are unities in any given number' (A VI iv 1393/LoC 235); and in another, explicitly titled *A Body is Not a Substance*, he argues that if body – understood as infinitely divisible extension or 'bulk', as by Cordemoy and the Cartesians – is held to be a substance, 'we will fall into contradiction as a result of the labyrinth of the continuum'. For 'first, there cannot be atoms, since they conflict with divine wisdom; and second, bodies are infinitely divided into infinitely many parts, but not into points. Consequently there is no way one can designate body as "one"; rather, any portion of matter whatever is an accidental unity, and indeed is in perpetual flux' (A VI iv 1637/LoC 259). We can see this position that matter is only an accidental unity emerging in a manuscript (*Infinite Numbers*) in early April 1676, contemporary with Leibniz's reading notes on Spinoza's *Letter on the Infinite*. There he writes: 'I doubt whether what is really divided, i.e. an aggregate, can be called one. It seems to be, since there are names invented for it' (A VI iii 503/LoC 99). When something becomes another thing, he continues, 'something must remain that pertains to it rather than the other thing, but this is not always matter. It can be mind itself, understanding a certain relation.'

Thus in responding to Spinoza's attack on the substantiality of a divided body, and in conformity with his own rejection of the unity of an infinite aggregate, Leibniz falls back on the nominalist position that an aggregate is an entity in name only, which he assimilates to a kind of Platonic phenomenalism, where material things are classified as phenomenal rather than substantial because they are always becoming and never remain self-identical. 'In philosophical strictness,' he wrote later, 'body does not deserve the name of substance, a view which seems to have been Plato's, who says that there are transient beings that never subsist longer than a moment. . . . body is not a true unity, only an aggregate, which the Scholastics call a being *per accidens*, a collection like a herd. Its unity comes from our perception.'[1] Thus bodies are phenomenal in two senses. First, they are merely beings by aggregation that are perceived as one thing, even though they are in fact (infinitely) many. They have no unity in themselves, but only a unity resulting from their being perceived as one thing. Second, they have no unity through time, because they do not remain self-identical through time. They are one thing after another, and therefore do not qualify as enduring things: they are not substances, but merely modifications of substances.

Nevertheless, as the aggregates or modifications of real substances (as opposed to mirages or illusions), bodies are *real phenomena*. This is not a contradiction in terms: they are phenomena, 'things that appear'; but they are real as opposed to illusory insofar as they are 'well founded' in substances external to the perceiver. A body is an aggregate of such external things, together with its appearance as one thing; and successive different aggregates constitute the body of the same substance through time insofar as they collaborate in the actions of that substance. In holding to the reality of things external to the perceiver, Leibniz is mindful of the doubts of his friend, the academic sceptic Simon Foucher, who subjected to critical scrutiny all arguments purporting to show that there is something outside of us. In response, Leibniz insisted that there are two absolute general truths about the existence of things: that we exist, and that there is something outside of us that is the cause of the variety of the things that appear to us. The first, he claimed, follows from the fact we think, as Descartes discovered with his *cogito ergo sum*. But the second follows from the variety contained in our thoughts, which could not have its origin in the thinker. For there would be no reason for the thinker to perceive these changes rather than others, contrary to the Principle of Sufficient Reason (A II i 245/AG 2). The reason ' "must be outside the perceiver, and therefore there are other things besides me' " (A VI iv 1395/LoC 239).

On the question of unity, then, Leibniz agrees with Spinoza in inferring from the actually infinite division of bodies that they are modes or appearances of something substantial that is not really divided. As he writes to Arnauld in April 1687, 'the essence of a being by aggregation is only a mode [*manière*] of being of the things from which it is composed. For example, what makes the essence of an army is only a mode of being of the men who compose it' (GP ii 96–7/WFT 124). But since he does not accept Spinoza's argument against plurality, he feels entitled to reject Spinoza's conclusion that bodies are all modes of the same substance. For Leibniz, 'every machine presupposes some substance in the parts of which it is made' (97/124), but since each body is infinitely divided into actual parts that are themselves bodies, there are infinitely many substances in it. The aggregate of substances is nothing but the substances themselves, whose appearance is the extended body.

As for mind–body interaction, Leibniz had been apprised of Spinoza's views by Tschirnhaus. Spinoza, he learned, was contemptuous of Descartes's belief that 'he could see clearly and distinctly that the mind acts on or is acted upon by the body' (A VI iii 385/ LoC 43), and had adopted a solution that was as simple as it was radical: there is no interaction between mind and body, because they are the same thing! 'The mind and the body are one and the same individual, which is conceived now under the attribute of thought, now under the attribute of extension' (Spinoza 1882: *Ethics* IIP21, IIIP2S). Mind, Spinoza claimed, is the idea of the body: it simply *is* the body under the aspect of thought. Thus when a body is dissipated, the mind no longer exists: 'our mind can be said to endure . . . only insofar as it involves the actual existence of the body' (VP23S). To soften this mortalist position, Spinoza allows that 'from the perspective of eternity (*sub specie aeternitatis*) there is an idea in God that necessarily expresses the essence of this or that human body' (VP22).

Leibniz's response is firm. In the *De Summa Rerum* manuscripts of April 1676 he writes: 'I do not accept Spinoza's opinion that the individual mind would be extinguished with the body, that the mind would in no way remember what had gone before, and that there would remain in the mind only what is eternal – the idea of the body, or its essence – the idea of *this* body, that is. If that were so,' he argues, 'the extinction of an individual mind would produce nothing new, for this essence already exists.' Moreover, 'that which then survives will in no way belong to us, for it will not be remembered' (A VI iii 510/DSR 61). Earlier he had reasoned that if a mind is what acts on itself, so that its nature consists in this sense of itself, then 'it seems this sense of oneself always exists . . . and I do not see how that sense can be impeded or destroyed'. Again, 'since the identity of the mind is not destroyed by some modifications, it cannot therefore be destroyed by any' (509/61). 'Is the idea the mind of the body?' he asks later the same month. 'That cannot be, since the mind remains while the body has been continually changing' (518/75). Again, 'whatever acts cannot be destroyed, for in any event it endures as long as it acts, and therefore will endure forever'. The contrast here is with the body, which is an aggregate, and therefore 'can be destroyed', whereas 'the soul which proportionately corresponds to it cannot be destroyed' (521/81).

Thus Leibniz's conception of the mind and its relation to body contrasts with Spinoza's in these respects. Where Spinoza conceives the body-mind as existing for a finite duration, Leibniz reserves such a finite duration for bodies insofar as they are mere aggregates, like a woodpile or a clock, which remain roughly the same thing until they fall apart. 'Every mind', on the other hand, 'is of unbounded duration' (A VI iii 476/LoC 51). An individual's possession of a mind or soul is, for Leibniz, precisely what distinguishes the *organic body* of a living being from a *mere aggregate*: the mind is that being's *principle of individuation*, that by which its continuously changing body qualifies as being the body of the same substance. On Spinoza's account, all individuals, 'though in different degrees, are animate' (*Ethics* IIP13S). Every body is a machine, a system of interrelated parts constantly undergoing collisions, by which it will eventually be destroyed when it can no longer sustain its characteristic ratio of motion-and-rest. The body of an animal is a well-organized such system, gaining and losing parts in its interactions with other bodies, as happens in the processes of ingestion and excretion. But on Leibniz's account the body of a living organism would have to be a machine in all its parts to infinity (see chapter 3), and only a mind or mind-like thing capable of expressing such infinite complexity could qualify as its principle of individuation.

In fact this idea of the mind as *expressing* all the causal relationships in which the body is involved is another point on which Spinoza's thought seems to have exerted a profound influence on Leibniz. According to Spinoza, a body acts and is acted upon by those surrounding it, and as long as it endures it will be in a series of states, each expressing its relations with those other bodies, with causal relations among its states expressed as sufficient reasons of one idea for another. Thus a Spinozan individual expresses divine attributes from its own vantage point in the universe – an idea that was to become a leitmotif in Leibniz's philosophy. As we saw in chapter 4, at the height of Spinoza's influence on his thought, and shortly before meeting him in The Hague, Leibniz wrote: 'things differ only modally, just as a town seen from a high point differs from a town seen from a plain' (A VI iii 573/DSR 95). The image of the town, and its different projections giving different representations of it, features prominently in his philosophy from this point onwards.

Spinoza's idea of expression is devoid of the connotation of analogy. But this is the very nub of Leibniz's conception of it: expression for him is a symbolic representation that preserves analogy, as can be seen in this passage written during his first months in Hanover in 1677:

> One thing is said to *express* another when the relationships that hold in it correspond to the relationships of the thing to be expressed. But there are various types of expression: for example, a model of a machine expresses the machine itself, a projective delineation of a thing onto a plane expresses a solid, speech expresses thoughts and truths, characters express numbers, and an algebraic equation expresses a circle or some other figure. What they all have in common is that solely from a consideration of the relationships of the expression we can arrive at a knowledge of the corresponding properties of the thing to be expressed. Hence it is clear that it is not necessary for that which expresses to be similar to the thing expressed, so long as a certain analogy is preserved between the relationships. (A VI iv 1370/L 207)

For Leibniz, moreover, it is the visual analogy of *point of view* that prevails. From the beginning, his main application of this concept of expression is in his account of *perception*: at any time each thing has a state that will represent its distinctive set of relationships to all other things existing at the same time, and this representation of all other coexisting things from its own point of view will constitute its perception of them. All other things in the universe will be represented, but the perceptions corresponding to them will be confused – that is, in the literal meaning of 'confused', fused together. For this reason, Leibniz wrote in 1676, 'sensible things cannot be understood perfectly by us, since infinitely many things come together in constituting them' (A VI iii 515/DSR 71). The perception of a colour, for example, although clear, is confused in just this way.

Only two months after meeting with Leibniz, Spinoza died unexpectedly (probably of a lung disease exacerbated by the dust from the lens-grinding by which he made his living). Through Schuller, Leibniz strove to procure his posthumous works for the library in Hanover, but he did not finally lay eyes on the *Ethics* and the *Treatise on the Improvement of the Understanding* until February 1678, a year after Spinoza's death. He was severely critical of the proofs Spinoza offered in the *Ethics*, but more sympathetic to the *Treatise*. Although dismissive of Spinoza's identification of the mind with the idea of the body,[2] Leibniz was very much taken with his conception of the mind or soul as a *spiritual automaton*.

In his *Ethics* Spinoza had written that 'the decisions of the mind are nothing but the appetites themselves, which therefore vary as the dispositions of the body vary' (IIIP2S). Leibniz had no quarrel with the idea that the appetites as conceived by an animate being (appetites which Spinoza and Hobbes identified as desires and aversions) must correspond to certain motions or changing dispositions in the body. As he later wrote to Bayle, 'the soul's tendencies towards new thoughts correspond to the body's tendency to new shapes and new movements' (GP iv 545/WFT 236). Spinoza, however, conceived this correspondence as an identity. Because the mind is the idea of the body, there is only one order of connection, whether Nature is conceived under the attribute of extension or of thought (*Ethics* IIP2S). Thus the causal relations among states of a body, viewed under the aspect of thought, will appear as sufficient reasons of one idea for another. Leibniz rejects the identity of the series of ideas ordered by sufficient reasons with the series of mechanical states, but retains the idea of a perfect correspondence. Only he will insist (as we'll explore in detail in chapter 8) that this perfect correspondence does not rule out free actions and choices in the case of a rational being.

Leaving aside for now the issue of freedom of choice, both thinkers insisted that the determinism they saw in individuals' actions is not incompatible with autonomy of action. 'A being is free', wrote Spinoza, 'which exists and is determined to action by the necessity of its own nature alone' (Spinoza 1882: IV, 265); Leibniz agreed, writing to Malebranche in 1679 that '*Whatever acts is free insofar as it acts*' (GP i 330/L 211). Spinoza explained this in terms of participation in causal activity. The more an individual understands the reasons giving rise to a given situation, the more control that individual has over the outcome of that situation, the more it participates in the nexus of causal influences, the individual itself being one of the contributing factors in the total cause. Leibniz concurs. As he writes in his *Monadology*, all creatures are said to act insofar as they are perfect, and to be acted upon insofar as they are imperfect: they are '*active* insofar as what is known distinctly in one serves to explain what happens in another, and *passive* insofar as the reason for what happens in one is found in what is known distinctly in another' (§ 52: GP vi 615/WFT 275).

Nevertheless, Leibniz did not accept that Spinoza had a satisfactory account of what an individual's causal activity consists in. For Spinoza's physics is Cartesian: the measure of a body's activity – the 'motion-and-rest' whose proportion is conserved in the body – will be Descartes's quantity of motion. The very phrase 'motion-and-rest' is an indication that Spinoza has not appreciated the problem of the relativity of motion with which Leibniz was wrestling, and is imagining bodies as parts of extended substance that have an absolute motion or rest relative to it: 'a body at rest', he writes in the *Ethics*, 'remains at rest until it is determined to motion by another' (IIP13L3C). But Descartes's rules of collision are not compatible with the relative nature of motion, a fact that Leibniz will point out in his first publication on physics in 1686. Already in the summer of 1676, prior to meeting with Spinoza, he had articulated the Full Cause Principle on which those arguments were based (see chapter 6). Thus he would have been able to demonstrate that Descartes's rules would result in there being more activity in the effect than in the cause, in contradiction to the impossibility of a mechanical perpetual motion. And this he does when he meets with Spinoza in December of that year. In a now lost fragment in which he comments on that meeting, he wrote: 'Spinoza did not see the defects of Descartes's rules of motion; he was surprised when I began to show him that they violate the equality of cause and effect' (Foucher de Careil 1854: lxiv).

The upshot of this is that the causal activity of individuals cannot be explicated solely in terms of motion. Moreover, if there is no absolute space, and motion is relative, then you cannot conceive bodies as modes of an extension relative to which they are at rest or in motion. So there must be something prior to extension that accounts for their reality, as well as for their activity. As we will see in chapter 6, reasoning from the Full Cause Principle, Leibniz was able to show in early 1678 that a body's ability to work, to produce physical effects, is measured not by quantity of motion (mv) but by *vis viva* ('living force'), whose measure is mv^2. Once he had satisfied himself that this is the quantity conserved in every interaction, and indeed in every isolated corporeal substance or aggregate of substances, he was able to represent individuals as the sources of their own actions. This allowed him to revert to the Aristotelian idea of an entelechy or actualizing principle in bodies, reconceiving substance as a 'primitive force' internal to bodies, from which all the external phenomena – mechanical forces, extended bodies and their motions – would result. No longer would he be obliged to call on God to guarantee the continuity of motion by His direct action, or ascribe the conservation of motion only to the world as a whole. Now appetition could be reconceived in terms of an internal principle bringing about a succession of changes according to a law specific to each individual substance.

With appetition thus reconceived in terms of a non-mechanical internal principle, Leibniz was ready to 'rehabilitate' substantial forms by refashioning the ideas of perception and appetition he had found in Bisterfeld: perception is reinterpreted in terms of representation, and appetition in terms of an internal principle bringing about change in such a way that the reason for the changes is in the subject performing the action. Individuals, rather than being mere 'expressive centres',[3] as in Spinoza's philosophy, could then be properly regarded as authors of their own actions. Their substantial forms would be the result of God regarding the universe from the point of view of the body at successive times, and creating in the body the organs of sense in which these representations are presented with varying degrees of clarity and distinctness, while at the same time creating in it appetites that take these existents from one perception to those succeeding it in an autonomous fashion. This is what Leibniz argues in a piece written around 1681:

Insofar as God relates the universe to some particular body, and regards the whole of it as if from this body, or what is the same thing,

thinks of all the appearances or relations of things to this body considered as immobile, there results from this the substantial form or
soul of this body, which is completed by a certain sensation and
appetite. (A VI iv 1460/LoC 261)

The Mature Theory: Minute Perceptions
and Innate Ideas

Leibniz's reform of metaphysics thus consists in the way in which
he weaves all the disparate strands of thought described above into
one new 'system'. The result is a highly original synthesis, even if
– partly because of the very complexity and diversity of the problems it was intended to address – it has convinced few people.

The problem of unity of bodies is solved by recourse to the Scholastic idea of a substantial form, radically reinterpreted so as to be
conformable to the mechanical philosophy. Bodies as purely material entities are not only divisible but actually infinitely divided.
They therefore have no unity in themselves, but only from being
perceived as one, and are different aggregates at each different
instant. There must nonetheless be real unities in every body, otherwise it would have no reality; and they must be immaterial,
otherwise they would be divisible and thus not substantial. These
unities thus perform the same role as the substantial forms in the
plurality of forms doctrine discussed in chapter 3, making actual
the matter they inform, and containing the information necessary
for the substance's lawful development.

Unlike the substantial forms of the Scholastics, however, these
forms do not act on matter: 'all the operations of substances, both
actions and passions, are spontaneous, and except for the dependence of creatures on God, no real influence of them on one another
is intelligible' (A VI iv 1620/LoC 311); rather, 'each individual substance, expressing the same universe in its own measure according
to the laws of its own nature, behaves in such a way that its changes
and states correspond perfectly to the changes and states of other
substances' (1621/313). This detailed correspondence, Leibniz
stresses, extends to the relation between soul and body: 'with each
pursuing its own laws and properties and operations, everything
conspires together most beautifully' – a thesis he calls 'the *hypothesis
of concomitance*', later to be renamed the Principle of Pre-established
Harmony. Because the states of substances and their phenomena

arise spontaneously and according to their internal laws, there is no need for the 'kind of special operation of God' to excite thoughts in the soul corresponding to the motions of the body, and vice versa, as proposed by the occasionalists (and Leibniz himself in the *Pacidius*), or for the 'real influence' ('the passing of I know not what from the soul into the body') supposed by others of his contemporaries. Given the unintelligibility of any interaction between the mental and the physical, or between any substances, the inner perceptual activity of substances has to run autonomously and in parallel to the outer world of physical phenomena.

Each substance, according to Leibniz, represents or 'expresses the whole universe according to its own situation and point of view, inasmuch as everything is related to it' (1618/309). Perceptions are these infinitely ramified representations in the soul or substantial form, and constitute a kind of cognition, although this may be extremely limited. 'This representation is conjoined with a reaction, i.e. an endeavour or appetite, according to this cognition of acting' (A VI iv 1508/LoC 287). This occurs when the organs of sense are acted upon: the body 'resists what endeavours to divide it, and this resistance is sensation' (A VI iii 510/LoC 117); in the body there is 'as much appetite in it as there is a force of acting, and as much sensation in it as there is a force of being acted upon' (A VI iv 1398–9/LoC 245). Every substance therefore has in it some vestige of divine omniscience and divine omnipotence, limited by its finite perspective and power: 'the multiple finite substances are nothing but different expressions of the same universe, according to the different respects and limitations proper to each one, just as one ground plan has infinitely many lateral perspectives' (A VI iv 1618/ LoC 309).

Although for Leibniz all substances are living beings, there are distinct kinds of substances or monads. There are the most primitive simple substances which only have perceptions and appetites in the very general sense explained, and which possess no distinct perceptions. Next there are animals, which have '*souls*, where perception is more distinct and accompanied by memory' (*Monadology* § 19: GP vi 610/WFT 270). Then there are humans, monads distinguished by the ability to reason, who therefore have *minds*. The memory that animals possess allows them to imitate reason to some extent, by providing an association to a sequence of actions they remember. Thus 'if we show dogs a stick, they remember the pain that it caused them, and they flee' (*Monadology* § 26: 611/271). But such sequences 'are only a shadow of reasoning', 'a passage from one image to another' (NE 51). Although we humans also reason in this way perhaps three-quarters of the time, we also possess reason, the ability to reflect. We perceive that we perceive (for which Leibniz coins the term 'apperception'), and these *reflective acts* 'enable us to think of that which is called "I"' (*Monadology* § 30: 612/271), as well as to arrive at necessary truths through reason.

Here Leibniz's metaphysics links up with his logic and theory of knowledge. We arrive at necessary truths through reflection on the contents of our mind; the relations we discover there are relations among possibilities, which exist in the divine mind and are mirrored in our own. 'Necessary truths', Leibniz tells Bierling in 1709, 'can only be proved from principles intrinsic to the mind, because the senses certainly teach us what happens but not what happens necessarily' (GP vii 488). This is the nub of Leibniz's response to Locke, who had rejected innate ideas by appeal to the Aristotelian dictum that all knowledge comes through the senses. 'There is indeed nothing in the intellect that was not in the senses', Leibniz replies, '– except the intellect itself' (488).[4] The proof of these intrinsic principles 'does not depend on instances, nor, consequently, on the testimony of the senses, even though without the senses it would never occur to us to think of them' (NE 50). In fact such truths of reason are proved by analysis, as we have seen, that is, by the Principle of Contradiction, since their opposite is self-contradictory. Truths of fact, on the other hand, are proved by the Principle of Sufficient Reason. 'Here the resolution into particular reasons could be continued endlessly', corresponding to the fact that the complete notion of an individual substance, as we saw in chapter 4, 'involves relations to the whole series of things', which are therefore reflected in the infinitely ramified perceptions in the soul.

In the *New Essays* Leibniz opposes Locke's comparison of our mind at birth to a 'blank slate' with the image of a block of marble: as the veins in the marble guide the sculptor's creation, so the innate principles are dispositions guiding and constraining the way we think (52). But he gives a more compelling analogy in response to Locke's image of the understanding as like 'a closet from which light is wholly shut out', save for some little openings through which visible images could pass into the room (144). Leibniz asks us to imagine that inside the room there is also a screen or membrane onto which these images are cast, one that is 'not uniform but diversified by folds representing items of innate knowledge' (144). The membrane, being under tension, 'has a kind of elasticity or force of acting, and even an action or reaction adapted as much to past folds as to new ones caused by the impressions of the images', its action consisting in an oscillation like that in a tensed cord vibrating in response to a musical sound. This is, Leibniz suggests, a reasonable analogy for the brain; the immaterial soul, on the other hand, represents all these oscillations 'and has perceptions of them' (145). The impressions will be compounded from endeavours reaching the brain from bodies all over the fluid universe, including the unimaginably minute endeavours from remote bodies. Corresponding to these compounded endeavours will be "confused perceptions", that is, perceptions fused together from lesser perceptions, including ones that are so faint that they will fall below the threshold of awareness, the insensible perceptions.

These insensible perceptions will play a large role in Leibniz's philosophy. He appeals to them in rejecting Locke's claim that the mind does not always think. For Locke and the empiricist tradition, thought consists largely in a passive reception of ideas through the senses. So when we are in a deep and dreamless sleep or a stupor, we are not thinking. But for Leibniz the mind is always active, resulting in a continuous sequence of perceptions. In such a state our soul does not sensibly differ from that of simple monads; but like them, we will continue to have perceptions, even if we are not aware of them. In fact, 'we never sleep so deeply that we do not have some feeble and confused sensation, and we would never be woken up by the loudest noise in the world if we did not have some perception of its beginning, which is small' (54). When perceptions or appetitions are 'either too small or too numerous, or else too unified, so that they have nothing by which they can be told apart', they are unaccompanied by awareness or reflection. Leibniz gives two examples: the constant noise of a mill or waterfall of which we cease to be aware, even though the sounds are still perceived (53); and 'the roaring noise of the sea, which impresses itself on us when we are standing on the shore', which must be a fusing together of the noises of 'a hundred thousand little waves' of which we are individually unaware (54).

Thus Leibniz has rightly been credited with being the first to recognize the significance of the unconscious. Where Descartes and Locke conceived the mind as always being aware of its contents while it is active, Leibniz recognized that conscious awareness of thoughts and ideas is only an aspect of the mind's activity when it is engaged in reflective thought. Even then the mind will still be unconsciously perceiving things external to it, and when we reason inductively like the lower animals, this kind of computation can occur subliminally, by the process of blind thought discussed in chapter 2. Conscious reasoning is, nonetheless, what enables us to reflect on our actions and thus be capable not only of mathematical and logical reasoning, unlike lower animals, but of moral judgement as well. This, so Leibniz thought, gives us a special fellowship with God not available to creatures lacking reason.

Leibniz also appeals to minute perceptions and appetitions in support of the Principle of Indiscernibles. For they 'determine our behaviour in many situations without our being aware of them, and deceive the unsophisticated with an appearance of an *indifference of equilibrium*' (56). We'll come back to this in chapters 7 and 8 below.

Leibniz's Theory of Substance: Objections and Replies

When Antoine Arnauld was first presented with the paragraph headings of the *Discourse* summarizing many of these theses, his initial reaction was dismissive. He charged that Leibniz's complete concept doctrine implied 'a necessity more than fatal', and was unconvinced by Leibniz's defence, matters to which we will return in chapter 8. Arnauld then turned his critical eye to Leibniz's reintroduction of substantial forms. He could not see why Leibniz ascribed indivisible and indestructible souls to animals: 'what will you say about worms which have been cut in two, and each part continues to move as before? If fire took hold of one of those houses where they keep a hundred thousand silkworms, what would become of those hundred thousand indestructible souls?' (4 March 1687: GP ii 87–88/WFT 121). Leibniz was unmoved: 'it is not necessary for the two halves [of the worm] still to be animated in order for them still to possess some movement . . . the soul of the whole insect will remain in just one of the parts', just as it was only in a microscopically small part before the insect was born and grew (30 April 1687: 100/126). 'You suppose that there remains no organized body in the ashes . . . whereas I suppose instead that naturally there is no soul without an animated body, and no animated body without organs; and neither ashes nor other masses seem to me incapable of containing organized bodies' (9 October 1687: 124/134).

Perhaps the harder problem for his critics to digest was Leibniz's claim that body is an aggregate of substances, since what can be aggregated can also be divided. Thus in 1698 his friend Johann Bernoulli challenged him to divide a portion of matter into the substances of which it is composed. Leibniz responded that 'there are as many individual substances in it as there are animals or living things or things analogous to them'; one could divide a flock of sheep into the individual sheep, and similarly the matter between the sheep and the matter in the sheep's bodies until one found further living beings, 'and so on to infinity'. Bernoulli pressed his point, arguing that in that case 'an individual substance would be a point with a form, not a quantity with a form, otherwise it could be divided into many substances' (GM iii 546–7). He thus misunderstood Leibniz's position on actually infinite division, where the division is such that there is no smallest part. Leibniz replied accordingly: 'there is no smallest animal or living thing, none without an organic body, and none whose body is not in turn divided into many substances. One will never, therefore, arrive at living points, or points endowed with forms' (GM iii 551/AG 168).

Leibniz's point here is that you do not arrive at monads by division of bodies. The body of a living being can be divided, as when a lizard loses its tail; but this does not divide the lizard insofar as it is a unified living being. What makes it a lizard is not the mere assemblage of its parts, but the way they act together to achieve its various functions: ingestion, excretion, reproduction, and so on. A substance does not cease to be the same substance when its constituents change, any more than a recipient of an organ donation would change identity on receiving someone else's organ; its body is reckoned to be the same body so long as it performs its functions. These are governed by its soul or substantial form, which takes it through its changes according to an internal law coeval with the universe. Leibniz's corporeal substances are indivisible, just like Spinoza's, not because their bodies cannot be divided, but because what makes them an enduring unity cannot. Now, we could of course be mistaken about whether a body – say the body of a dog – is a body with a substantial form or soul. Perhaps dogs are very clever machines, as Descartes proposed. But, Leibniz insisted, there had to be true substances with organic bodies at some level, otherwise things would be aggregates of aggregates without end, without there being any true substances for them to be aggregated from.

Now Leibniz's claim that what is truly one cannot be divided makes it seem as though the unities from which bodies are aggregated are souls or immaterial forms, which seems impossible to understand. When Father Michel Angelo Fardella makes such an objection to him in conversation in Venice in 1690, Leibniz denies holding that a body is composed from or is an aggregate of souls, and explains that it is rather constituted by an aggregate of substances, not substantial forms. But these are not its parts, 'since a part is always homogeneous with the whole'. He elaborates using an analogy with points in a line:

> just as there is no portion of a line in which there are not infinitely many points, so there is no portion of matter which does not contain an infinity of substances. But just as a point is not a part of a line, but a line in which there is a point is such a part, so also a soul is not a part of matter, but a body in which there is a soul is such a part of matter. (A VI iv 1673/AG 105)

Some commentators have alleged that there is a change in Leibniz's metaphysics from a commitment to the reality of *corporeal substances* in his middle years to a reductionism in his later years (roughly, after 1704) where all that exist are *simple substances* or *monads*, interpreted as purely immaterial substances. This is a controversial issue in Leibniz scholarship, and it is unlikely that I will resolve it to anyone's satisfaction in two paragraphs. But there are several points that seem to tell against such a radical change of view, even apart from Leibniz's continuing endorsements of the reality of body and the absence of any text announcing a conversion to idealism.

First, it never was Leibniz's view that matter is, strictly speaking, *composed of* unities: he preferred to speak of its being *constituted* by them, in the sense that every part of matter presupposes them. Substances are centres of force, as we shall see below, and one manifestation of this force is bodies' resistance to penetration. The extension of a body is constituted by the diffusion of this passive force. Thus to say that bodies are aggregates of substances is to say that every actual part of a body presupposes substances as constituents.

Second, monads are no less the entelechies of living bodies in the *Monadology* than substantial forms were in earlier writings. A monad consists in the enduring potentials for acting and being acted upon, and Leibniz refers to it variously as a simple substance, or the entelechy of a body. It is necessarily indivisible, so it cannot be material. On the other hand, unless it could manifest itself in the material phenomena and motions that we see around us, there would be no point in introducing it. It must have a material body through which its activity is expressed in motions, and through which its passivity is expressed in being acted upon. For nothing can be acted upon if it does not possess a body, and if it cannot be acted upon, it will have no sensation. So it seems to me that there is no opposition between monads and corporeal substances: a monad is an enduring centre of activity and passivity that is at any time the entelechy of some body; and taken together with its body, it can be referred to as a corporeal substance.

There is, however, one respect in which Leibniz toyed with adjusting this position in the last decade of his life. This was on the issue of substantial union. The Jesuits had rejected occasionalism because it reduces the union of soul and body to a mere concomitance between the perceptions God wills in the soul and the corresponding changes He wills in the body (LDB 59). This is incompatible with the Catholic interpretation of the Eucharist, in which there is a genuine change of substance of the bread into the substance of Christ (transubstantiation). In his correspondence with the Jesuit Des Bosses, Leibniz explores whether his philosophy can supply an acceptable solution. On his own view, the bread is not a substance: it is at best a quasi-substance, whose reality consists in the reality of its constituent monads, with its unity supplied in perception. He suggests that this is adequate to support the Lutheran interpretation of the Eucharist he favours, which required only that the body of Christ 'be present' when the bread is received: the monads constituting Christ's body could be substituted for those constituting the bread, with the phenomena remaining the same (to Des Bosses, 8 September 1709: GP ii 390/LDB 153). But when Des Bosses objects that the same phenomena cannot be accidents of different substances, Leibniz proceeds to explore whether it is possible after all for the constituents of a body to be united into a real unity. To achieve this he posits a 'substantial bond', a thing that is neither itself a substance, nor an accident, but 'something substantial' that unites the constituent monads into what the Jesuits regarded as a corporeal substance, namely either the bread or Christ's body. But the attempt fails (largely as a result of Des Bosses's acute criticisms), and Leibniz reverts to his standard metaphysics, 'restrict[ing] composite or corporeal substance to living things alone, that is, solely to organic machines of nature' (to Des Bosses, 29 May 1716: 519/375–7).

But Leibniz's reform of metaphysics came hand-in-glove with his creation of the new science of dynamics, and it is to this that we should now turn in order to throw further light on his revised conception of substance.

6

Dynamics
The Physics and Metaphysics of Action

The fundamental connection between Leibniz's conception of substance and his dynamics is the definition of substance as *something that acts*; if a thing acts, then there must be a physical quantity that expresses this activity. Now, Leibniz had such a conception of substance from the first, but as we saw in chapter 3, his attempt to explicate this by taking *conatus* or endeavour as the expression of this activity of bodies was not a success. His dynamics can be seen as built around a sustained attempt to remedy this defect by identifying activity as *force*, and the measure of the expression of this force as proportional to mv^2.

Of course, the scientific terminology in this period was still fluid, and we now take force to be proportional to mass and acceleration, corresponding better to Newton's conception of it, while using one of Leibniz's other terms for his 'power' or 'force', namely energy.[1] Although *dynamics* was the name Leibniz coined for the study of force in his sense, it is now applied to the study of Newtonian forces. But there is more to this than a dispute over names: no one before Leibniz had conceived the need for a whole new subfield of rational mechanics distinct from statics, based on new, more general principles. The success of Leibniz's innovation can be gauged from what he achieved, delineating two cornerstone concepts of classical physics that do not appear in Newton's work: on the one hand, *energy* – including its correct dimensions, its equivalence to work done, the principle of the conservation of energy, and the gist of the distinction between potential energy and kinetic energy – and, on the other, *action* – including its correct dimensional equivalence to energy times time, and the first articulation of the principle of least action.

All these developments pertain to physics. Leibniz, however, insisted on their relevance to metaphysics, claiming that his advances in this realm opened the 'gateway to the true metaphysics' (to De Volder: GP ii 195/LDV 131), and were instrumental to its reform. The forces occurring in his physics he called *derivative forces*: as we shall see, they can be of two kinds, *active* and *passive*. The derivative passive forces manifest themselves as the resistance bodies have to being penetrated or to being put in a new state of motion; the derivative active forces are those 'brought about by the collisions of bodies with each other' (GM vi 236), among which are the forces of elasticity, centrifugal force and *vis viva* (living force). All such derivative forces, however, are understood by Leibniz to be modifications or limitations of underlying *primitive forces*, which he takes to be enduring powers in corporeal substances that also have a tendency toward actualization. Thus he conceived the active forces as modifications of a *primitive active force* or enduring tendency to act that 'is inherent in every corporeal substance as such' (236), and the passive forces as modifications of a *primitive passive force*, or an enduring tendency to resist changes of state. Understood in this way, primitive active force may be understood as what the Scholastics called the substantial form or soul, and primitive passive force as what they called *primary matter* (236–7), so that when these two forces taken together constitute a substance that is a true unity, it makes what Leibniz calls a monad (GP iv 511).

Although Leibniz's insistence on the metaphysical import of his dynamics is one of the most distinctive features of his thought, commentators have generally regarded his claims for such a connection as overblown. In Russell's estimation, for instance, 'the relation of Leibniz's dynamics to his metaphysics is hopelessly confused', and his claims for their interconnection are nothing but a 'false boast' (Russell [1900] 1937: 89). At the root of the difficulty is Leibniz's identification of primitive force as the entelechy of a substance, while insisting that the physical forces acting among bodies, the derivative forces, are modifications or limitations of that force. For, as we saw in the previous chapter, the activity of the entelechy is simply its appetition or tendency to proceed from one perception to another according to its internal law. But it is very hard to see how *physical* forces among bodies can be regarded as modifications of the *mental* activity of appetition, and this does appear to be 'one of the weakest points in [Leibniz's] system', as Russell suggests (89).

Part of the confusion Russell sees, though, arises from his own misconceptions about Leibniz's intentions. He supposed that Leibniz was aiming to 'reduce the whole series of dynamical phenomena to subjective series of perceptions', and that this was made impossible by his further assumption of 'the subjectivity of space' (99). But space was certainly not subjective for Leibniz, as we'll see in chapter 7; and it is also important to understand that 'mental' for Leibniz did not connote pure subjectivity. In explaining primitive force in terms of appetition, Leibniz was following a Platonist paradigm that was shared by most of his contemporaries, where what is active in nature is construed as necessarily mental or spiritual, since matter in itself is essentially passive. This had led many of his contemporaries – such as Severinus, More and Cudworth – to eschew mechanism, populating nature with causally active immaterial spirits. Even Newton proposed to supplement mechanism with immaterial 'active principles', such as those causing gravity and fermentation (*Optics*, Query 31: Newton 2004: 136). To many mechanists, though, the only alternative seemed to be to preserve the mechanical philosophy by ascribing all causal activity to God – as had the Cartesian occasionalists. Leibniz (characteristically) chose a middle way, situating a spontaneous activity in matter everywhere, but without interaction, in such a way that it did not detract from the mechanical explanation of phenomena. The appetition he posited in non-sentient beings was only an analogue of what we experience as the desires and aversions of our mental life. The latter could only be experienced by a substance with the required organs of sense, just as the confused representation of the rest of the universe constituting the state of a bare monad is only an analogue of perception, since it would not result in any sensation without the required organs of sense.

In this chapter I shall try to explain how Leibniz saw the connection between his dynamics and his metaphysics. As we shall see, it is through his searching analyses of the nature of body and motion that he diagnoses the problems with mechanism, and comes to see what is needed to complete its account of nature. His metaphysical analysis of body demonstrated that its essence is neither extension nor motion alone, but required a conception of activity that is not reducible to motion; the laws governing its behaviour could not be deduced from its merely mechanical qualities.

The Insufficiency of Mechanism

Nowadays so much credit is given to Newton for the creation of classical mechanics that it is hard to see how things were before his intervention. In fact, as Newton duly acknowledges, much of his conceptual apparatus had already been established by others, particularly Galileo, Wren, Wallis and Huygens. As we saw in chapter 3, the latter three had corrected Descartes's laws of impact, recognizing that only quantity of motion in a given direction is conserved in collisions.[2] They had adopted Descartes's principle of inertia, as expressed by Huygens in his *Horologium Oscillatorium* (*Pendulum Clock*) of 1673: 'if there is no gravity, and if air does not obstruct bodies' motions, each of them will continue the motion it has received with equable velocity in a straight line' (Huygens 1673: 21). They had also adopted Galileo's way of composing a resultant motion out of uniform motion in one direction and the action of gravity in another by completing the parallelogram of motions. There remained some ambiguity about mass or bulk, which was usually just equated with the body's 'magnitude', and many mechanical philosophers followed Gassendi in regarding anitypy or impenetrability as an additional basic quality of matter. But by and large Leibniz's contemporaries were content to infer matter's properties and laws from the phenomena, and did not see the need to derive the laws of mechanics from first principles. On this, Huygens, Wren and Wallis followed Galileo, and so did Newton. In fact, Newton would convert what Leibniz regarded as a shortcoming into a virtue of experimentally grounded natural philosophy, thus initiating the positivist epistemology that still pervades modern physics. In the second edition of his *Principia* of 1713, smarting from Leibniz's criticisms of action at a distance as an occult quality, Newton declared that principles and laws of nature are not assumed or derived from metaphysical considerations, but are 'deduced from the phenomena and made general by induction' (Newton [1687] 1999: 943). Leibniz's project, by contrast, was driven by his ambition to establish physics on firm principles, and the need for definitions from which the possibility of the thing would be evident. In keeping with the mechanist criterion of intelligibility, all the phenomena had to be explicable in terms of matter in motion, together with mind.

By these standards, Leibniz found mechanism's foundation wanting on several counts. First, there is nothing in body (understood geometrically) to offer any resistance to a change of state, nothing that would ground its impenetrability or its resistance to a change in its motion (inertia). Second, if motion is understood as change of situation, then it is entirely relative, and assigning causes of motion becomes arbitrary. Third, if only quantity of motion in a given direction is conserved, then motion would be lost in every collision of bodies that is not perfectly elastic. To these criticisms were added difficulties arising from the composition of the continuum: given the actually infinite division of body, no existing body can have a perfect shape: its contours will be fractal. Again, since the division differs moment by moment, no body remains the same for more than an instant. Likewise, given the arbitrarily small impacts on any body in a plenum, no body can remain in the same state of motion for longer than an instant, so that motion too is ephemeral. Finally, given the non-existence of anything truly homogeneous or continuous, as well as the relativity of space, extension itself cannot be taken as primitive.

To see how these criticisms lead Leibniz to his dynamics, we should first recap some of the main features of his first theory of activity, the endeavour theory. As we have seen, in Cartesian physics bodies are distinguished from one another by their differing motions, so that a body is a volume of extension all the parts of which have a certain motion in common. Leibniz insisted that this would have to be an instantaneous motion, an endeavour. Since the particular composition of endeavours distinguishing a body will differ from one moment to the next, it is therefore a momentaneous being, different at each instant – a conclusion Leibniz will continue to hold throughout his mature work. Moreover, since on the endeavour theory every point of an extended body is definable only by the endeavour proportional to it in an instant, actual extension also comes down to endeavour. Body is thus reduced to pure activity, defined in terms of endeavour.

As pure endeavours, however, bodies would have no means to resist motion impressed on them. Initially, as we saw in chapter 3, Leibniz attempted to get around this by distinguishing concrete motion from motion in the abstract. He thought he could account for the fact that in practice bodies resist motion by taking into account their elasticity, explained in terms of collisions of their internal parts. But he could not get the theory to agree with experience. In a further attempt of December 1675, noting the 'compensation' implicit in the fact that the same quantity of motion (in a given direction) is conserved ('if the magnitude of a moving body is increased, its speed is diminished'), he remarks that 'although this has been derived from the phenomena, no one has shown its origin in nature itself' (A VI iii 466/LoC 31). 'We have assumed by a kind of prejudice that a greater body is harder to move, as if matter itself resisted motion. But this is unreasonable, since matter itself is indifferent to any place whatever, and thus to change of place, or motion' (466/31). So Leibniz tries to derive this resistance to motion from a notion of matter as that which is extended or fills space, and motion as change of place. But, as he relates a few years later, all such attempts to account for this compensation of magnitude by speed – 'as when we see the same boat carried downstream the more slowly the more heavily it is laden' – were in vain, and he realized that 'this so to speak inertia of bodies cannot be derived from the initially supposed concepts of matter and motion alone' (A VI iv 1980/AG 249).

Consequently, Leibniz reasons, the founding of mechanism in a concept of body as pure extension in motion is inadequate. If bodies were pure extension and offered no resistance to motion, you could move a large body (say of 3 units of bulk) from rest to a given speed by having a small one (say of 1 unit) collide with it at that speed, and then, by splitting the large body into three parts, you would have quadrupled the ability to do work. As Leibniz later explained to Sturm, 'the greatest body could be moved by a very small one, with no slowing down of the latter, and there would be an acting without passion, the effect would be more powerful than the cause, and a perpetual mechanical motion would be possible'. Clearly, since this does not happen, there must be 'something other than extension and impenetrability in bodies' (A II iii 99).

A second difficulty confronting the endeavour theory that we met earlier arises from the relativity of motion. If motion is understood purely geometrically, that is, as change of situation, then when A moves away from B at speed v, it is equally true that B moves away from A at speed v in the opposite direction. As Leibniz wrote in the *Discourse on Metaphysics* of 1686, if motion is considered purely geometrically, then 'when several bodies change situation among themselves, it is not possible to determine, solely by a consideration of these changes, to which among them the motion should be attributed' (GP ii 444/WFT 71). This he called 'the equivalence of hypotheses', a position from which he never wavered.

The reason this is a difficulty is that it contradicts all our normal attributions of true versus apparent motion. 'No one doubts', Leibniz wrote in a manuscript of 1676, 'that the coach moves over the ground rather than the ground under the coach' (*Mechanical Principles*: A VI iii 104–5). We usually attribute motion to one of two bodies in relative motion 'because we have seen it receive a blow, or because it is dislocated and deformed, or shows signs of having received some other blows and of having had a change wrought in it as a result of this' (104). When we can't, the attribution of true motion may be more complex. This is the case with the Copernican hypothesis, according to which it is the Earth that moves, both around its own axis and around the Sun. Leibniz explains the ways in which 'the beauty and simplicity of the Copernican System easily attracted all the most talented people onto its side': 'many imaginary circles, many eccentric circles, and many anomalies vanish'; but also the hypothesis of the annual motion of the Earth – that is, that it 'changes its situation to the fixed stars' – 'would certainly be sufficiently corroborated' by such phenomena as changes in the apparent diameter of the fixed stars and parallax (105). Thus when it comes to explaining the phenomena, there will be a most intelligible hypothesis as to which bodies should be regarded as unmoving (here, the fixed stars), and which are moving with respect to them.

Leibniz assumes that for a given set of phenomena there will be one true hypothesis that accounts for them in the best way. Other hypotheses will be possible which also account for them, but these will give successful explanations of the phenomena only accidentally. Here Leibniz follows Kepler's defence of Copernicanism against the criticisms of Tycho Brahe (1546–1601) and Nicolaus Reimers Ursus (1551–1600). Kepler distinguished between merely *geometrical hypotheses*, which are in numerical agreement with the phenomena, and *true hypotheses*, which depict all the phenomena accurately and also give a causal explanation of them.[3] Because of the relativity of motion, there will be a geometrical equivalence between supposing a body *A* moving with speed *v* colliding with a stationary body *B*, and supposing body *B* moving with an equal and opposite speed to collide with body *A*, provided the speeds of all the other bodies are also adjusted accordingly. But that is to conceive the matter purely geometrically: with respect to causes of motion, there will not be an equivalence. 'Thus if one person supposes that a solid moving in a fluid stirs up various waves, another can understand the same events to occur if, with the solid at rest in the middle of the fluid, one supposes certain equivalent motions of the fluid in various waves.' Nevertheless, of course, 'that hypothesis which attributes motion to the solid is infinitely simpler than the others, and the solid is therefore judged to be the cause of the motion' (A VI iv 1620/LoC 311).

Leibniz will therefore agree with Newton when he argues in the *Principia* (against Descartes) that there cannot just be apparent motions without there being true ones. But he will not agree 'that the causes that distinguish the true motions from the relative ones are the forces impressed upon bodies to generate motion' (Newton [1687] 1999: 412). For according to Leibniz, when two bodies collide, the same force of impact will occur whether the first is moving with speed $\underline{v}$ toward the second, or the second with speed $-v$ toward the first, and all action is by contact. When all the other bodies around them are brought in to the picture, however, there will be a simplest or most intelligible hypothesis concerning which bodies are to be regarded as at rest, and which truly in motion. The causes of motion will then be assignable consistently with this true hypothesis. Leibniz's understanding of cause is thus crucially different from the one Newton employs. The key to understanding it is Leibniz's insistence on the lack of anything passing from one substance to another in a causal interaction: 'Causes are not derived from a real influx, but from the providing of a reason' (A VI iv 1620/LoC 311). An influx of something from one substance into another is unintelligible on the mechanical philosophy, and this will form the basis of Leibniz's rejection of Newton's idea of gravitational attraction. A merely relative motion is an extrinsic denomination, they both agree. But where Newton sees the true motion as being a motion generated in absolute space, Leibniz conceives it as determined by the most intelligible, and therefore true, hypothesis. Although the motions of bodies relative to one another at any instant will be represented in the perceptions of the substances they contain, that body will be said to act as opposed to be acted upon to which there is better reason to attribute the cause of the motion. Thus Leibniz's philosophy of cause is consistent with his philosophy of action.

A related point on which Leibniz criticizes Cartesian mechanism is on teleology, or end-directed action. Descartes had banished such final causes from his natural philosophy (*Principles* I § 28). But as Leibniz had shown in his work in optics, it is possible to construe end-directed actions in such a way that no reference is implied to any intentions or knowledge on the part of the systems involved. The optimal path of a reflected or refracted light ray will be such as to make it the *most determinate*, which will be either a maximum or a minimum. There is no assumption here that the ray 'knows' this best path: 'it is not the ray itself, but the founding nature of optical laws that is endowed with cognition, and foresees what is best and most fitting' (A VI iv 1405/LoC 257). The application of final laws is not only compatible with mechanical explanations, but often easier, especially when a detailed knowledge of causes is unavailable.

Third, there is the difficulty that if the only conservation law in mechanics is the one Huygens, Wren, Wallis and (later) Mariotte had established – the conservation of quantity of motion in a given direction – then motion is always being lost in the universe. For example, if two inelastic bodies of equal mass – Leibniz gives the example of 'two balls of clay wrapped in paper, suspended from threads' (A VI iv 1980/AG 249) – collide head-on with equal and opposite velocities $\underline{v}$ and $\underline{-v}$, they will come to a standstill. This means that their quantity of motion is not conserved: if each had a (scalar) quantity of motion mv, then their total quantity of motion before the collision would be $2mv$ and after the collision it would be 0. It is true, as Huygens and Wren had argued, that the quantity of motion in a given direction is conserved, because $m\underline{v} + (-m\underline{-v})$ = 0. Nevertheless, where before the collision we had two moving bodies, afterwards we have none. That is an extreme case, but it is easy to see that in any inelastic collision some motion would be lost if only the Huygens–Wren–Wallis law was in play.[4]

Leibniz's breakthrough in resolving these difficulties was his articulation of what I have called his Full Cause Principle, the principle that the full cause must be contained in the entire effect, to a consideration of which we now turn.

The Full Cause Principle and the Conservation of Force

Leibniz first articulates this principle in *On the Secrets of Motion* dating from the summer of 1676. Subsequently he will describe its discovery as the 'Ariadne's Thread' that helped him emerge from the labyrinth, although it was not for another year and a half that he was able to use the principle to identify the quantity conserved in collisions as *vis viva*, or mv^2. He conceives it as a metaphysical principle underlying mechanics analogous to the principle in geometry that the whole is greater than the part:

> Any full effect, if the opportunity presents itself, can perfectly reproduce its cause, that is, it has forces enough to bring itself back into the same state it was in previously, or into an equivalent state. In

order to be able to estimate equivalent things, it is therefore useful that a measure be assumed, such as the force necessary to raise some heavy thing to some height. . . . Hence it happens that a stone that falls from a certain height can, if it is constrained by a pendulum, and if nothing interferes and it acts perfectly, climb back to the same height; but no higher, and if none of the force is removed, no lower either. (Hess 1978: 204)

Here Leibniz is generalizing from what Huygens had established in his *Pendulum Clock* of 1673. He knew from Huygens' experiments that pendulums could not be made to rise to a greater height than they had fallen through; and that the more all sources of friction could be reduced, the more nearly such bodies would return to the same height through their natural inertia.[5] Leibniz was seeking a principle from which this phenomenon could be inferred. Reasoning that the falling through the height under its own weight could be regarded as the cause of a pendulum's subsequent motion at the bottom of its swing, and that the force of this motion could then be regarded as the cause of its attaining the same height, Leibniz identifies the Full Cause Principle as the general principle of which this is an instance. At the lowest part of its swing, he reasons, the pendulum must have sufficient force to take it back up to the top again, assuming all frictional forces are removed. Thus if the motive force is taken as the full cause, then the height the body is raised through can be taken as the entire effect.

In early 1678 Leibniz was able to infer a measure for this force as follows. At first he had worked with the accepted measure of the force of a body's motion, mv. This seemed reasonable: the motive force would depend on the mass of the body, and also on how fast it was moving. But Huygens had proved in Proposition III of the *Pendulum Clock* that for a given mass in free fall the distances of fall are proportional to the squares of the times of fall, or 'the squares of the velocities acquired at the end of these times' (36). Thus the correct measure of this motive force, Leibniz realized, should be proportional not to mv, but to mv^2. Finding some resistance to this argument among his correspondents, he published a version of it in the new scientific journal, the *Acta eruditorum*, in March 1686, his *Brief Demonstration of a Memorable Error of Descartes and Others*. . . . Assuming it would take the same quantity of force to raise a 1 pound body A to a height of 4 ells as to raise a 4 pound body B to a height of one ell, he then investigates whether these will produce the same quantity of motion by falling through these heights. Using

Galileo's result that the velocities produced by falling bodies are as the square roots of the heights through which they fall, he infers that the velocity produced by A's fall is twice that produced by B's, say, $2v$ as opposed to v. Multiplying by their masses, we see that A's quantity of motion, $1 \times 2v$, is only half B's, $4 \times v$. Thus motive force cannot be equivalent to quantity of motion, but 'is rather to be estimated by the quantity of the effect which it can produce, e.g. by the height to which a heavy body of a given magnitude and kind can be raised' (GM vi 118/L 297). (Leibniz leaves implicit here that in this case force will therefore be proportional to mv^2; although he makes this explicit elsewhere.)

According to the equality of cause and effect, this also means that a body of mass m that is raised through a height h sufficient for it to acquire the motive force mv^2 by falling through that height, *even when it is not yet in motion*, must have a force in it equal to mv^2. Such a force Leibniz came to call a *dead force*, in contrast to the force in a moving body, which he called *living force* (in Latin, *vis viva*). In modern terms, the dead force here is the potential energy of the body, and the living force is (twice) its kinetic energy. (The factor of $\frac{1}{2}$ does not factor into calculations done in terms of proportions: $KE_1 : KE_2 = m_1 v_1^2 : m_2 v_2^2$). Thus Leibniz was led to posit a universal conservation of force, or what we now call the *conservation of energy*: living force may be converted into dead force, but in an isolated system no force is ever gained or lost: 'that which is absorbed by the minute parts is not absolutely lost for the universe, although it is lost for the total force of the concurrent bodies' (GM vi 231).

Now given that Leibniz has apparently inferred this principle from two results already stated by Huygens, one might wonder what more is involved in the generalization. Why couldn't Huygens have derived it himself? The answer lies in Leibniz's commitment to the inherent elasticity of matter, and the need to explain this mechanically. Huygens assumed that when two perfectly hard bodies (like his pendulum bobs) collided head-on, then, since they were impenetrable, they would have to reverse direction, but with their relative speed unaltered. One can show that in such a case the total mv^2 will be the same before and after the collision.[6] With soft bodies, however, some motion is lost in the collision, so the relative speed will be reduced, and mv^2 will not be conserved. Huygens, then, could allow that mv^2 is conserved in the case of perfectly hard bodies, like the atoms he assumed, but could regard this simply as a result of the conservation of relative speed, while rejecting a conservation principle for *all* bodies.

Leibniz, however, held that the total force is always conserved. According to his analysis of collision, 'all reflection arises from elasticity'. As had been shown by Mariotte's experiments, 'when A and B collide, the resistance of the bodies conjoined with their elasticity causes them to be compressed by the collision, and the compression is equal in each of them, whatever hypothesis is made [about which is in motion]' (GM vi 251/WFT 172–3). This would apply even to Huygens' pendulum bobs, or any other bodies acted on in a collision: 'their repercussion or flying apart arises from their own elasticity – that is, from the motion of the ethereal fluid matter permeating them – and so from an internal force, that is, one existing within them' (251/173). Thus as the bodies collide, their living force is converted by degrees into an elastic force in each body as it becomes deformed, and then, as the bodies rebound, the force is converted back into living force. The elastic force itself consists in the force of the individual particles of the ethereal fluid. This scheme also applies to bodies that are not perfectly elastic, where 'the force is taken up by their internal parts, which are themselves elastic, and so it does not perish, but just becomes insensible' (GP ii 169/LDV 71).

Thus, given Leibniz's interpretation of cause as the ability to do work, his Full Cause Principle is effectively what we now call the First Law of Thermodynamics: when a closed system has work done on it so that its internal energy is increased, this internal energy gives it an ability to do work that is equivalent to the work that was originally done on it, provided there is no interaction or heat transfer; in short, a perpetual mechanical motion is impossible. On the other hand, though, the dependence of Leibniz's law of conservation of force on the hypothesis that matter is inherently elastic offered scope for its detractors, as we shall now see.

Further Development: Application and Reception

Leibniz's criticisms of Cartesian physics in his *Brief Demonstration* of 1686 provoked predictably hostile responses from its defenders. The Abbé Catelan insisted on Descartes's behalf that Leibniz erred in leaving out of account the time during which the velocities are acquired: it will require greater force to raise 4 pounds through 1 foot the more quickly this is done. The basic idea is that if a force results in a change of motion, then the same change of motion could be produced by half the force if it acts for twice as long: slightly anachronistically, $\Delta mv = Ft = \frac{1}{2}F \times (2t)$.[7] Similarly, Denis Papin

objected that if gravity acts by the impacts of small ethereal particles, then the force a body needs to overcome in rising to a certain
height will depend on the number of particles it encounters during
the time of ascent, and thus be proportional to its velocity, not to
the square of its velocity (A III v 296).

Leibniz countered these criticisms by insisting on three basic
principles: the interpretation of force as ability to do work, the Full
Cause Principle interpreted as conservation of this force, and his
Principle of Continuity. Regarding the first, he noted that it was
supposed even by Descartes in his correspondence with Mersenne,
and – steamrollering over distinctions actually made by Descartes
between the concepts of force applicable in free fall and in statics
– he created further logical arguments to show how Cartesian principles would lead to perpetual motion. According to him, when
his opponents assimilated the forces exchanged in collisions to the
forces acting in a balance – as, incidentally, does Newton in his
Principia ([1687] 1999: 428–9) – they were mistakenly taking a proportion between dead forces and velocities that applies in statics
also to apply to collisions, where the correct measure of the cause
must be equivalent to 'some absolute effect, such as when a weight
is raised to a certain height' (GP ii 154/LDV 29), and thus (by the
above argument) proportional to mv^2.

Here, Leibniz asserts, there is an important distinction to be
drawn between force and action (154/29): when a living force is
sustained over time, it is not the force but the *action* that is proportional to time. As he writes to De Volder, 'action is nothing but
the exercise of forces through time, i.e. as force multiplied by time'
(174/81). This allows Leibniz to give an a priori demonstration of
his conservation principle. In terms of his own concrete example,

(1) The action of covering 2 leagues in 2 hours is twice that of covering 1 league in 1 hour; (2) the action of covering 1 league in 1 hour
is twice that of covering 1 league in 2 hours; (3) [therefore] the action
of covering 2 leagues in 2 hours is four times that of covering 1 league
in 2 hours. (173–4/79–81)

Thus if the actions are as forces multiplied by times, and the times
are the same, then the forces are also in the ratio 4:1. Moreover, the
velocities of completing the two actions in (3) are in the ratio 2:1, so
the forces are as the squares of the velocities.

Against Huygens' notion that his infinitely hard atoms would
instantaneously change their direction of motion on impact, Leibniz

appealed to his law of continuity. 'If it is supposed that there are atoms – that is, bodies of maximal hardness and inflexibility – then it is clear that change would happen through a leap, or momentaneously,' he wrote in the unpublished second part of the *Specimen of Dynamics*. This is absurd, even putting aside the difficulties about infinite firmness itself, for there would have to be 'a momentaneous change from motion to rest, without any intermediate degrees' (GM vi 248/WFT 170). Consequently, as he had written to Huygens in 1692, '[your atoms] cannot obey the laws of motion, for if two equal atoms with equal and opposite velocity collide head-on, their force will be lost, since it would seem that it is only elasticity which makes bodies rebound' (A III v 393). Rest, he concludes in the *Specimen of Dynamics*, 'can never arise from motion (and even less can motion in the opposite direction), without passing through all the intermediate degrees of motion' (GM vi 249/WFT 170), as happens in an elastic collision.

On Leibniz's understanding of collisions, the living force characterizing bodies moving freely is converted by infinite degrees into a dead force represented by a differential of velocity, dv, which he calls a *solicitation*. Thus if motion is represented by a line r traversed by a body in a given time, 'the velocity is expressed by an infinitely small line $[dr]$, and the element of velocity, which is solicitation of gravity or centrifugal conatus, by a line infinitely many times infinitely small $[ddr]$' (Bertoloni Meli 1993: 131). In this way, for example, when a body is constrained to move in a circle, its tendency to move off freely along the tangent manifests itself as a centrifugal force which, as Huygens had already explained, is balanced by an equal and opposite reactive force from the surrounding matter. The solicitation to move away from the centre is balanced at each instant by a force that is experienced as gravity. When a heavy body has been falling or a stretched bow has been springing back for some time, however, it possesses a living force which 'arises from infinitely many continued impressions of dead force' (GM VI 238/WFT 159).

With these points in mind, we can consider Leibniz's reactions to Newton's celebrated *Principia* (1687), which he encountered while in Vienna in 1688. This presented a significant challenge to Leibniz's emerging dynamics, and at the same time stimulated him to develop some of the points already discussed. Newton firmly rejected vortices in the heavens, and instead inferred the existence of a centripetal inverse square force from a mathematical description of the phenomena. In Leibniz's eyes, great though the merit of Newton's mathematical achievement undoubtedly was, this amounted to an implicit rejection of any mechanical cause of gravity in favour of some sort of non-mechanical virtue. Noting the impressive numerical agreement with the phenomena achieved by Newton, he set about trying to reproduce his mathematical results while giving a causal explanation of gravity consistent with mechanism. Working very fast in Vienna on his way to Venice, he constructed a solution to the problem of planetary motion using his new methods of the differential calculus, which he published as *An Essay on the Causes of Celestial Motions* (the *Tentamen*) in the *Acta* of Leipzig in February 1689.

Leibniz was not in fact able to account for the cause of gravity in the *Tentamen*, or to derive Kepler's Third Law (his subsequent attempts met with serious difficulties). Nevertheless, what he achieved there was quite remarkable. Leaning heavily on the authority of Kepler, he split the elliptical motion into two components: a 'harmonic motion', in which the planet is swept around in such a way that its velocity is inversely proportional to r, and a 'paracentric motion, as if it had a certain gravity or attraction, namely an impulsion towards the Sun' (Bertoloni Meli 1993: 132). For the harmonic motion he was able to prove Kepler's Second Law, stating the proportionality of the areas swept out by the rotating radius vector of a rotating planet to the times of transit. Then, by an adroit use of his newly introduced idea of differentials, he gave an analytic derivation of the inverse square law in terms of a differential equation – one of the very first uses of a differential equation in physics:

$$ddr = \left[a^2/r^3 - a/r^2 \right] dt^2$$

Here dt is the element of time, a is a constant (the *semi-latus rectum* of a conic section, $\frac{1}{2}L$), r is the distance of the orbiting body from the Sun at a focus of the ellipse, and the term ddr represents the solicitation toward the Sun.[8] Since for harmonic motion the centrifugal *conatus* $C = v^2/r$ and $v \propto 1/r$, we have $C \propto 1/r^3$. So Leibniz interpreted the first term on the right as the centrifugal *conatus* due to the harmonic motion, and the second term as the solicitation due to gravity, which follows the inverse square law. In circular motion, $r = a$ and $ddr = 0$, so these two terms balance one another; in elliptical motion there is an imbalance between them, resulting in the force taking the planet either beyond or inside the circular orbit.

Leibniz pretended he had only read a review of the *Principia* before composing the *Tentamen*. As noted in chapter 1, this was a strategic blunder. The essay might well have had the same impact had he presented it for what it was: a reworking of Newton's result to make it compatible with a mechanical explanation, and at the same time an example of the power of his differential calculus. But the stakes were perhaps too high. Leibniz was convinced that Newton's purely geometric approach needed replacing by an account that allowed for a mechanical explanation of the cause of gravity, and to have had his own derivation of the inverse square law riding on the back of what he saw as a geometrical hypothesis – not to mention a faulty ontology of space, time and motion, as we shall see below – would have made a feebler case for the inadequacy of Newton's approach.

The Metaphysics of Activity and Perfection

The reaction to his publications made it clear to Leibniz that he was unlikely to have much success in persuading his contemporaries of the implications of his dynamics for his theory of substance. This can be seen in his correspondence with Burchard de Volder, with whom his friend Johann Bernoulli had put him in touch. De Volder was intrigued to learn that Leibniz had argued that all matter is inherently active, and wanted above all an explanation of how to derive this activity from the nature of corporeal substance. But Leibniz was reluctant to dive into a confrontation with De Volder's evidently Cartesian conception of substance as extension (together with a conception of activity as consisting in endeavour) if he could not first secure the latter's recognition of the inadequacy of a Cartesian physics pursued in terms of mere composition of endeavours.

First, Leibniz gives the argument we discussed above that mass cannot be derived from extension and motion alone. It is necessary also to bring in a certain power that bodies have to oppose motion, which results in their not being able to be set in motion without a loss of force in the impelling body; this is the *natural inertia* introduced by Kepler. This inertia consists in a resistance to change of state in a body that is being acted upon (the patient), a power that limits the ability of the body acting upon it (the agent) to transfer all its activity to the patient. Such a power, Leibniz urges De Volder to accept, is clearly something in matter that is not reducible to geometrical notions alone.

Then Leibniz rehearses the arguments treated above about the elasticity of matter and the law of continuity, his distinctions between dead and living force, and between force and action. He is also moved to allow that action may be resolved in two different ways: either as the product of powers and times, or as the product 'of effects (i.e. spaces traversed) and velocities'. That is, depending on the phenomenon in question, action may be as mv^2t or as mvs. As Leibniz explains, this makes sense dimensionally, since v is as s/t: or, as we would say, the dimensions of action are $[ML^2T^{-1}]$ for both resolutions (GP ii 202/LDV 149). After many arguments back and forth (and with a decisive intervention from Bernoulli), De Volder finally assents to Leibniz's measure of force, accepting also his physics of forces and even the elasticity of matter, at least as a hypothesis. But De Volder cannot see why anything more is required: why could one not have a physics of Leibnizian derivative forces superposed on Cartesian substances – portions of extension with mass m, quantity of motion mv, dead forces such as centrifugal *conatus* v^2/r, gravity and elasticity conceived as solicitations, and living force mv^2?

This takes the discussion into deeper philosophical waters. For Leibniz the admission of the conservation of force is tantamount to an acceptance that matter contains substances that are intrinsically active. Force 'is an attribute from which change follows, whose subject is the substance itself' (170/73). But substance cannot consist in extension, which is an incomplete concept. Extension, Leibniz insists, must be the extension *of* something. It is the diffusion of something throughout all its parts, and is therefore further resolvable 'into plurality, continuity and coexistence (i.e. the existence of parts at one and the same time)' (170/73). What is diffused is a force of resistance to penetration, and when this is continuously diffused over a region, that volume is extended. By continuity here Leibniz means that between any two points there are more (denseness), so that there is no part of the region that has no resistance to being penetrated. Abstract extension has no such resistance; only a space seeded with entelechies has that, and only such a filled space is actualized.

This force of resistance is one aspect of *passive force*, the other being its resistance to change of motion, or inertia (which, as we saw, is necessary in order to account for the correct rules of collision). It is a derivative passive force characterizing coexisting parts of a body, and thus it is *force at a given time*. All derivative forces are like this, Leibniz explains – they are accidental entities, whose value changes from one instant to another. They therefore presuppose something enduring of which they are evanescent modifications: namely the primitive passive and active forces that together constitute substance. Primitive passive force is the enduring power in corporeal substance to resist being penetrated or moved, and, Leibniz claimed, is what the Scholastics were groping toward with their concept of *primary matter*. Its modifications are the infinite parts into which matter is folded at any instant, each with its own inertia and degree of resistance: this is *secondary matter*, or bodies. Similarly, motions and derivative active forces are modifications of a primitive force, the *first entelechy*, corresponding to the soul or substantial form; they should be attributed to secondary matter (171/77).

De Volder wanted to discover how the activity of bodies follows from the nature of corporeal substance, and how this relates to the physics of forces. What Leibniz shows him instead is that physical forces are modifications of the first entelechy, identified with soul or form, whose activity consists in its production of its perceptions; and that in collisions no force is actually exchanged, but we determine which body is truly moving and acting according to the most intelligible hypothesis. This is all too idealistic for De Volder, who accuses Leibniz of 'doing away with body' (272/313), and loses interest in further correspondence. Still, there is more to be said concerning substance and activity in connection with Leibniz's idea of an *entelechy*, and this is worth examining.

In the *Monadology* Leibniz writes: 'one can call all simple substances or created monads *entelechies*, for they have in themselves a certain perfection' (§ 18: GP vi 621/WFT 270). Literally translated, he notes, entelechies are *'perfection-havers'* (*en* = in, *telos* = perfection, end, *echein* = have); 'they are only limitations, proportional to the perfection they possess' (§ 48: 615/274). Every possible existent, Leibniz maintains, has a degree of perfection, and a claim to existence that is proportional to this. In *On the Ultimate Origination of Things* he even talks of these possibles as 'striving for existence' in proportion to the degree of perfection they contain (GP vii 303/AG 150). Here the striving is to be understood as occurring in the divine mind prior to creation, as equivalent to the weighing up of the claim to existence each thing has. Of course, no possible thing has a claim to existence except insofar as it fits with others: it is the combination of possibilities and possible series that contains the most perfection that is brought into existence, and the existence of any given possible thing will exclude the existence of others. Leibniz gives an analogy with a game where tiles of various shapes and sizes are placed on a board according to certain rules, with the object of leaving as few empty places as possible. As in practical affairs, where 'one prefers the maximum effect at minimum cost, so to speak', so the creation of the best of all possible worlds is a problem of maximization: 'a certain Divine Mathematics or Metaphysical Mechanism is used in the very first origination of things' (304/151). The best of all possible worlds that God chooses to create is the world in which perfection is maximized. But this does not imply that any individual in that world (or any sequence of its actions) is more perfect than other similar ones that can be imagined; simply that the world in which it fits is the best possible.

Nevertheless, Leibniz believed, this divine maximization explains why the sequences of actions of created things are optimally determined in time. Action involves an expenditure of force (energy) to achieve a certain effect in a given time, and is thus proportional to energy and time. The Principle of Perfection applied to individuals seeking to achieve a given end, therefore, will involve this action's being optimally determined. From the fact that 'action is either minimized or maximized', Leibniz writes in 1707, 'one can derive several important results, such as the paths followed by bodies attracted to one or several centers of force'.[9] This is the gist of the Principle of Least Action later popularized by Maupertuis (as we'll see in chapter 9).

It is in this metaphysics of entelechies that we can see the connection between substance and activity in Leibniz's dynamics. All matter is active, and so contains a substance consisting in primitive force, construed as an active principle or entelechy. The instantaneous measure of a body's activity is energy; and the effect of the activity is action, its ability to do work over time. Each individual substance in the universe is an entity striving to maximize its own perfection in relation to all the others. In conscious beings, this is experienced as an appetite for what is best. But all beings, conscious or not, will exhibit an optimization of their actions, reflecting the architectonic Principle of Perfection. It is not necessary that they act this way, but for them to act differently would imply greater imperfection. Thus over any duration, a body endeavours to optimize its expenditure of energy, resulting in an optimization of action.

We will return to the questions of optimization and perfection in chapter 8, in connection with Leibniz's moral philosophy. But first we should discuss a third axis of Leibniz's reformed metaphysics that constitutes one of his greatest intellectual accomplishments, his philosophy of space and time.

7

The Philosophy of Space and Time

It is often said that Leibniz denied the reality of space and time, holding them to be mere relations among appearances and not part of fundamental reality. On this reading, monads would be timeless entities occupying some Platonic realm of being, independent of the phenomena we experience, and having no situation in space. Reality would be outside of time and space, and the spatially ordered things and successions of events of our common experience would be reduced to mere appearances.

Such a picture, I contend, is a serious misreading of Leibniz's philosophy. Certainly, he held that space and time (considered in themselves) are ideal and not actually existing entities. Nevertheless, he was far from denying that coexisting things are really spatially ordered, or that the states of monads really succeed one another in time. Space and time, he maintained, are systems of relations among the things or states they order, but they are 'real relations or orders of existing'. What he wanted to oppose was the notion that they could exist independently of those things or states.

Of course, Leibniz had some specific targets he was opposing. One was the Cartesian philosophy, which took extension to be equivalent to material substance. For Leibniz it could not be, since as a passive, homogeneous thing, extension lacks the essential attributes of a substance, as we saw above. Later, his target was the Newtonian view, derived from Gassendi and the Stoics, that time and space are absolute, possessing a kind of existence independently of the things in them. This is one of the main topics he disputed with Newton's ally, Samuel Clarke, in their famous controversy, which was terminated by Leibniz's death in November

1716. Clarke's publication of this correspondence in 1717 (with a fifth reply added by Clarke to which the deceased Leibniz could not respond) did much to ensure that the German philosopher's views were always taken seriously by later scientists. 'I hold space to be something merely relative, as time is,' Leibniz told Clarke, and, despite the triumph of Newtonian physics, most scholars have taken Leibniz's side in this debate. Notably, Ernst Mach in the late nineteenth century, and empiricists in the twentieth, followed him in rejecting Newton's absolute space and time. This has taken on special significance in that Einstein acknowledged Mach's influence on this point in helping him to create his Special Theory of Relativity.[1] But Leibniz had rejected absolute space prior even to hearing of Newton's views on space, arguing that it is incompatible with the relativity of motion implicit in the correct laws of collision of bodies.[2]

It should not be thought, however, that Leibniz's contribution to the philosophy of space and time lay solely in his arguments against taking them as absolute or self-existing. The idea that they were relational had precedents in some of Descartes's own views, as well as in Aristotle and the medieval nominalists. But Leibniz went much further, developing constructive theories of space as the order of situations, or of simultaneously existing things, and time as the order of successive things. His theory of space, moreover, was given an elaborate formal treatment in the new science he had devised, Analysis Situs or the Analysis of Situations: a more fundamental geometry than Euclidean geometry in which the situations of bodies one to another would be represented directly. Hardly any of Leibniz's work on this new geometry was published until recently. Even so, the very idea of such a more general geometry was to prove most fecund for a number of subsequent scholars. Although there was not much more for them to go on than Leibniz's early description of his idea in a 1679 letter to Christiaan Huygens, this sketch of a more fundamental science of situations, together with his views on the continuum, served as an inspiration first for Grassmann's vector algebra in 1844, and then for Poincaré, Brouwer and others in their creation of combinatorial topology in the late nineteenth century (as noted in chapter 4).

Leibniz's Nominalist Approach to Relations

The reading of Leibniz as relegating space and time to mere relations among appearances is in keeping with the idealist picture of him discussed in chapter 1. But it also draws support from a certain reading of his philosophy of relations. For Leibniz construed space and time as relations, yet he also held that relations are '*concogita-bilia*', entities which result from the related things being thought of together, rather than existing independently of them. Like other nominalist thinkers, Leibniz regarded relations are mere *results*, which follow from substances having certain properties. Thus if Plato is wise and Socrates is wise, then in this respect they are similar. So, when you think of Socrates as wise and Plato as wise, their similarity in this respect is a simple result which does not have to be independently posited. The relation of similarity *supervenes* on the subjects having these properties.

According to Russell, Leibniz was compelled to take this position as a result of his commitment to a subject–predicate logic. Since Leibniz held that in every true proposition the predicate is contained in the subject, he was obliged to rephrase relational statements accordingly. In some of his logical papers we can see him attempting rewritings of this kind. Thus Leibniz paraphrases 'Paris loves Helen' as 'Paris is a lover and by that very fact Helen is a loved one'. Accordingly, Russell reasoned, Leibniz would regard all relational statements as eliminable in favour of statements attributing absolute properties to subjects, corresponding to the fact that the relations would not exist unless someone thought of those substances' properties together. Thus, according to Russell's reading, 'relations, though veritable, are the work of the mind' (Russell [1900] 1937: 14), a view which he referred to as Leibniz's 'denial of relations'. In a similar vein, Benson Mates has claimed that Leibniz would reduce a statement attributing a spatial relationship between two subjects, such as 'Theaetetus is taller than Socrates', to two statements in subject–predicate form, say, 'Theaetetus is six feet tall' and 'Socrates is five feet tall' , since it cannot be false if they are true (Mates 1986: 217–18). Thus, claims Mates, Leibniz was committed to a version of nominalism which 'refuses to accept . . . abstractions like heat, light, justice, beauty, space or time' (173): all that exist are individual substances and their accidents, among which are certain non-relational qualities, like 'is tall' or 'is today', on which spatial and temporal relations supervene, or can be read off by a discerning mind (227).

There is no doubt that Leibniz was a nominalist about relations, and held them to supervene on related things, but it is not clear that he regarded this as making them subjective or unreal.[3] As we saw in our discussion of his nominalism in chapter 2, Leibniz rejected abstract entities as things existing in their own right. But he did not reject statements involving them as expressing truths. Such truths would involve a true predication of an accident to a concrete substance, and this would be reflected in the fact that the complete concept of the individual substance would contain the appropriate predicate: for instance, Julius Caesar's complete concept would contain the predicate 'crossed the Rubicon'. This fact in turn would have its basis in the modifications of Caesar's substance at that time. Such a reading tallies with Leibniz's portrayal of bodies and their motions, which were also characterized by him as 'results' of the underlying monads and their changing states. For, as we saw in previous chapters, the point of supposing monads is to ground the reality of phenomena, not to reduce them to mere appearances. And there is a strong analogy in Leibniz's philosophy between the status of aggregates and that of relations. The reality of a body consists in the reality of the constituent monads from which it is aggregated, while body as an entity conceived independently of these constituents is a mind-dependent phenomenon (like a secondary quality). Similarly, the reality of a spatial relation between bodies is to be found in the modifications of the coexisting substances that constitute them, while the relation conceived apart from those substances is something ideal. But the fact that relations are ideal entities does not detract from their being used to express truths, and in fact these truths are guaranteed by their having counterparts in the Divine Mind. It is this that enables Leibniz to characterize space and time as 'real relations', as we shall see below.

In fact, Leibniz's denial of the independent existence of space and time is better conceived as being in the tradition of medieval nominalism (or, to be more accurate, nominalism/conceptualism) than as anticipating modern idealists like John McTaggart (1866–1925), who asserted the unreality of time and space. This can be clarified by a comparison with the views of William of Ockham, the English nominalist whose name is immortalized in 'Ockham's razor', and who was revered by Leibniz as the cream of the Scholastic philosophers. Ockham insisted that 'a plurality of things should not be posited without necessity', and went about systematically applying this 'razor' to eliminate entities to which our language might seem to commit us prior to analysis. Insisting that all that exist are enduring things (*res permanentes*) and their accidents, he would then set about determining whether other entities had to be supposed to exist in addition, and then apply his famous razor to answer in the negative. Regarding time, for example, he reasons that 'time is composed of non-entities, because it is composed of the past which does not exist now, although it did exist, and of the future, which does not yet exist; therefore time does not exist' (Ockham 1984: 496). But might not the present at least exist? Ockham responds: 'of the present, nothing exists but the instant, which is neither time nor a part of time' (496). He then proceeds to prove that an instant, being neither substance nor accident, 'does not imply the existence of anything distinct from enduring things'. It is not a substance (an enduring thing) because it is always going out of existence; it is not an accident because there is no candidate for the substance of which it could be the accident (543). This does not prevent us from making true statements involving time, though. The statement that two processes last for the same time, for example, could be parsed in terms of a coincidence between the endpoints of their durations, these durations being concrete particulars and the endpoints their modes. Thus Ockham denies the existence of either time or instants distinct from enduring things. But, of course, since the constituents of his world are enduring things, he certainly does not deny that things endure, or that accidents temporally succeed one another.

The similarity with Leibniz is quite striking. Like Ockham, Leibniz is committed to the basic constituents of the world being enduring substances, and to regarding statements involving abstract things (*abstracta*) as abbreviations for ones involving concrete things (*concreta*) only. For him the world consists in monads and the modifications they have from one instant to another, and whatever results from this: 'For there can be nothing real in nature but simple substances and the aggregates that result from them' (GP ii 282/LDV 331–3). Insofar as a substance is a primitive force, as we saw in chapter 6, its modifications are the derivative forces existing at each instant, and it is in these that the reality of bodies and motions consists: 'accidental or changeable active forces, and motions themselves, are certain modifications of some substantial thing' (171/77). And concerning the reality of time, Leibniz avails himself of arguments almost identical to Ockham's. In his dispute with Newton and Clarke, the latter had claimed that duration exists eternally. To this Leibniz retorts:

> Everything which exists of time and duration, being successive, perishes continually. And how can a thing exist eternally if, to speak precisely, it never exists at all? For how can a thing exist if no part of it ever exists? Nothing of time ever exists except instants, and an instant is not even a part of time. Anyone who considers these

observations will easily comprehend that time can only be an ideal thing. (To Clarke, V § 49: GP vii 402/L 705)

The similarity of Leibniz's brand of nominalism to Ockham's extends to his philosophy of relations. He wants to eliminate the need to posit abstract entities such as instant, height, space and time, by showing how statements involving them can be rewritten in terms of expressions such as 'is simultaneous with', 'is congruent with', and so forth. Thus as he writes in a fragment *On the Reality of Accidents*, written probably in 1688:

> Up to now I see no other way of avoiding these difficulties than by considering *abstracta* not as real things but as abbreviated ways of talking . . . and to that extent I am a nominalist, at least provisionally. . . . It suffices to posit only substances as real things, and, to assert truths about these. Geometricians, too, do not use definitions of *abstracta* but reduce them to *concreta*: thus Euclid does not use his own definition of *ratio* but rather that in which he states when two quantities are said to have the same, greater, or lesser, ratio. (A VI iv 996)

Leibniz gives the same example of Euclid's use of *ratio* almost thirty years later in his controversy with Clarke about the nature of space. Just as Euclid, 'not being able to make his readers well understand what ratio is in the sense of the geometricians, defines what are the same ratios', so Leibniz, rather than posit places as existing entities which a body must occupy, is 'content to define what is the same place' (Fifth Paper § 47: GP vii 402/L 704). Bodies have situations to one another, he says, and these are concrete particulars, like the durations of enduring things. To occupy the same place is to have the same situation relative to other bodies – or at least, since two different subjects cannot have precisely the same individual affection, to have situations which agree in exactly the relevant respect.

There is a salient contrast here with the linguistic reductions drawn attention to by Russell and Mates. They suggest that on that model Leibniz would parse 'Theaetetus is taller than Socrates' as 'Theaetetus is six feet tall' and 'Socrates is five feet tall'. But Theaetetus' *being six feet tall* is a relational accident of Theaetetus, so it cannot be said that this kind of reduction 'eliminates relations' in any meaningful sense. In fact, given what was said above, it seems that Leibniz would not have been inclined to take Theaetetus' height as an irreducible accident, but would instead, like Ockham, have rewritten statements about his height in terms of relations of comparison between concrete particulars, the extended bodies of Theaetetus and Socrates. Thus the kinds of linguistic reductions suggested by Mates for spatial and temporal relations appear to go in the wrong direction, and tell us little about Leibniz's ontology of relations.

Where Leibniz does discuss the status of relational accidents such as situations is in connection with 'extrinsic denominations'. An extrinsic denomination is a property attributed to a thing by reference to things external to it, whereas an intrinsic denomination attributes to the thing a quality internal to it, such as a modification. Situation, as we shall see, is a prime example of an extrinsic denomination, since a body can only have a situation by reference to other bodies coexisting with it. On this subject Leibniz holds a very distinctive position, namely that *there are no purely extrinsic denominations* (A VI iv 1645): 'there is no denomination so extrinsic as not to have an intrinsic one for its foundation' (GP ii 240/LDV 239). From this it follows that there can be no change in an extrinsic denomination without a corresponding change in some intrinsic modification of the individual. To use one of Leibniz's favourite examples, 'no one becomes a widower in India because of the death of his wife in Europe unless a real change occurs in him' (GP vii 321–2). Just how unusual this thesis is can be seen by comparing it with traditional views about the reality of relations. A traditional nominalist about relations would hold that a change in relation would result from changes in the intrinsic denominations of one of the individuals, here the change involved in the death of the man's wife; but this would not involve a change in the man. Not even a realist about relations, though, would maintain that the new relational accident of being a widower implies any intrinsic change in the man who becomes widowed. But this is what Leibniz asserts to be the case, believing it to be a consequence of 'the connection of all things', the thesis (discussed in chapters 2 and 5) that every individual substance represents everything else that is coexistent with it, the representation being its state or perception.

Thus relations of situation, such as one thing's being in front of another, supervene on the modifications of the two individuals concerned. Nevertheless, Leibniz maintains, 'they can truly inhere even if no one thinks of them', since they subsist (along with possibles and eternal truths) in the divine intellect. The fact that this is so is then the foundation of the reality of space: it is an order of coexistents that results from the fact that God has created a world in which every existent necessarily reflects all things coexisting with it from its own point of view, in such a way that these representations all harmonize perfectly. Similarly, we shall see, the reality of time, the order of successives, is founded in the fact that each state or representation of any substance involves the reason for (or is a condition for) all those subsequent to it. Thus the intrinsic modifications on which spatial and temporal relations supervene are, ultimately, these modifications or states of monads. But the fact that these constitute objective orders of coexistence or succession that do not depend on individual perceptions is a consequence of the order that God has imposed on any possible world He could create. Leibniz describes this foundation of the reality of space and time as consisting in 'divine magnitude', namely the divine attributes of immensity and eternity, as we shall now see.

Space and Time, Immensity and Eternity

Leibniz contended that space and time, insofar as they are continuous, are not existing things but ideal entities. This contention is apt to seem more unusual to us than it would have to his contemporaries. For in the Scholastic tradition, space was distinguished from extension, and time from duration – distinctions that were lost after Newton, who regarded space as another word for extension, and time for duration. Traditionally, though, extension and duration were regarded as attributes of extended and enduring things, whereas space and time were abstractions. We can see Leibniz urging Clarke to recognize this distinction in their dispute over the ontic status of space and time: 'Things keep their extension, but they do not always keep their space. Each thing has its own extension, its own duration; but it does not have its own time, and does not keep its own space' (V § 46: GP vii 399/L 703). Moreover, although one could also have abstract concepts of extension and duration, space and time were regarded as differing from these in that they were taken to be *measures* of extension and duration. As such, they would be *quantities*, and would therefore have to be continuous. The spatial extent of a body would be judged by comparison with a standard length, and estimation of the duration of a process would involve comparison with the duration of a further motion taken as standard – such as that of the Sun's apparent rotation. Thus even though Descartes and his followers had diverged from tradition in regarding material substance as being constituted by what they considered its essential attribute, extension, they nevertheless upheld the traditional distinction between the attributes of extension and duration, and their measures, space and time. Thus in his *Principles of Philosophy* Descartes wrote: 'in order to measure the duration of all things, we compare the duration of the greatest and most regular motions which give rise to years and days, and we call this duration *time*' (AT viii A 27/CSM i 212). Similarly, in his controversy with Gassendi he insisted upon the difference between 'the duration of the enduring thing' and 'time considered in the abstract'; the latter is the mathematical construct, and is therefore truly continuous. We can see Leibniz taking Malebranche to task for not acknowledging this distinction in his dialogue *Conversation of Philarète and Ariste* (1712, revised 1715): 'Duration and extension are attributes of things, but time and space are considered to be something outside of things, and serve to measure them' (GP vi 584/L 621–2).

Now, even in his earliest work, Leibniz had distinguished space as an indeterminate quantity from the extension of the matter contained in it. For 'although [space] involves magnitude and figure, it does not involve a determinate magnitude and figure' (GP iv 107/L 111). It is continuous, and therefore perfectly homogeneous. In this respect it is like primary matter, which can also be conceived as a homogeneous whole prior to any divisions in it. Thus in a letter to his Leipzig professor Thomasius in 1669, Leibniz describes how matter has quantity, but 'is *unbounded*, as the Averroists call it, or *indefinite*'. As a continuous entity, 'matter is not cut into parts, and therefore does not actually have boundaries in it' (A VI ii 435/LoC 337). Here Leibniz is appealing to Aristotle's distinction between continuity and contiguity: the parts of a thing whose adjacent extremities are together are *contiguous*, that is, merely touching; whereas those whose adjacent extremities are one and the same boundary are *continuous* (Aristotle, *Physics*, Books 5 and 6, i.e. E and Z).

The same goes for space. In fact, Leibniz argues, this means that space is indistinguishable from matter if you ignore the resistance of bodies to being penetrated or being moved. In December 1675 he wrote:

> If I imagine in space, instead of an *extensum*, a perfect fluid which is at rest, but which, when another body is floating in it, moves to keep the place filled, then I mean nothing other than empty space. It would be matter if the motion of the body were retarded by its motion. (A VI iii 466/LoC 31)

Space, consequently, is an *extensum* – an extended entity – containing no actual parts. If it has no bodies in it, then, like primary matter, it will 'not actually have boundaries in it'. But by the same token, insofar as it contains bodies that are moving within it, it will be divided into parts along with the matter it contains. This means that while space in the abstract includes all possible divisions into parts, space conceived through time is a constantly changing partition, whose fluctuating boundaries are determined by the motions of the bodies within it. Such a conception is explicitly spelled out by Leibniz in some manuscripts written in March 1676, in his last year in Paris:

> Supposing space to have parts – that is to say, so long as it is divided by bodies into empty and full parts of various shapes – it follows that space itself is a whole or entity accidentally, that it is continuously changing and becoming something different: namely when its parts change, and are extinguished and supplanted by others. (A VI iii 391/LoC 53)

In a continuation of this passage, Leibniz distinguishes between space, which has constantly changing parts, and an eternally existing 'something in space that remains through these changes'. This he identifies as 'the immensity of God, an attribute that is one and indivisible, and at the same time immense' (391/55). This is a traditional doctrine: God gives reality to space by virtue of being locally present to all created things. Thus divine immensity is the 'basis of space', which 'is not divisible, as space is'; likewise, 'eternity is something indivisible, since it is the necessity of existing, which does not express succession, duration or divisibility' (391/55). (This wording, incidentally, bears close comparison with Spinoza's philosophy, which, as noted in chapter 5, Leibniz was studying assiduously with Tschirnhaus at this time.) This unchanging basis of space, 'the *immensum*', Leibniz writes a month later, is the indivisible 'extended per se'; when 'bulk or mass' is added to it, 'there result spaces, places and intervals, whose aggregates give Universal Space' (A VI iii 519/LoC 119–21). Thus universal space is an aggregate of places; it is a result of the addition to the *immensum* – which he also calls 'real space' – of actually divided matter. Leibniz compares it to a net which 'continually receives a different form, and thus changes' (519/121). The vehicle for such changes is the matter within each part or cell of this net, which he conceives as being inherently elastic.

On this picture, space is a constantly changing network or aggregate of places produced by the differing motions of bodies: all that endures of space through time is the partless *immensum*. An immediate implication of this, however, is that there is no immobile background space, such as Leibniz had previously taken for granted in his treatment of the laws of collision of bodies. As he later recalls, his doubts about 'whether there exists in nature such a being as we call space' (Leibniz 1991: 810–11), coupled with his abandonment of his prior laws of collision, led him to abandon his notion of absolute motion as a change of location in this absolute space. Thus by 1677 we find Leibniz explicitly asserting the relational nature of motion and space, and in a manuscript of 1678–80 describing time as a 'relation of things with each other' (namely *before*, *after* or *simultaneous with*: A VI iv 1397/LoC 243). As for continuity of motion and existence of bodies, for a period Leibniz takes refuge in the occasionalist solution that motion occurs through God's continual re-creation of the world at successive moments, with different divisions into actual parts at different moments. This changes with his new philosophy of substance in 1678: henceforth bodies may be thought of as aggregated from prior unities – i.e. enduring substances – whose passive force accounts for their elasticity and resistance to penetration, and whose active force accounts for their continuance through time.

Now one might have thought that once he had formulated his relational theories of space and time, Leibniz would have jettisoned the 'real space' of his Paris meditations. That he did not can be seen most clearly from a fragment written in the late 1680s, which begins by taking for granted the relational theory:

> Time and place, or duration and space, are real relations, i.e. orders of existing. Their foundation in reality is divine magnitude, to wit, eternity and immensity. For if to space or magnitude is added appetite, or, what comes to the same thing, endeavour, and consequently action too, already something substantial is introduced, which is in nothing other than God or the primary unity. That is to say, real space in itself is something that is one, indivisible, immutable; and it contains not only existences but also possibilities, since in itself, with appetite removed, it is indifferent to different ways of being dissected. But if appetite is added to space, it makes existing substances, and thus matter, or the aggregate of infinite unities. (A VI iv 1641/LoC 335)

Here we see that, as in the papers of 1676, space and time owe their foundation in reality to divine magnitude, that is, immensity and eternity. Immensity or real space is characterized as 'one, indivisible, immutable'; it is only divided into parts by the addition of actually divided matter. Only now what has to be added is not matter directly, but endeavour, equated with appetite; when this is added to space, 'it makes existing substances, and thus matter, or the aggregate of infinite unities'. Space, considered in itself, 'contains not only existences but also possibilities'; it is only a particular order of existing things when it has been divided by the motions or endeavours within it. This should be compared with what Leibniz publicly replied to Bayle in 1702: 'But space and time taken together constitute the order of possibilities of the one entire universe, so that these orders – space and time, that is – relate not only to what is actually is but also to anything that could be put in its place, just as numbers are indifferent to the things numerated' (GP iv 568/L 583). Thus space and time are intrinsic to all possible worlds because they are based in the divine attributes of immensity and eternity, which belong to the divine essence; particular existents, on the other hand, depend on God's will to create them in the order in which they appear. As Leibniz writes in the *New Essays*: 'However, where space is in question, we must attribute immensity to God, and this gives parts and order to his immediate operations. He is the source of possibilities and of existents alike, the one by his essence and the other by his will. So that space, like time, derives its reality from him' (NE 155). Thus we see that real space is like primary matter in that it lacks all forms and is 'indifferent to different ways of being dissected'. It is only the addition of the endeavours or appetitions belonging to each of the infinite individual substances that produces boundaries and shapes in space, and constitutes it as a particular order of existents created by the divine will. But in order to see how space can be conceived as a real manifold divided by the parts of matter in it, and at the same time be called relational, we need to proceed to Leibniz's Analysis Situs, the Analysis of Situation.

Space as the Order of Situations

The most important thing to understand about Leibniz's relational theory of space is that its primitives are not relations like 'to the left of', but *relations of situation*, or, more simply, situations. They are the *situs* (situations) of Leibniz's celebrated theory of Analysis Situs. This is not immediately obvious, since the latter is a branch of his *universal characteristic*, and is usually conceived as a mathematical theory that does not have any direct bearing on physics or the metaphysics of space. In fact, however, a situation denotes a given arrangement of bodies, modelled on the arrangement of the vertices in a geometrical figure. In the late 1670s, Leibniz conceived the idea of a new kind of geometry in which such situations are directly represented by symbols, without recourse to the Cartesian coordinates and equations of ordinary analysis. He wrote a large number of drafts for this Analysis Situs in 1679, returning to the project intermittently till the end of his life, but without ever producing a finished theory.

The idea of Analysis Situs, as Leibniz wrote in one of these drafts, is to represent 'situation directly and immediately, so that, even if the figures are not drawn, they are portrayed to the mind through symbols; and whatever the empirical imagination understands from the figures, this calculus derives by an exact calculation from the symbols' (*On Analysis Situs, c.* 1693: GM v 182–3/L 257). Consider, say, a tetrahedron. The apex of the figure has a determinate situation with respect to the other three vertices at its base, determined by the angles at each vertex, the proportions among its edges, and the distance between any two vertices. These same angles and distances will likewise determine the situation of any of the vertices to the rest. Again, the same situation between the four vertices could be represented by drawing lines from them to some arbitrary reference point, and then taking the angles between these lines, the proportions between them, and the distance from any one of them to the reference point. Leibniz's source here is probably Hobbes, who gives the same two equivalent characterizations of situation in his *De Corpore* (Hobbes 1668: Part II, chapter 14, §§ 21–2). In the first sense, a situation corresponds to a cell of Leibniz's infinitely divided space; in the second sense, every figured body in space has a situation with respect to a given point of view.

So far this may not seem promising, since these lines, proportions and angles would have to be embedded in a three-dimensional Euclidean space (a 3-space). But Leibniz's approach is to abstract from the figures basic relationships that do not depend on anything concerning their composition, but only on coincidence of their boundaries. Once these abstract relations are represented algebraically, they can be regarded as embodying these relationships independently of the Euclidean lines and surfaces in which they had been depicted. Proceeding in this way, Leibniz hoped eventually to be able to 'extend the characteristic to things which are not subject to the sensory imagination' (GM ii 27/L 253).

The three basic relations in Leibniz's Analysis Situs are *equality* (A = B), *similarity* (A ~ B) and *congruence* (A ≏ B). Two figures are similar to one another when they cannot be discerned from one another when considered in isolation. If they are similar and equal, they will be congruent. This depends on a fundamental distinction between *quality*, which can be conceived in things individually, and *quantity*, a determination of which can only be made by comparison: 'Quantity can be grasped only when the things are actually present together, or when some intervening thing can be applied to both', whereas 'quality presents something to the mind that can be recognized in a thing separately and can then be applied to the comparison of two things without actually bringing the two together' (*On Analysis Situs*, c. 1693: GM v 179/L 255).

Congruence, however, is the most fundamental relation, as the relation of situation is based on it. We have already seen that rather than defining situation, Leibniz prefers instead to define what it means for two things to have the same situation: a situation of two bodies A and B (written A.B) is the same as the situation of two other bodies C and D if A can be made to coincide with C and B with D: that is, if and only if they are congruent, A.B ≏ C.D (*Characteristica geometrica*, 1679: GM v 150). Thus the extremities of two equal straight-line segments have the same situation, as do the vertices of two triangles with equal sides. On this basis Leibniz derives several properties of situations, such as reflexivity (A.B ≏ B.A) and the reduction of A.B.C ≏ A.C.B to A.B ≏ A.C (157). A point is defined as 'what has situation and does not have extension', whereas space, on the contrary, is what has extension but no situation. (Formally, 'if A is in X, and because of this A ≏ X, then A will be a point'; whereas, if A is a point, then space is all those points Y such that A ≏ Y.) (*In Euclidis PROTA*: GM v 183). A point is not just that which lacks parts: it also has situation, 'otherwise an instant of time would also be a point, as would a soul' (183). And anything that has situation is situated with respect to everything else. This allows Leibniz to construe space as *constituted by points, but not composed of them*. Since each point has its situation to all the others, this is what an instantaneous space consists in: it is a system of relations of situation, an *order of situations*.[4]

Two centuries later Moritz Pasch, Giuseppe Veronese and Giuseppe Peano will use the kinds of combinatorial properties of congruence derived by Leibniz to define it algebraically. Similarly, Poincaré, Brouwer, Hermann Weyl (1885–1955) and James W. Alexander (1888–1971) will use a combinatorial approach to defining a very general topological space, beginning with 'simplexes' and 'complexes' that correspond closely to Leibniz's situations. But Leibniz does not achieve such generality. Part of the reason for this is that for him space is inherently *metrical*: it is defined in terms of congruence, and congruence involves quantity or distance. Thus although his conception of space as constituted by an ordering of situated points prefigures the modern conception of space as a manifold of points endowed with structure by ordering relations, Leibniz does not in fact anticipate the affine and topological spaces of modern mathematics.

But perhaps the deeper reason for his not anticipating these more general spaces is that, unlike later thinkers, Leibniz still conceives space as an abstraction from existing extended things, rather than as a self-standing entity. Thus the distance involved in congruence is in the first instance that between situated bodies, bodies *in extenso*, and only derivatively in the space abstracted from them. It is not an attribute bestowed on things by virtue of their being in an intrinsically quantified space, as Francesco Patrizi (1529–97) and, following him, Newton, conceived it. Moreover, Leibniz could not have accepted a space built on merely nominal definitions; he wanted real definitions of its terms, and this required philosophical analysis. Now quantity, as we have seen, can only be determined by comparison, that is, when 'things are actually present together', i.e. coexist with other things at the same time. Thus situation is a mode of coexistence: 'A *Situation* is nothing but that state of a thing by which it happens that it is understood to exist in a certain way with other *extensa* at the same time; that is, the mode of co-existing' (Leibniz 1995b: 276–7). Coexistence was conceived by Leibniz in terms of simultaneous perception: all coexistents must in principle be perceivable together:

> When we conceive two points as simultaneously existing, and ask why we say they are simultaneously existing, we will think the reason is that they are simultaneously perceived, or at least that they can be simultaneously perceived. Whenever we perceive something as existing, we thereby perceive it to be in space, that is, we perceive that there can exist indefinitely many other things absolutely indiscernible from it. (228–9)

In this way, Leibniz tried to give phenomenological derivations of lines, distances, extension and space, all in terms of simultaneous perceptibility. 'What is perceived when two points are simultaneously perceived', he argued, 'is a *straight line*, that is, the path of a point' (228). Later, in the *Initia rerum* of 1714, he would define distance in terms of the simplest order through intermediate coexisting perceptions: 'this simplest order is the shortest path from one to the other, whose magnitude is called *distance*' (GM vii 25/L 671). And from the mid-1680s:

> We call *extension* whatever we observe as common to all simultaneous perceptions; and we call an *extensum* that by the perception of which we can perceive several things simultaneously; and this for some indefinite reason. Hence an *extensum* is a continuous whole whose parts are simultaneous and have a situation among themselves, and in the same way this whole behaves as a part with respect to another whole. A continuous whole is that whose parts are indefinite; space itself is such a thing, abstracting the soul from those things that are in it. (A VI iv 565/LoC 271)

Here we are dealing with abstract or mathematical space, in which the things entering into relations of situation are mutually *indiscernible*. We are discussing what all perceptions must have in common, but not the specific contents of the perceptions of actual phenomena. The actual situations of phenomena, on the other hand, are expressed more or less confusedly in the perceptions of each monad. Thus, although the representation of a plurality of coexistent objects regarded as indiscernible gives rise to the perception of a homogeneous extension, a purely extrinsic interrelation of positions, the relations among the actual phenomena must be expressed in the perceptions, which are intrinsic modifications of the substances. As Leibniz expresses it in a piece written in about 1696,

> Thus to be in a place seems, abstractly at any rate, to imply nothing but position. But in actuality, what is placed must express place in itself; so that distance and the degree of distance involves also a degree of expressing a remote thing in the thing itself, a degree of affecting it or of receiving an affection from it. So, in fact, situation really involves a degree of expressions. (*On the Principle of Indiscernibles*: C 9/MP 133)

Leibniz amplifies on these points in his fifth letter to Clarke, where he shows how to account for motion in space. When we come across a number of things existing simultaneously, we 'observe in them a certain order of coexistence, according to which the relation of one thing to another is more or less simple' (§ 47: GP vii 400/L 703). This is their *situation*, which involves, as we have seen, the path between them; and the simplest such path is the shortest, namely the straight line, whose magnitude is their mutual distance. The order according to which these situations are disposed is the figure with these bodies as its vertices, say, A.C.E.F.G. Now let us 'suppose or feign' that the situation of C, E, F and G, and so on, with respect to each other remains invariant (they are *fixed existents*), and that B comes to be situated with respect to them just as A was, so that their relations of situation agree. Now B will be said to be 'in the same place' as A was, 'and that which comprises all those places is called space'. 'This shows', Leibniz adds, 'that in order to have an idea of place, and consequently of space, it is sufficient to consider these relations and the rules of their changes, without needing to fancy any absolute reality apart from the things whose situation we consider' (400/703). More formally, B will be in the same place as A if and only if B.C.E.F.G $\simeq$ A.C.E.F.G, and this place will be the equivalence class of all situations Y.C.E.F.G congruent to A.C.E.F.G. Space 'is that which results from places taken together' (400/703). Here Leibniz adds that of course A and B cannot have precisely and individually the same relations of situation; rather,

> these relations agree only. For two different subjects, as *A* and *B*, cannot have precisely the same individual affection, it being impossible that the same individual accident should be in two subjects or pass from one subject to another. But the mind, not contented with an agreement, looks for an identity, for something that should be truly the same, and conceives it as being extrinsic to the subject; and this is what we here call *place* or *space*. (401/704)

Here we see that a relation of situation is characterized as an individual accident of the body possessing it; this is situation as a *concrete situation*, what is manifested as a phenomenon. This will correspond to a particular degree of expressions in the substance. Once one represents these relations as a network or complex of lines and boundaries, one has abstracted away from the individual accidents, and represented the lines as if self-standing and external to the bodies, that is, as places. Space is 'an order of situations', and 'abstract space is that order of situations when they are conceived as being possible' (415/714).

Leibniz's theory of space is evidently quite complicated. In a nutshell, it is that space is an order of situations. These situations are the mutual arrangements of bodies, their distances and angular relations to one another at a given time. Each such situation of a body is grounded in the substance whose body it is, and involves a 'degree of expressions' of that substance in its perception of all others, where the perceptions of that substance are from the point of view of its sense organs. Such a space is instantaneous, the order of simultaneously existing things. Abstract space is the order of all situations conceived as possible; it is an abstraction from existing extended things, and is therefore an ideal entity. Every possible thing must be situated with respect to other existing things, and the foundation for this ordering is divine immensity (i.e. God's being locally present to all created things). Finally, distinct from both instantaneous space and the purely mathematical abstract space is the absolute space in which motions can be represented. This depends on the fiction of certain bodies remaining in the same situation, and representing motions as continuous transformations of the situations of other bodes relative to them. We can imagine bodies tracing paths in such an enduring space (what we now call spacetime), but this is 'a mere ideal thing', consisting 'only in the truth of relations and not at all in any absolute reality' (402/704).

Time as the Order of Successive Things

Time, according to Leibniz, is the order of succession, that is, the order according to which all successive things are disposed. This is analogous, obviously, to his definition of space as an order of situations. Just as space in the abstract encompasses all possible situations, so time in the abstract encompasses all possible successions, and whereas the concrete situations of particular bodies are founded in the modifications of substances, so concrete successions are the particular orders of changes of those modifications. And whereas the basis of space is the divine attribute of immensity, so that of time is the divine attribute of eternity.

According to many readings of his philosophy, this can only mean that Leibniz denied the reality of time altogether. To be sure, there are changes among the phenomena; but among things as they are in themselves – the monads – there are only differences of states, and the states are but the perceptions of those monads. Thus time pertains only to appearances, and there is no change or time in monads themselves. On such grounds, Bergson, for example, claimed that Leibniz was led to 'regard the temporal aspect of things as a mere illusion' (Bergson 1911: 353). And Russell – despite his disparagement of almost everything else Bergson said about time – agreed on this point, arguing that Leibniz was committed to the unreality of time as a result of his 'denial of relations'.

As we saw above, however, the truth is more nearly the exact opposite. From the beginning, Leibniz had stressed the *connection of all things*, and in his *Dissertation* he had echoed Bisterfeld in seeing this connection as founded in relations, in the intrinsic relatedness of things. When he begins to fashion his reform of metaphysics in the late 1670s, Bisterfeld's notion of each thing's *perception* of 'what is congruent to it, and what is not' is recast in terms of representation: each state or perception of a substance represents or expresses the whole of the rest of the universe simultaneous with it. Thus those states or perceptions are simultaneous which are *harmonious* with one another, that is, do not contradict one another. *Appetition*, meanwhile, is construed in terms of the active force constituting each created substance, 'which brings about change, or the passage from one perception to another' (*Monadology* § 15: GP vi 609/WFT 269). This passage from state to state, moreover, is in accordance with the individual law of the series. As Leibniz explains to Clarke, 'the nature of every simple substance, soul, or true monad, is such that its following state is a consequence of the preceding one' (V § 91: GP vii 412/L 711). That is, one state precedes another in time, a is earlier than b, if b is a logical consequence of a. Thus precedence in the 'order of reasons' correlates perfectly with temporal priority.

Some critics have objected that this correlation reduces time to logic: change in time consists merely in difference of location in the order of reasons. Burchard de Volder raises an objection of this kind. When Leibniz explains to him that the persistence of the same law of the series in a succession of monadic states is 'what produces our belief that the subject of change, or monad, is the same', and is 'exactly what I say constitutes it as the same substance' (GP ii 264/ LDV 291), De Volder responds that he cannot understand 'how any succession can follow from the nature of a thing, viewed in itself' (260/283). In a series of numbers, for example, 'nothing is thought of as successive'. To this Leibniz replies, 'I do not say that every series is a temporal succession, but only that a temporal succession is a series, which has in common with other series the property that the law of the series shows where it must arrive in continuing its progress' (263/289). He grants that it is indeed impossible to see how such a succession follows from the nature of a substance if one has a conception of the nature of a substance like De Volder's, where this nature is not individual, but abstract and mathematical. But on his view, 'all individual things are successions or are subject to succession'. When God elects to create the world, He creates individual substances that are intrinsically active, 'spiritual automatons', which spontaneously change from one state to another by this inherent dynamism: 'the nature of a substance necessarily requires and essentially involves some progress or change, without which it would have no force to act' (GP iv 485/WFT 151).

Thus the objection that temporal precedence reduces to logical precedence ignores the crucial role of active force, that which brings one state out of those that precede it. Without such a force, the universe would indeed be static – it would be so many possible states arranged in a certain order. With it, monadic states are temporally ordered by virtue of being produced in their logical order, but as a result of the activity of the substance they really do succeed one another in time: substance necessarily involves change, since it is essentially something that acts.

In a manuscript from the 1680s, Leibniz formulates his theory of time as follows. A state that is logically prior to other states is, in his terminology, 'prior by nature' to them, and therefore prior in time to all those derivable from it. Moreover, because each state represents the whole world from its own point of view, simultaneous states in a given world must all be compatible with one another, and states in a given world that are not simultaneous must contradict one another:

> And therefore that is *prior by nature* whose possibility is more easily demonstrated; or, that which is more easily understood. Of two states one of which contradicts the other, that is *earlier in time* which is prior by nature. Two incompatible or contradictory existents differ in time, and that is earlier or later in time which is prior or posterior by nature. (A VI iv 181)

In a second formulation from the same period, Leibniz writes:

> Now that is understood to be earlier which is simultaneous with the cause, that later which is simultaneous with the effect. Or the earlier is understood as that which is simpler or what is the requisite of the other. For I have defined a requisite as a condition simpler by nature than that whose condition it is. (A VI iv 628/LoC 273–5)

To such formulations, though, objections have been made as follows. In correlating time with the internal law of each substance or monad, Leibniz presupposes an *intrinsic monadic time* for each substance. If each substance has its own law and its own force, it would seem to have its own law of succession. In the words of Nicholas Rescher, in addition to the 'public time obtaining throughout the system of monads in general' and determined by inter-monadic harmony, there would be 'the essentially private, intra-monadic time of each individual substance continuing, by appetition, through its transitions from state to state' (Rescher 1967: 92). But this objection underestimates the strong connection holding among the states of all the monads in each possible world. Each state involves the reason for any later state of the same monad, but because this later state must harmoniously represent the coexisting states of all the other monads in the same universe, the earlier state involves the reason for all those states too. As Leibniz explains to Clarke in 1716,

> Since the nature of every simple substance, soul, or true monad, is such that its following state is a consequence of the preceding one; it is there that the whole cause of the *harmony* is to be found. For God has only to make a simple substance be once and from the beginning a *representation of the universe*, according to its point of view; since from this alone it follows that it will be so perpetually, and that all simple substances will always have a harmony among themselves, because they always represent the same universe. (V § 91: GP vii 412/L 711–12)

In other words, the fact that a state is a representation of the same universe from its own point of view guarantees that there exists a unique class of possible monadic states that are in harmony with it, and therefore simultaneous with it. Thus the law of one monadic series, in determining uniquely a succession of states of that monad, *thereby* also determines a unique succession of all the sets of simultaneous states of the other monads in the same universe.

This feature is made explicit by Leibniz in his mature account of his theory of time in the *Initia rerum* of 1714. There he begins by stating that the states of simultaneous things are harmonious in that they 'do not involve each other's opposite', while earlier states of the same thing 'involve the reason for' later ones:

> *If many states of things are assumed to exist, none of which involves its opposite, they are said to exist simultaneously.* Thus we deny that the things that happened last year are simultaneous with those happening this year, since they involve opposite states of the same thing.
> *If one of two states that are not simultaneous involves the reason for the other, the former is held to be the earlier, the latter to be the later.* My

earlier state involves the reason for the existence of my later state. (GM vii 18/L 666)

It is here that he introduces what has been called his 'axiom of connection': 'And since, because of the connection of all things, my earlier state involves the earlier state of the other things as well, it also involves the reason for the later state of these other things so that my earlier state is in fact earlier than their later state as well' (18/666). This axiom guarantees that the states in all the differing series corresponding to different individual substances in the same world 'line up'; without it, there would be an infinity of different temporal successions or times, as Rescher had charged. Coexisting states must line up, of course, since all the substances in a given possible world must be *compossible*. That is, the states of differing substances existing at the same time must reflect the same universe, and so cannot involve any determinations that are incompatible with one another. Adam cannot be eating an apple that Eve has just thrown away.

This account has all the ingredients needed to construct time as a *total ordering*: it guarantees, in Leibniz's own words, that *'whatever exists is either simultaneous with, earlier than, or later than some other given existent'* (18/666). For one state to be at the same time as another is just for it to be a member of an equivalence class of all those states that are simultaneous with one another (because they contain no contradictory determinations); for one state to be earlier than another is for it to contain the reason for that state or for one simultaneous with it. Times are therefore purely relational: a time is identified relative to what occurs at it, not by reference to an instant presupposed as existing independently of it.

In his dispute with Newton and Clarke, Leibniz constructs a *reductio ad absurdum* argument on this basis (III § 6: GP vii 364–5/L 682–3). Suppose, he says, that if instead of creating the world when he did, God had instead created it a year earlier, with all the relations and intervals between events remaining the same. On Newton's view, creation would have had to have occurred at the instant of absolute time $t_0 - 1$, instead of at t_0 (with t measured in years). But there is no way to distinguish these times except by reference to the things occurring in them, since all the instants of absolute time are exactly alike: since $t_0 - 1$ and t_0 both denote the instant of creation, 'there is no mark or difference whereby it would be possible to know that this world was created sooner' (V § 55: 405/ 706–7). Applying the Principle of the Identity of Indiscernibles, the two situations are therefore identical. This proves that the instants of absolute time are ideal things: they are only nominally, but not really, distinct. Creation could not take place a year earlier on the relational view, since the instant of creation is identified by what happens in it, and by its relation to what happens at all other times.

This account of time as an ordering of succession is based on the idea that a given possible world is determined by its own 'law'. This would correspond to the set of divine decrees that would go into the making of that particular universe – the 'laws of general order of that possible universe' (to Arnauld, 14 July 1686: GP ii 51/WFT 107). This gives us what Leibniz described to Clarke as 'real times' (V § 27: GP vii 395/L 700): the concrete orders of succession of the things existing in that universe. Time in the abstract, on the other hand, would be the order of all possible such successions, relating 'not only to what is actually is but also to anything that could be put in its place' (GP iv 568/L 583), as noted above. That states are temporally ordered is a feature of all possible worlds, and is based in the divine essence, a real order depending on divine eternity. But the particular temporal order of existing things depends on God's will.

So far this account does not include a basis for determining the quantity of time. Now on Leibniz's account, *'Quantity or magnitude is that which can be recognized in things only by their compresence or simultaneous perception'* (GM vii 19/L 667). This invites a potentially damaging objection, for if the determination of quantity depends on things being perceived simultaneously, it is inapplicable to successive things. The Newtonians, who posited time as a self-existent magnitude, did not fail to perceive this weakness. Thus (with Newton's tacit approval) Clarke objected that time as a quantity must be something more than just an order: 'the order of things succeeding each other in time is not time itself, for they may succeed each other faster or slower in the same order of succession, but not in the same time' (Clarke to Leibniz, IV § 41: GP vii 387/L 695). In his reply, Leibniz appeals to a conception of magnitude as the number of constituents interposed: 'For if the time is greater, there will be more successive and like states interposed, and if it is smaller, there will be fewer' (V § 105: 415/714). Likewise in the *Initia rerum* he had written of determining nearness and distance *'in time as well as in space'* in terms of a 'maximally determined' or 'simplest path' through interposed constituents, but he gave no account of how a simplest path in time could be determined. In order for this to work, the 'like states interposed' would have to be the durations of similar phenomena, such as the uniform motions used for clocks (GM vii 18/L 666–7).[5] But the comparison of motions will necessarily involve change of place through time, that is, the determination of a simplest path or a straight line in spacetime, which Leibniz did not attempt.

Subsequent developments have shown that Leibniz was on the right track, even if the obstacle is the assumption that lies at the very heart of his theory: that there is a unique set of events simultaneous with any one event in the universe. If one drops his axiom of connection, and reinterprets 'containing the reason for' in terms of its being possible for a physical process to go from one event to another, then it is possible to construct axiomatically the basis for the Minkowski spacetime of Einstein's physics, including its metric structure, as was first shown by A. A. Robb. But this would have required Leibniz to relinquish the notion that each state represents the whole universe simultaneous with it – the representation of the infinite in a unity that is at the core of his metaphysics.

Now let us turn from these scientific considerations to a consideration of Leibniz's moral and political philosophy, including his views on law and on theology. To us this may seem like a radical change of subject. For Leibniz it was not: just as his views on space and time were bound up with his conception of God's action in the world, so, as we will see, his attempts to provide firm foundations for the theory of justice, theology and morals were part and parcel of the same project that motivated his reforms in physics.

8

Morals and Politics

There is perhaps no respect in which Leibniz has been more maligned than for his morals, whether for his moral philosophy, his own moral character, or both together. This began with Voltaire's lampooning of him in *Candide* (1759) as the puffed-up and ridiculously unworldly Dr Pangloss. No matter what calamities beset his pupil Candide and himself, Pangloss trots out the pseudo-Leibnizian aphorism, 'All is for the best in this best of all possible worlds!' Thus in one blow, Voltaire (born François-Marie Arouet, 1694–1778) represents Leibniz's political philosophy as an apology for the status quo, and his theology as an apology for God's mistakes. Russell adds to this scorn for Leibniz's theology and politics an impugning of his moral character, as noted in chapter 1, accusing Leibniz of betraying his own better logical philosophy for a fawning political conservatism in an effort to ingratiate himself with nobility. And this character assassination has been continued by Matthew Stewart (2006), who not only portrays Leibniz as completely unprincipled, but even insinuates his connivance in the murky circumstances surrounding Spinoza's death.[1] Lastly, even professional philosophers sympathetic to Leibniz have not thought well of his moral philosophy. To most contemporary philosophers his definition of justice as 'the charity of the wise' is apt to seem as old-fashioned as his out-of-style wig, while his concerted efforts to answer 'the great question of freedom and necessity, above all in the production and origin of evil' (GP vi 29/T 53), is seen as a disappointing failure, a half-baked attempt to make free will compatible with causal determinism.

I think all of this reaction would have been very surprising and bitterly disappointing to Leibniz, had he lived to experience it. It is not just the slights on his character or the fact that the criticisms of his views misunderstand what he saw himself as attempting to achieve; what would have hurt more would have been the charges of moral insincerity. For there is a sense in which Leibniz's moral vision was at the heart of all of his own political and religious initiatives, from the juridical reforms he strove to undertake under Baron von Boineburg's wing, through his persistent attempts to achieve church reunification, to his interventions on behalf of those Jesuits who respected the natural theology of the Chinese.

Justice, Natural Law and Voluntarism

To see how the criticisms of Voltaire, Russell and Stewart badly misread Leibniz, we could do worse than go back to the beginning of his career, when he had just left Leipzig for the Catholic court of Mainz. First, however naïve Leibniz might have been about politics on arriving in Mainz, it is hard to imagine that he would have remained so for long after starting his collaboration with a man of the world such as Boineburg. Raised as a Lutheran, Boineburg had been obliged to undergo a conversion to Catholicism in order to serve as Secretary of State for Archbishop von Schönborn at Mainz, and had then taken part in all the complex political negotiations following the Peace of Westphalia until 1663. After incurring the Archbishop's displeasure, Boineburg was thrown into jail and then expelled from Mainz, but in 1668 he managed to reconcile with Schönborn, a reconciliation sealed by the marriage of his daughter to the Archbishop's son. From then until his untimely death in 1673, he collaborated with his young protégé on a variety of political projects. One of these was the famous *Egyptian plan*, mentioned in chapter 1, a diplomatic effort to divert the Sun King's military ambitions for some of the German states bordering France by suggesting he invade Egypt instead. The Leibniz who arrived in Paris clutching his latest draft of this Machiavellian proposal – with the ink hardly dry on its hundreds of pages of arguments – could scarcely be mistaken for a young Pangloss.

On the other hand, it is odd for someone with as little principle as Stewart makes him out to have that Leibniz never did follow Boineburg's lead in converting to Catholicism: not to enter Schönborn's services, nor as a result of the entreaties in the 1680s of the

Landgrave Ernst von Hessen-Rheinfels, who had hoped Arnauld would succeed where he had failed, and not even when he was offered a position as custodian of the Vatican library in 1695. A position in Rome would have been enormously attractive to Leibniz, who was by then desperate to escape the provincialism of the Hanoverian court for the wider world of learning and culture. But, as his most recent biographer writes, 'for all his little subterfuges and equivocations in prolonging his travels to the south, Leibniz was not prepared to bend his principles and convert to Catholicism, despite the great attraction of settling in such an intellectually stimulating environment' (Antognazza 2009: 306).

And when we look at what Leibniz was thinking in those early years of theorizing with Boineburg, a very different picture of him emerges from the deeply conservative moralist derided by his critics. Indeed, if there is one figure who dominates his thinking in these years it is the English radical philosopher Hobbes. We have already seen how much Leibniz was influenced by Hobbes in his conception of thought as a kind of computation, and also in his early *conatus* physics and philosophy of mind. But the same impulse and method that informed those researches also informed Leibniz's approach to reforming jurisprudence and grounding moral philosophy – namely going to the very heart of the New Philosophy to extract its guiding principles, and then showing how on this foundation a philosophy could be fashioned that was not only serviceable and progressive, but also in keeping with Christian values. And in the case of morals, Leibniz identified this principle as *self-interestedness*: people do not choose to do anything that they do not perceive to be to their advantage or use. We see Leibniz pinning his colours to this mast very explicitly in a letter to Conring of 1670, where he adopts the same defiant commitment to the cause of modernism that we saw in his later letters to the same correspondent in 1678 (see chapter 1 above):

> I suppose with Carneades (and Hobbes is of the same opinion) that to be just without any gain for oneself (current or future gain) would be the height of foolishness. The Stoics and the Sadducees are very far away from human nature when they boast that virtue is desirable in itself. So every just thing must be a privately beneficial thing. (A II i 47)

For Conring, an established Aristotelian professor, forty years Leibniz's senior, such views must have seemed scandalous. Carneades, the ancient Greek Sceptic, had argued that because there is only self-interest, a belief in justice is folly. Hobbes had argued that individual self-interest could best be promoted in society by the establishing of the state, through a kind of social contract. Whereas in the state of nature, Hobbes maintained, one has the right to do whatever one thinks necessary for self-preservation irrespective of the effect that action has on others, in a political state self-protection is best achieved by entering into a contract with others in which the right is transferred to the sovereign. Laws are part of such a contract, and justice is the obligation to keep contracts. Moral obligations, on the other hand, are only binding in the context of the security and assurance that the state provides. Thus the existence of a powerful state is a necessary condition of morality and perhaps also justice. Hobbes is therefore not only a legal positivist, in that he does not think that morality is a fundamental condition of legality, but also a reductivist concerning morality: he thinks it is always based in self-interest, although in a civilized state self-interest is determined by the social contract. Such views would be opposed by Aristotelians like Conring, who would have seen sociability as an innate feature of human nature. On the one hand, in following Aristotle they would have been trying to define justice as a kind of mean (perhaps between self-love and altruism); on the other, they would have been intent on defending a Christian conception of justice in terms of loving one's neighbour.

Now Leibniz, too, was opposed to legal positivism. In his doctoral thesis at Altdorf (1666) he had argued that positive law only derives its justification from a contract through which natural rights have been transferred to the sovereign, in which context natural law is not applicable. Therefore when positive law is insufficient to decide certain cases – the *casus perplexi* that were the subject of the thesis – we should return to the principles on which that law is based. Natural reason provides the mechanism and procedures for the solution of such cases, while natural law – in particular, principles of strict right and equity – provides the substantive content that guides such decisions.[2] Here he was much influenced by his reading of Hugo Grotius (1583–1645) – 'the incomparable Grotius', as he calls him more than once (D iv 276/PW65; GP vi 53/T 77) – and it will be worth dwelling on this for the light it throws on the young Leibniz's orientation. For Grotius had anticipated Hobbes by insisting that a people can, over time, give up their rights to a ruler in return for a just and peaceable society, so that the institutions resulting from these incremental transferrals of rights can eventually coalesce into the state. But where Hobbes and Grotius agree about the transfer of rights by a social contract, the key difference lies in Grotius' insistence that the warrant for the contract comes ultimately from rights based on natural law. For Hobbes, by contrast, the rights we give up in acceding to the social contract are *rights of nature*, consisting in the 'blameless liberty of using our own natural power and ability'[3] for our own self-preservation. But since such 'a right of every man to every thing' is of little use if someone else 'as strong, or stronger than himself, hath right to the same', the social contract is determined not only by contingent historical circumstances, as in Grotius, but at bottom by relationships of power. The same applies to divine justice: 'God in His natural kingdom hath a right to rule, and to punish those who break His laws', Hobbes wrote, 'from His sole irresistible power' (*De cive* xv, 5). Thus for Hobbes all justice, divine as well as human, is ultimately established through power, reminiscent of the 'might is right' doctrine of Thrasymachus in Plato's *Republic*.

In opposing Hobbes on this, Leibniz followed Grotius' lead. This can be seen in comments he made later in life (*c.* 1706) on the philosophy of law of his contemporary, Samuel Pufendorf (1632–94). To the latter's definition of law as 'a command by which the superior obliges the subject to himself, in order to conform his actions to what it prescribes' (D iv 279/PW 70), Leibniz objects that it commits him to the Hobbesian position that there is no justice in the state of nature. Moreover, it follows from this that someone who possesses supreme power will not be doing anything unjust even 'if he proceeds tyrannically against his subjects, if he robs them at will, crushes and kills them through torture, or if he makes war on others without cause' (279/70). Nor can Pufendorf escape the consequences of this position by appealing to the fact that only God has such supreme power, and that the tyrant would still be sinning in His eyes. For this merely pushes the question of the origin of justice back one step further, making God's will the sole reason for something's being just.

This position on divine justice, known as *voluntarism*[4] (from *voluntas*, Latin for will), was well stated by Jacques-Bénigne Bossuet (1627–1704), Leibniz's opponent in matters theological: 'that everything God wills becomes the best because his will is the cause of all the good and all the best that exists in nature' (*Traité du libre arbiter*; quoted from PW 8). Leibniz consistently opposed voluntarism throughout his life, insisting that God's understanding of the good is prior to His will. If what is good and just is so simply because

God has willed it, then whatever has been decreed by God (or the gods) is good and just by definition. In *Meditation on the Common Concept of Justice* from around 1703 (probably written for Duchess Sophie, who liked this kind of humour), Leibniz allows himself a ribald joke: noting the Emperor Claudius' decree that 'in a free republic, farting (*crepitus*) and belching should be free', he writes, 'it would follow that if Claudius had made the god Crepitus one of the authorized gods, he would have been a god worthy of worship!' (PW 47/L 562). In thus opposing voluntarism, Leibniz acknowledges Grotius, 'who observed that there would still be a natural obligation even if it were granted – what cannot be granted – that God does not exist, or if divine existence were left out of consideration' (D iv 279/PW 71).[5] Such obligation, Grotius had claimed, 'proceeds from the essential traits implanted in man' (Grotius 1625: Prol. § 12).

There are two implications of this position, and Leibniz followed Grotius on both counts. First, in its commitment to *naturalism*: natural law must be determined by a study of the rational and social aspects of human nature, and not by appeal to divine revelation. Second, in its *Platonism*: if God wills justly, then He wills according to the same standard of justice as do we, one based in reason, not in an arbitrary will. Moral norms and the nature of justice, Leibniz concludes, 'do not depend on God's free decree, but rather on eternal truths, objects of the divine intellect, which constitute, so to speak, the essence of divinity itself' (D iv 280/PW 71).

All of which brings us back to Leibniz's letter to Conring of 1670: why, if he opposed voluntarism (and this opposition was there from the beginning), did he side with Hobbes on self-interest? The answer is that Leibniz did not see acting in one's self-interest as being opposed to acting in the interests of others. Grotius had criticized Carneades for saying that 'every creature is led by Nature to seek its own advantage', objecting that people desire to live 'peaceably and in a community' (Grotius 1625: 79–81). Leibniz did not dispute that we act out of self-interest any more than had Hobbes, but did not regard this as incompatible with sociability or morality.[6] Here his views were in tune with Gassendi's moral philosophy, which consisted in a defence of Epicurus' doctrine that people are naturally inclined to be happy. 'Happiness, or a life free from pain and misery,' Gassendi argued, 'are the things that influence and direct all our actions and purposes in order to obtain them' (Schneewind 1990: 355). To suppose that such a view is in conflict with Christian moral teaching, he maintained, is a misunderstanding. An enlightened pursuit of self-interest involves a respect for the interests of others too. Thus the maxim 'Don't do to anyone else what you would not have them do to you' is described by Gassendi as 'the first natural law' (366). For 'not only is there nothing more natural or according to nature than society, and society being not able to subsist without this precept, it ought also to be esteemed natural; but also because God seems to have imprinted it in the hearts of all men' (366). Similarly, Leibniz explicitly takes Grotius to task for opposing Carneades in his *Elements of Natural Law* (1669–71) (A VI i 431). Grotius has not established from principles and definitions how man's inclination for society is supposed to follow from human nature, or how it is supposed to be contrary to acting in one's own interest.

In the subsequent drafts of the *Elements*, Leibniz sets about trying to do just that. Crucial to the success of this undertaking was his adoption of the notion of endeavour (*conatus*), which played such a founding role in the philosophies of both Hobbes and Spinoza. Although it is purely an endeavour for self-preservation that they take as basic, their methodological decision to make endeavour foundational is what gives their definitions causal force, ensuring a philosophy that is compatible with determinism. In keeping with this, Leibniz defined justice as 'a constant endeavour (*conatus*) toward the common happiness while preserving one's own' (454). Now his problem was to set things up in such a way that both acting in one's own interests and acting in others' were equally consequences of the definitions. After several tries, and with close attention to Hobbes's account of the affects (emotions) in *On Man*, Leibniz finds the solution in 'a true definition of love': 'We love a thing whose happiness causes our own pleasure' (457). In this definition, private advantage and love of one's neighbours are reconciled in one affect, love. Natural law is reconciled with Christian love of one's neighbour:[7]

> Since then justice requires that the good of others is sought for its own sake, [and] since to seek the good of others for its own sake is to love others, it follows that love is of the nature of justice. Justice will therefore be the habit of loving others (or of seeking the good of others for its own sake, [or] of taking pleasure in the good of others). . . . Justice is the habit of loving all human beings. (464–5)

As Antognazza comments (2009: 114), from this beginning it is but a short step to Leibniz's mature definition of justice as '*caritas sapientis'*, the charity of the wise. He first articulates this definition in a letter to Duke Johann Friedrich in May 1677 (A I ii 23), but it becomes the cornerstone of his moral philosophy from then on. The logical steps from the desire for happiness and the 'habit of love' to the 'charity of the wise' are laid out by him in a chain of definitions in 1681:

> *Justice* is *the charity of the wise.*
> *Charity* is general *benevolence.*
> *Benevolence* is the habit of love.
> *To love someone* is to delight in that person's happiness. (GP vii 73)

Leibniz presents a very similar line of reasoning in *Felicity*, a short tract from the 1690s, where he claims that 'Justice is charity or a habit of loving conformed to wisdom' (Grua ii 579/PW 83).

There is, of course, development in Leibniz's views on politics and justice during the course of his career. Thus whereas the *New Method for Learning and Teaching Jurisprudence* of 1667 (D iv 159–229) appears compatible with conventional contractarianism, he makes little appeal to social contract theory after he has formulated his own position in 1671. He cedes that common security is the foundation of the state, but hopes that 'one can obtain something more for people than security, namely happiness' (to Falaideau, 1705: PW 29). Again, whereas his earlier writings on international relations were dominated by the hope that the Republic of Christendom could be restored, in his preface to the *Codex iuris gentium* of 1693 (a collection of medieval documents supporting the position of the Holy Roman Empire against the claims of the French), he shows a new inclination to accept the existence of sovereign nation states, and even allows that there is something to Hobbes's view that 'between different states and peoples there is perpetual war' (D iv 287/PW 166). There is nonetheless considerable continuity. For in that same preface he repeats the threefold distinction between different degrees of natural right he had given in the *New Method*: the strict right that applies in commutative justice; the equity or charity that applies in distributive justice; and the piety or probity that applies in universal justice – 'whence come the most general and commonly accepted principles of right: to injure no one, to give each his due, and to live honestly (or rather, piously)' (295/171–2). Moreover, he derives all this from the very same conception of justice he had delineated in his youth: 'Justice is the charity of the wise, that is, charity which follows the dictates of wisdom' (294/171). Since everyone desires happiness, and loving others gives them pleasure, justice is the habit of loving others, a habit wise people will adopt. His position thus blends features of several main ethical theories into a typical Leibnizian synthesis: everyone desires happiness (Epicurus); this involves charity toward others (Christ); charity is a virtue of a wise person (Aristotelian virtue ethics); divine justice is based on the same standard as human justice, one existing in the divine understanding, not resulting from an arbitrary will (Plato, Grotius); and this is all grafted onto a Hobbesian–Spinozist foundation, where people's actions are determined by a constant endeavour, an endeavour toward other people's happiness as well as their own.

Determinism, Freedom and the Lazy Fallacy

Given this naturalistic foundation, where human actions are determined by endeavours, Leibniz has committed himself to a moral philosophy as deterministic as Hobbes's. But why should Leibniz want a moral philosophy compatible with determinism? The short answer is: because, as a Christian, he believes in God's omniscience. As an omniscient being, God must know everything, including all future events: He must have complete foreknowledge. And in order for this to be possible, everything, including all future events, must be predetermined; otherwise, God would not know what He was creating.

This, however, immediately creates a problem for another central Christian belief, that of freedom of the will: if God has preordained everything that we do, in what sense do we have freedom to do otherwise? This apparent paradox spawned a number of attempted solutions by his contemporaries, of which Leibniz was well aware. In the *Theodicy* he mentions Conrad Vorst (1569–1622) and Thomas Barton (d. 1681–2) as leaning toward denying that God has knowledge of all events in detail, and, in particular, of future events (GP vi 34/T 58; 100/121–2). This aligned them with the Socinians, a dissident sect that denied the divinity of Christ, and also held that human free will would be impossible if God knew all contingent events, including future ones. The Molinists, on the other hand, proposed that human freedom is possible in cases where there is a perfect equilibrium between two alternatives, so that the will is able to select one without its being predetermined (128/148–9). Finally, Pierre Bayle, whose criticisms prompted Leibniz to write the *Theodicy* in reply, held that since reason is unable to resolve the incompatibility between divine foreknowledge and free will, one must instead take recourse to faith.

Leibniz believed that all these responses were premised on a misconception, and this is where he found Hobbes's arguments decisive, as we shall now see. In his Reflections on Hobbes's *Freedom, Necessity and Chance*, appended to the *Theodicy*, Leibniz lists some of the 'very reasonable things' that Hobbes had established:

> He shows very clearly that nothing comes about by chance, or rather, that chance only signifies the ignorance of causes that produce the effect, and that for each effect there must be a concurrence of all the sufficient conditions, anterior to the event, not one of which, evidently, can be lacking when the event is to follow, because they are conditions; and that the event no more fails to follow when these conditions all occur together, because they are sufficient conditions. Which comes down to what I have said so many times, that everything happens through determining reasons, the knowledge of which, if we had it, would make us know at the same time why the thing has happened and why it did not go otherwise. (389/394–5)

This, in fact, is a very clear statement by Leibniz of his debt to Hobbes. It was in Hobbes that Leibniz found the proof of the Principle of Sufficient Reason, discussed in chapter 4 above, according to which everything that exists has requisites for its existence, and the sum of all these requisites is the sufficient reason. Leibniz was also well aware of Hobbes's view that human freedom consists in the absence of coercion or external constraint, and that this is compatible with determinism. Willing does not consist in some uncaused choice, but in choosing a course of action for some reason, and in a process of deliberation this reason is what determines one's will. The will is just the last or resultant endeavour in a composition of opposing aversions and desires in a deliberation. So, provided it is not coerced by external factors, the process of willing is free.

Spinoza took a similar line. In a reply to Tschirnhaus (via Schuller) in 1674 (Letter 58), Spinoza asks him to imagine that a stone, set in motion by an external cause, and continuing to move with the same quantity of motion, 'thinks and knows that it endeavours, as far as it is able, to continue to move'. Such a stone, 'being conscious only of this endeavour, and not at all indifferent, will believe itself to be free, and to persevere in motion from no other cause than because it wills to' (Spinoza 1882: iv, 266). It is similar with 'that famous human freedom everyone brags of having', which consists only in people being 'conscious of their appetites and ignorant of the causes by which they are determined'.

Whether or not Tschirnhaus showed Leibniz this letter in Paris, he certainly apprised him of Spinoza's view of freedom, as recorded in Leibniz's notes on their conversation in February 1676:

> [Spinoza] claims to demonstrate things about God: that He alone is free. He thinks freedom consists in an action or determination's not resulting from an extrinsic impulse, but solely from the nature of the agent. In this sense he is right to say that God alone is free. . . . Man is free to the extent that he is not determined by any external things. But since this is not the case in any act, man is in no way free – although he participates in freedom more than bodies do. (A VI iii 384–5/LoC 41–3)

So Leibniz agrees with Spinoza: only God is completely free, because He alone is free of any external constraint. Man is not absolutely free, because all his acts are constrained; nevertheless, he is free to the extent that he knowingly participates in his own acts. At this juncture, as he wrote in 1689, 'I was very close to the opinions of those who hold that everything is absolutely necessary, believing that it is enough for freedom that we not be subject to coercion even though we are subject to necessity, and not distinguishing what is infallible, or known certainly to be true, from what is necessary' (A VI iv 1653/L 263).

Later the same year, after his meetings with Spinoza, Leibniz finally recognized the threat to morals implicit in Spinoza's understanding of this position. As we saw in chapter 4, he had not initially realized that Spinoza understood his view to rule out objective contingency. On his way back to Hanover, however, reading copies of Spinoza's letters to Oldenburg that the latter had given him in London, he fastens on Spinoza's claim that 'all things follow necessarily from God's nature', and remarks: 'If all things emanate necessarily from the divine nature, then all possible things exist with equal ease, unfortunately for the good and the bad. Therefore moral philosophy is destroyed' (GP i 124).

This has led many to wonder why Leibniz was so slow to perceive the threat. To answer this, we need to remind ourselves of what had attracted him to the determinism of Hobbes and Spinoza in the first place. This was his conviction that there must be a determining reason for any of our acts. But when we freely decide something, that decision is the determining reason; therefore, Leibniz reasoned, determinism is not contrary to our being able to decide freely, but necessary for it. To suppose otherwise, as had Vorst, Barton, the Socinians and the Molinists, is to commit a fallacy, one that had already been identified by the Stoics. As Leibniz explains in the *Theodicy*,

> People in almost every age have been troubled by a sophism that the Ancients called the 'Lazy Argument', because it would tend toward doing nothing, or at least having no care for anything, and following only the inclination for pleasures of the moment. For, they would say, if the future is necessary, what ought to happen will happen, whatever I might do. (GP vi 30/T 54)

There's an apocryphal story by Diogenes Laertius concerning the founder of the Stoics, Zeno of Citium, who was about to flog his slave for stealing. The slave, aware of the Stoics' doctrine that everything is necessitated, protests: 'But, master, I was fated to steal!' 'And I', replied Zeno, 'am fated to flog you for it!' The fallacy, as Leibniz explains, is as follows:

> It is false that the event happens whatever one may do: it will happen because one does what leads to it; and if the event is written, the cause that will make it happen is written too. Thus the connection of effects and causes, so far from establishing the doctrine of a necessity detrimental to conduct, serves to destroy it. (33/57)

Thus Descartes's attempt to prove that freedom of the will consists in its actions being 'altogether undetermined' is mistaken in principle (90/112). Our actions are not free from external causes; our feeling that they are arises from our not being sensible to their causes. 'It is as though the magnetic needle', Leibniz writes, 'took pleasure in turning itself to the north; for it would believe that it was turning independently of any other cause, not being aware of the imperceptible movements of the magnetic matter' (130/150–1). In a letter to Spinoza (Spinoza 1882: iv, 263), Tschirnhaus had objected that he could easily have refrained from writing to him; he could have so chosen on a whim, just to demonstrate his freedom. Here Leibniz sides with Spinoza: even such a whim, he writes in the *New Essays*, 'weighs in the balance and makes pleasing to people something which would otherwise not be; so that their choice is always determined by their perception' (NE 182). 'We do not will what we wish to,' he concludes, 'we will what pleases us.'

Leibniz's uncompromising stand here makes it seem as though the will, being completely determined by its desire for what seems most pleasing, is in no way free. But, he believes, this is a false opposition: freedom is opposed not to determinism, but to necessity. A free act must be contingent, which means that it cannot be necessitated. But 'determination should not be confused with necessity' (178). Thus it is not enough to say that freedom consists in absence of coercion if our actions are still necessitated: a free act must also be genuinely contingent.

Necessity, Certainty and Hypothetical Necessity

This brings us to a consideration of how Leibniz's criterion of contingency, described above in chapter 4, enabled him to escape Spinoza's necessitarianism. As we saw, Leibniz thought he had made room for contingency by establishing that there are possible things that God chose not to create. Now possible existents are those individuals whose complete concept contains no contradiction, so that if there are such individuals that are incompossible with existing things (as he took himself to have established), this proves that there are uncreated possible worlds. This is enough to establish, against Avicenna and Spinoza, that the existing world is not necessitated.

Now, given this existence of alternative worlds, and the Creator's free will to choose among them (something Spinoza would have rejected as anthropomorphism), the notion that this is the best of all possible worlds follows logically from the hypothesis of God's perfection. For whatever the defects of the world as it appears to us, we can be certain that God created the best, since otherwise either He would not have foreseen what He should have foreseen, or must have been impotent to prevent it, or He did not willingly choose the best. But each of these alternatives is incompatible with one of His attributes, either His being omniscient, omnipotent and omnibenevolent or His having free will. There is no metaphysical necessity here, since God is free not to create anything, and also not to create the best. On the other hand, Leibniz thinks that to create is better than not to create, since something is better than nothing; and since God is omnibenevolent, He wants to create the best. So, given His free will and His perfection, He is morally bound to create the best of all possible worlds. As Leibniz writes in the *Theodicy*,

> The decree to create is free: God is prompted to all good; the good, and even the best, inclines Him to act; but it does not necessitate Him:

for His choice does not render impossible that which is distinct from
the best; it does not make what God refrains from doing imply a
contradiction. There is therefore in God a freedom that is exempt not
only from constraint but also from necessity. I mean, metaphysical
necessity; for there is a moral necessity that the wisest is obliged to
choose the best. (GP vi 255/T 270)

God is not in fact entirely free from constraint, since He cannot
create what is impossible. But possibilities are in His understanding, and prior to His will. His will, on the other hand, is determined
to choose the best by His wisdom, which identifies what is best, and
His goodness, which inclines him to choose it. Thus there is a clear
distinction between 'metaphysical necessity, which admits of no
choice, presenting only one single object as possible, and moral
necessity, which constrains the wisest to choose the best' (333/345).
Leibniz also expresses this distinction between metaphysical and
merely moral necessity in terms of the traditional distinction
between *absolute* and *hypothetical necessity*: it is not absolutely necessary for God to have created this world, but it is necessary on the
hypothesis that He wills the best. Similarly, it is absolutely necessary that there are no four-sided triangles or any other impossible
entity, but it is only hypothetically necessary that any given contingent entity does not exist: it is necessary on the hypothesis God has
chosen to create the best of all possible worlds, the one containing
the most perfection.

The appeal to hypothetical necessity did not convince Arnauld,
however, who claimed that it still implied an absence of free will
on the part of any human agent. For suppose God is free in just this
way, and creates him with his own individual concept. Since,
according to § 13 of the synopsis of the *Discourse on Metaphysics* that
Leibniz sent him in 1686, 'the individual concept of each person
involves once and for all everything that will ever happen to him',
this would still make it impossible for him, given God's creation of
him in this world, to do anything that was not in his concept.
Leibniz had in fact anticipated this objection in the body of the
Discourse, which for some reason he had not sent Arnauld. If it is
certain that Caesar will cross the Rubicon, he writes, and God
creates that particular Caesar with that individual notion, and not
someone who happens to be like him in most respects, in what
sense can Caesar be said to have willed freely that he would cross
the Rubicon? Surely, Leibniz writes, it will be insisted that Caesar's
'nature or form corresponds to that notion, and since God has

imposed this character on him, it is thereafter necessary for him to comply with it' (*Discourse* § 13: A VI iv 1547/WFT 64). To this he responds: 'what happens in accordance with its antecedents is certain, but it is not necessary; if anyone did the contrary, he would not be doing anything impossible in itself, although it is *ex hypothesi* impossible' – that is, impossible on the hypothesis that that person has the individual notion and nature that he does in fact have. 'As if', he adds in his letter to Hessen-Rheinfels, 'notions or previsions made things necessary, and as if a free action could not be included in the notion or perfect view that God has of the person to whom it pertains' (12 April 1686: GP ii 17/WFT 98).

Here Leibniz could have appealed to the symmetry between foresight and hindsight. If we suppose Arnauld had freely decided to remain celibate (as he said he did), it is nevertheless certain in hindsight that he did so decide. Given his complete concept, there would be a contradiction in his not deciding to remain celibate; but this only gives us hypothetical necessity. Such contingent truths are *certain*, because God is able to foresee them intuitively: 'the certainty and perfect reason for contingent truths is known only to God, who grasps the infinite in one intuition' (A VI iv 1616/LoC 305). But these truths are not *logically necessary*, since their opposite is not self-contradictory: the reasons for them (involving 'the whole succession of the universe') are not accessible to us.

Leibniz explains his position in an entertaining dialogue recording a conversation he had with Baron Dobrzensky in 1695, who cannot see how his freedom is compatible with God's infallible foresight. For if I were to commit some crime, he says, 'it is infallible that I will commit the sin that he has foreseen. It is therefore necessary that I will sin, and it is not within my power to abstain from it. Thus I am not free' (Grua 361/AG 112). To this Leibniz replies: 'It must be admitted, sir, that we are not altogether free; only God is free, since He alone is independent. Our freedom is limited in many ways: I am not free to fly like an eagle or swim like a dolphin, because my body lacks the necessary means. One can say something similar about our mind' (362/112). But 'this does not prevent us from having a certain degree of freedom that beasts do not have, that is, our faculty of reasoning, and of choosing according to how things seem to us'. And regarding divine foresight, Leibniz writes, 'God foresees things such as they are, and does not change their nature.' Contingent events 'remain so, notwithstanding the fact that God has foreseen them. Thus they are assured, but not necessary' (362/112). This conclusion is repeated in the *Theodicy*:

[God's] decree changes nothing in the constitution of things: it leaves them just as they were in the state of mere possibility, that is to say, it changes nothing either in their essence or nature, or even in their accidents, which are already represented perfectly in the idea of this possible world. Thus what is contingent and free does not remain any less so under the decrees of God than under His prevision. (GP vi 131/T 151)

Spontaneity, Freedom and Divine Concurrence

Of course, more than bare contingency is necessary to account for human freedom. As C. D. Broad comments, 'The fact that Vesuvius erupted and destroyed Pompeii in AD 79 would be held by Leibniz and by many other philosophers to be contingent, but no one regards it as a free act on the part of the volcano' (Broad 1975: 27). This is perfectly true, but Leibniz does not equate contingency with freedom; he merely takes it as a precondition for a free act. If a person acts freely, then the act must be contingent, and not logically necessary. As Leibniz notes in the *Theodicy*,

We are not prevented from having a free mind when we deliberate, as would happen if someone gave us a potion that made us lose our judgement. There is *contingency* in a thousand actions of Nature; but when there is no judgement in one who acts, there is no *freedom*. And if we had judgement that was not accompanied by any inclination to act, our soul would be an understanding without will. (GP vi 122/T 143)

Our inclination to act is our appetition, the *conatus* or endeavour that we have toward what we perceive to be the best. This inclination to choose what we think is best does not make that choice logically necessary. But without the judgement involved in perceiving which of various alternative courses of action seems to us best, we do not act freely. We would be in the position of the magnetic needle discussed above, which endeavours to point north, but is unaware of what causes it to do so. Thus, according to Leibniz's account, a third condition must be satisfied for us to act freely, apart from freedom from external constraint and contingency, or the existence of alternatives: we must also have the ability to perceive these alternatives and to make a judgement as to which is the best for us. This is what sets us apart from lower animals: our faculty of reason.

As we saw in chapter 5, Leibniz explains reason in terms of the mind's ability to act on itself in such a way that it is aware that it is the same ego. For this we need not only an organ in which our endeavours can be contained (the brain), and the ability to retain them (memory), but also the ability to compare them and anticipate their effects on our future actions. Our mind needs to have the ability to act on itself as itself: in other words, to act in favour of endeavours that it perceives as leading toward what's in its interest. And these endeavours toward what's in its interest are going to be teleologically defined in terms of what the mind judges as being for the best.

We can throw some light on this aspect of Leibniz's thought by contrasting it with opposing views. In their famous controversy, Samuel Clarke grants Leibniz the Principle of Sufficient Reason, but insists that 'this sufficient reason is often nothing other than the mere will of God' (Second Reply § 1: GP vii 359/L 680). This is the voluntarist view we saw Leibniz rejecting above: if God's will is sufficient reason for His actions, then he cannot fail to be just, and is therefore unworthy of praise. But Clarke takes issue with Leibniz's comparison of the will with 'a balance, where reasons and inclinations take the place of weights' (GP vi 308/T 321), arguing that if the will could not act without a predetermining cause, 'this would tend to take away all power of choosing, and introduce fatality' (GP vii 359/L 680). Thus, on Clarke's view, in order to be called free, the will must be able to act independently of any cause. A balance pressed equally on both sides cannot move at all; whereas, according to Clarke, the mind, being active, has a 'self-motive principle' by virtue of which it can break the equilibrium of indifference. It may have 'very strong and good reasons' for acting, even 'when there may be no possible reason to determine one particular way of doing the thing to be better than another' (Fifth Reply §§ 1–20: GP vii 422).

For Leibniz this is self-contradictory: if the mind has reasons for its choice, then there must be a possible reason for it to choose one alternative as the best. The mind 'acts by virtue of its motives, which are its dispositions to act' (Fifth Paper § 15: 392/L 698).[8] Clarke's claim that the mind can act in defiance of its motives is 'to divide the mind from its motives, . . . as if the mind had, besides motives, other dispositions to act by virtue of which it could reject or accept the motives' (Fifth Reply, § 15). In contrast to this libertarian 'freedom of indifference', Leibniz espouses a conception of freedom based on the *autonomy* of the agent: when someone acts in accordance with what appears to be best, that person is acting freely. Essential to this conception of autonomy is the idea of *spontaneity*, the idea that the reasons for the agent's actions come from within the agent itself.

According to Leibniz's metaphysics of pre-established harmony, spontaneity is guaranteed. Each individual substance is the source of its own actions, which it produces according to its own individual law: 'everything in it arises from its own nature', he writes in the *New System*, § 14, 'with a perfect *spontaneity* as regards itself, and yet with a perfect *conformity* to things outside it'. As we saw above, Leibniz found a similar view in Spinoza, where an individual is free to the extent that she is author of her own actions. The difference that Leibniz claims to be crucial is that he has articulated how these actions are not necessitated, and how an individual endowed with reason can act freely. 'Why', he asks, 'couldn't God give to the substance at the outset an internal force which could produce in it in an orderly way everything that is going to happen to it, as in a *spiritual* or *formal automaton*, but a free one, in the case of a substance endowed with its share of reason?' (GP iv 485/L 458).

By endowing each substance with its own force and principle of activity, Leibniz was intent on avoiding the view of Malebranche and others that ascribed all causal activity to God. He was trenchantly opposed to any doctrine that could imply that God is the cause of sin, or that the damned have been predestined, both of which consequences he rejected as contrary to God's goodness. God desires that all people should be saved, Leibniz argues, prior to creating anything (His 'antecedent will'); but when all the consequences of all actions are taken into account, He wills the world containing the most perfection (His 'consequent will'). This world will necessarily contain some sin and some evil, but the least possible. God concurs with the individual wills of people by creating the world in which they exist and act; but he is not responsible for their actions, because they are the source of their own free actions. Nevertheless, a spiritual automaton does not exist independently of God: its existence is not given at creation, but is something continuously in process, requiring God's continuous creation. Thus 'all its actions come from its own depths, except for its dependence on God' (to Arnauld, 23 March 1690: GP ii 136/WFT 136).

This is an important point, as Leibniz is often seen as just providing a version of occasionalism by reducing causation to a correspondence. For he agrees with the occasionalists that mind does not act on body, and that this is an appearance produced by the perfect correspondence between the things that minds will to happen, and the physical effects that ensue. But he does not agree that the mental acts or their physical concomitants have to be individually caused by God. In this, Leibniz follows Descartes in appealing to the traditional distinction between two types of causes: the cause needed to bring things about (e.g. beavers causing a dam to be built through their actions), and the cause needed to conserve things in their existence (beavers, dam and the whole of the created world). Descartes had argued that 'the same force and action is plainly needed to conserve any thing at each moment it endures as would be needed to create it anew if it did not yet exist' (AT vii 49/ CSM ii 33), so that conservation is equivalent to continuous creation. The constancy of God's conserving activity, he argued, requires an overall conservation of this force. Leibniz disagreed with him about the measure of this force, as we saw in chapter 6, but not about the necessity for such a force to sustain things in existence, and the equivalence of conservation with continuous creation. A created substance, he writes in the *Theodicy*, 'depends continually on divine operation' and 'would not continue to exist if God did not continue to act' (G vi 343/T 355). But for Leibniz a substance is a thing that acts, and exists through acting. Thus, for him, divine operation is the source not only of the existence of each created substance, but also of its power to act. The force possessed by each created substance throughout its existence can therefore be regarded as a kind of divine spark, or limitation of divine omnipotence. Still, although a thing must exist and have the power to act in order to act, the cause of its existing is not the cause of its acting. In addition to possessing the power to act, as we have seen, a substance also needs to contain the reason for its actions. Thus, in contrast to occasionalism, for Leibniz a substance may be said to be the cause of its own actions insofar as it contains within itself both the reason for those actions, and the force or power to bring them about.

Pierre Bayle gave Leibniz's system of pre-established harmony a respectful consideration in the article in his famous *Dictionnaire* entitled 'Rorarius'. But he was not convinced by what Leibniz had to say about spontaneity. He asks us to imagine a dog enjoying some food while a man comes up behind it and strikes it with a stick. 'I cannot understand', he wrote, 'the series of spontaneous internal actions which could make a dog's soul feel pain immediately after having felt pleasure, even if it were alone in the universe. . . . I also find the spontaneity of this soul', he continues, 'wholly incompatible with its feelings of pain, and in general with all feelings that displease it' (GP iv 531/L 494). Why would the dog's soul find its state in feeling pain more perfect, or more in its own interest, than continuing to feel pleasure? Leibniz's reply is that the dog is *not* all alone in the universe. The perception in the dog's soul is very complex, a confusion of perceptions of everything in the material world; it represents all this, including 'the man positioned behind the dog getting ready to hit it while it eats', 'but feebly, by small confused perceptions and without apperception, that is, without the dog noticing' (GP iv 532). The better the soul understands the whole situation, the more it can be said to act, as opposed to be acted upon. Its soul contains the reason for continuing to eat more distinctly, and the reason for being hit much less distinctly; so the dog acts on the food, but is acted upon by the stick. It has acted in a way that it thought suited its own best interests, even though if it had judgement it would regret its action. Meanwhile, however, its action will, when taken together with everything else happening in the same universe, lead to a greater perfection in the universe as a whole.

Theological Projects

In keeping with his motto for the Berlin Academy, 'Theory with practice', Leibniz developed these theoretical views with an eye to their practical application in the theological disputes of his time. This was already the case with the *Catholic Demonstrations* project that he undertook with Boineburg, which they hoped would provide a natural theology that could serve to bring about reconciliation of the various faiths. Leibniz made further attempts at church reunification with Gerhard Molanus, first together with the Catholic Bishop Rojas, and then again in Vienna in 1700, negotiating with two prominent Catholic theologians close to Louis XIV, Jacques-Bénigne Bossuet and Paul Pellisson (1624–93). But Bossuet was intransigent, refusing to revisit any of the dogmas decided upon at the Council of Trent. Particularly troubling to Leibniz was the insistence that even those who were ignorant of the teaching of the Church were damned. As we have seen, he regarded this as based on a fallacious interpretation of determinism, and as incompatible with a loving God, 'who condemns only those whose will is evil' (GP vi 38/T 62). This was the same position Leibniz had taken in the dispute among the Jesuits over ancestral rites in China, where he sided with Matteo Ricci (1552–1610) in interpreting them as civil ceremonies rather than a religious cults (Leibniz 1994: 61), for which the Chinese sages should not be damned. Leibniz also interpreted what he could learn of the classical Chinese texts as showing that their *Li* could be interpreted as the Supreme Reason, from which the primitive entelechies or substances constituting the spirits in men or genii emanate (93–7).

Leibniz made other applications of his theory of substance to religious controversies. We saw in chapter 5 how he attempted to adapt it in his correspondence with Des Bosses to serve as a basis for the Jesuits' conception of the Eucharist. But his proposal there (that Christ's substance in the bread could be explained by super-added substantial bonds) was never more than half-hearted: Leibniz did not believe that anything further than substantial presence was required for a defensible interpretation of the Eucharist. On the other hand, he did believe his theory of substance adequate to resolve the doctrinal differences between Calvinists and Lutherans. Such a rapprochement became important as the Protestant states began to feel the threat of forced Catholicization, and in 1697 Leibniz and the Brandenburg chaplain Daniel Ernst Jablonski (1660–1741) were charged with preparing a brief for negotiations between Hanover and Brandenburg on the reconciliation of Lutheranism with Calvinism. In his part of the brief, Leibniz argued that Calvinists and Lutherans could be united on the issue of the Eucharist. In opposition to the Zwinglians' claim that Christ's body is in heaven and cannot be in two places at once, Leibniz argued that Calvin, like the Lutherans, taught that the substance of Christ's body is literally present in the Eucharist, and is perceived to be so, but that this happens supernaturally. Leibniz thought he could account for this with his conception of substance as force, with a substance exhibiting itself through its operations. For although a substance would operate in only one place naturally, it could operate in more than one place supernaturally.

But all these attempts at reconciliation were frustrated by events beyond Leibniz's control, above all by the deaths of key patrons. His *Catholic Demonstrations* project was scuppered by the deaths of Boineburg in 1672, Schönborn in 1673 and Johann Friedrich in 1679, and his later efforts by the deaths of a supportive pope, Innocent XI, in 1689, and then of Pellisson in 1693 and Rojas in 1695. The brief he had prepared with Jablonski was not officially transmitted to Berlin until 1704, too late to have effect, and its fate was sealed by the deaths in 1704 of two of its main promoters, the irenic Calvinist Paul von Fuchs, and Leibniz's friend and patron in Berlin, Sophie Charlotte.

More enduring were Leibniz's attempts to refine the traditional proofs of the existence of God. These were central to the *Catholic Demonstrations*, and his subsequent attempts to improve upon the proofs of his predecessors are well known. Descartes had revived St Anselm's proof that a most perfect being must exist, since its essence contains existence (A VI iv 1617/LoC 307). As noted in chapter 2, Leibniz objected that this demonstration (now known as the Ontological Argument) is incomplete, 'for it is assumed without proof that a most perfect being does not involve a contradiction' (1617/307). He accepts that a perfect being, if it is possible, necessarily exists, since existence is a perfection, and the concept of a most perfect being will include all perfections. If it is possible, it cannot not exist, since it contains existence in its concept; therefore it necessarily exists, provided it is possible. But it still needs to be proved that such a being is possible. Leibniz supplies the proof as follows: since the perfections, including existence, are all simple, positive attributes, they cannot contradict one another. So a most perfect being (God) is possible. It follows that God exists. The inference depends on what Leibniz describes as 'the pinnacle of Modal Theory' (A VI iv 315/LoC 307): if it is possible that God necessarily exists, then God does necessarily exist.[9]

The necessary existence of God contrasts with the contingent existence of created things. As we have seen, their concepts do not contain the reason for their own existence. This provides the means for another proof of God's existence. The reason for a contingent thing's existence lies in its requisites, in other things in the series of things preceding it. 'But even if the providing of reasons for contingents were to go on to infinity, a reason for the whole series would still have to be found outside the series' (1617/307). In his notes on a similar proof he finds in Spinoza's *Letter on the Infinite*, Leibniz proves this by a *reductio*. Suppose the reason for the series lies within the series; then even if we subtract members from the series of causes one by one, 'what remains must still be the reason for those following it. Hence it follows that the whole series . . . could be subtracted from itself, while leaving intact the reason for existence we assumed in it, which is absurd' (A VI iii 282/LoC 117). Thus there will be no reason for the existence of contingent things unless there is a necessary being, that is, one whose reason for existence does not lie outside itself, and which contains the ultimate reasons for the existence of all other beings. This is a version of what is traditionally called the Cosmological Argument, according to which the series of causes in the cosmos all have causes outside themselves save the First Cause, namely God. Like Spinoza's argument, Leibniz's does not suffer from the defect of supposing that an infinite series of causes must have a first cause. It depends only on the Principle of Sufficient Reason applied to the series of contingents itself, together with the premises that a necessary being contains the reason for its own existence, and ultimately for all others, since their causes 'are resolved into God's attributes' (A VI iv 1617/LoC 305).

A third traditional argument for God's existence is the Argument from Design, according to which the design of the universe implies a creator who designed it. Leibniz invokes this argument in his appeal to 'God the Designer' who creates the 'machine of the universe' (*Monadology* §§ 89, 84: GP vi 621–2/WFT 280), 'a first-rate geometer who prefers the best constructions of problems' (A VI iv 1616–17/LoC 305). So he could certainly be criticized for his anthropomorphism, as he would be by Spinoza. But there are two respects in which Leibniz's conception of the Argument from Design could be regarded as an improvement over traditional versions. The first is in his conception of the machines of nature as being of infinite complexity (chapter 3). Thus not only are they of admirable design, but it is not obvious how they could arise naturally; so, assuming they have not always existed, they require a creator with infinite knowledge and power. Secondly, there is Leibniz's more sophisticated conception of teleology discussed in chapter 6. There is no assumption on his part that any one thing taken in itself exhibits optimal design. Perfection is a comparative affair for contingent existents. A possible individual has a claim to existence that is proportional to its perfection, but its perfection is its degree of fit with others. So relative lack of perfection – sin, evil – will exist, but it will be minimized in the world that God creates. It is a consequence of God's choice of the best – the Principle of Perfection – that the world will exhibit optimal design. Thus the created world as a whole may be for the best – given the alternatives – but that world is one in which each individual will seek to maximize its own perfection, and the wisest among them will constantly endeavour toward other people's happiness as well as their own.

Russell was speaking as an atheist when he said of Leibniz that, despite the whole tendency of his temperament and his philosophy 'to exalt enlightenment, education and learning, he preferred to support Sin and Hell, and to remain, in what concerned the Church, the champion of ignorance and obscurantism' (Russell [1900] 1937: 202) This slighting remark tells us more about how radically the conception of 'enlightenment' had changed in the two centuries or so between Russell and Leibniz than it does about the morals of his subject or his purported conservatism. What fired Leibniz's optimism was his belief that human subjects, acting freely according to what they considered would be in their best interests, would nevertheless be acting in accordance with God's providential plan. His belief that God had created the world for the best, far from being a manifesto for political quietism, as Voltaire preferred to understand it, was for him both a logical consequence of God's benevolence, omniscience and omnipotence, and a reason for our loving God. But it was also the basis for his confidence in human nature, and thus for all his practical projects for improving the human condition:

> Every enlightened person must judge that the true means of guaranteeing forever his own individual happiness is to seek his satisfaction in occupations which tend toward the general good; for the love of God, above all, and the necessary enlightenment, will not be denied to a mind that is animated in this way. . . . Now this general good, insofar as we can contribute to it, is the advancement toward perfection of humankind . . . . (quoted from Rutherford 1995: 61)

Thus, as Don Rutherford comments on this passage, our acceptance of the fact that this is the best of all possible worlds 'should lead to neither self-satisfaction nor resignation' but should instead 'manifest itself as an active, progressive attitude, in which we apprehend the world's inherent tendency toward an ever greater perfection and accept our own role in it . . .' (61). This is the reason why Leibniz's practical philosophy, far from being 'the worst part of his philosophy', as Russell charged, resonated with Enlightenment thinkers like Diderot, despite their rejection of his theology.

9

Leibnizian Posterity

Few philosophers have impressed posterity as much as Leibniz. He has inspired or been admired by thinkers as different from one another as Diderot and Kant, Russell and Cassirer, Feuerbach and Mach, Cantor and Weyl, and Borges and Deleuze. The fact that each of them has understood his philosophy differently is a reflection of the nature of Leibniz's contribution, a cornucopia of profound insights and suggestions for new directions, but with no grand work of synthesis to define a philosophical system. Where Diderot picked up on Leibniz's idea for an encyclopaedia and put it into brilliant effect, Kant discerned in Leibniz's probing of Locke's empiricism the seeds for his Critical Philosophy. Where Russell saw Leibniz as having anticipated Frege's and his own attempts to found philosophy and mathematics in logic, his contemporaries Hermann Cohen and Ernst Cassirer seized on Leibniz's idea of infinitesimals as intensive magnitudes – scorned by Russell – to build a neo-Kantianism based on a priori categories revisable by science. Where Feuerbach's study of Leibniz informed aspects of his materialist view that the human subject exists in relation to material conditions, Mach found support for his phenomenalism, and for a rejection of absolute space and time that would inspire Einstein's relativity theories. Where Cantor was enthused by Leibniz's vision of the world as an actual infinity of metaphysical points, Brouwer and Weyl built on Leibniz's views on space and the continuum to found a new science of topology without assuming a manifold of points at all. Where Leibniz's labours in obscure metaphysics were an inspiration for Borges to create amazing literary labyrinths, for Deleuze they contained crucial insights into the importance of the concepts of expression, difference and repetition. But all this was later.

In the years immediately after his death, the reception of Leibniz's philosophy was far less rosy. It was dominated by the priority dispute with Newton over the invention of the calculus, which had turned ugly in the last years of Leibniz's life. Newton, suspecting (rightly) that Leibniz had composed his *Tentamen* only after reading the *Principia*, had allowed himself to become convinced that Leibniz had plagiarized his calculus and dressed it up in his own symbols. This squabble had a serious political backdrop, and the episode came to be coloured by the jingoistic championing of Newton as a kind of English prophet, whom God had granted discovery of the three Laws of Nature much as Moses had been chosen to receive the Ten Commandments. Alexander Pope epitomized this elevation of Newton to semi-divine status in his memorable couplet:

Nature and Nature's laws lay hid in night,
God said, 'Let Newton be,' and all was light.

Of course, Leibniz had his supporters on the European mainland, but this was somewhat compromised by a second controversy, the '*vis viva* controversy'. This controversy had been started by Leibniz himself with his attack on the Cartesian measure of 'force'. In hindsight the dispute appears very muddled, since by 'force' Leibniz meant the ability to do work, which we now call energy, but which both he and his Cartesian opponents equated with 'motive force', which is no longer regarded as a viable physical quantity. Moreover, the question whether the quantity that is conserved is the Cartesian 'quantity of motion' mv or the Leibnizian 'living force' mv^2 now seems idle, since both momentum ($m\underline{v}$) and kinetic energy ($\frac{1}{2} mv^2$) are conserved in elastic collisions, according to classical physics. In effect, this is to say that the issue was resolved in Leibniz's favour, since he acknowledged the conservation of both these quantities (the first of which he called 'quantity of progress', although Newton's term stuck). But it took the diligent efforts of the continental physicists who created classical physics – du Châtelet, d'Alembert, Euler, Maupertuis, Laplace and Lagrange – to sort it all out. At any rate, the controversy did not help Leibniz's cause in France in the short term, since Cartesianism was dominant in the universities.

More damaging to Leibniz's reputation in France, however, were the stinging attacks from Voltaire. As mentioned in the previous chapter, no one who read his witty satire *Candide* (1759) would forget the figure of Dr Pangloss ('Dr Explain-it-all'), or fail to associate it with Leibniz's 'best of all possible worlds'. Formerly an admirer of Pope's optimism, Voltaire had become radically disillusioned with it on witnessing the horrifying aftermath of the Lisbon earthquake in 1755, and had now become a scourge of optimism, especially the kind of apology for the status quo advocated by the likes of Noël Pluche in his bestselling *Spectacle of Nature* of 1754. Saddling Leibniz with such political quietism is, of course, neither accurate nor generous. As we have seen, the whole point of the *Theodicy* was to explain how it was possible for the actual world to have been freely created by God as the best possible despite its containing imperfections and evil, not to pretend that they didn't exist. Still, no satire is successful if it does not contain an element of truth – after all, Leibniz did seem to have an explanation for everything! – and the image stuck.

But at least as damaging as Voltaire's lampooning of Leibniz as Pangloss was his earlier comparison in his *Letters Concerning the English Nation* (1733) between the progressive English mentality and that existing on the continent. Like Maupertuis, who followed in his footsteps soon afterwards in 1728, Voltaire was instantly converted from the vortex theory espoused by Descartes and Leibniz to Newtonianism. 'Vortices', he wrote, 'may be call'd an occult Quality, because their existence was never prov'd; Attraction on the contrary is a real Thing, because its Effects are demonstrated, and the Proportions of it are calculated'(Voltaire [1733] 1994: 75). Voltaire's equation of the religious tolerance he saw in England with the empiricist method in the sciences left him with little patience for metaphysics. 'Can you really maintain', he railed, 'that a drop of urine is an infinity of monads, and that each one of these has ideas, however obscure, of the entire universe?' (Voltaire 1879: vol. xxii, ch. ix, 434). Voltaire bequeathed this anti-metaphysical attitude and veneration of Locke's empiricism to a younger generation of French intellectuals. Chief among these was Étienne Bonnot de Condillac (1714–80), who in his *Traité de systèmes* did much to cast Leibniz as a builder of a baroque, fanciful metaphysical system steeped in theology. 'He believed he was explaining phenomena', he wrote in his chapter on Leibniz, 'while employing only the unphilosophical language of metaphors' – a sure sign, said Condillac, that he had no idea what he was talking about (Condillac 1798: 95). This kind of criticism shaped much of the Enlightenment's conception of Leibniz, whose position in the court and defence of theology had set him on the side of the Establishment. Locke, of course, had already politicized epistemology, casting support for the doctrine of innate ideas as an implicit defence of the divine right of kings, and the non-publication of Leibniz's *New Essays* ensured that his perceptive remarks about the innateness of the faculty of the intellect rather than its contents were unknown to his rival's followers. Thus for Condillac and many of his fellow *philosophes* of eighteenth-century France, Leibniz's metaphysics and his politico-theology were two sides of the same coin, both to be rejected as part of their campaign against the ruling elite.

All this was largely ideological, however, and did not necessarily reflect Leibniz's actual influence. A good instance of this is d'Alembert's *Encyclopédie* article on 'Conservation des forces vives'. Although the very terms and content of the discussion are quintessentially Leibnizian – dead and living forces, the falsity of the Cartesian equation of force with quantity of motion, the correct estimation of force, and its relation to action – d'Alembert attributes the discovery of these relationships to Huygens, Johann Bernoulli, Daniel Bernoulli, Maupertuis, Clairaut and himself, rather than to Leibniz. But this probably only reflects d'Alembert's view that scientific principles should be established without any appeal to metaphysics. For in other *Encyclopédie* articles on Action, Analysis, Binary Arithmetic, the Characteristic, Final Causes, the Law of Continuity, Cosmology, the Calculus, Living Forces, Geometry and Mechanics, d'Alembert does not fail to acknowledge Leibniz's profound contributions. In 1740 Émilie, the Marquise du Châtelet (1706–49), published an influential physics textbook (*Institutions de physiques*) in which she demonstrated that the Dutch scholar Willem s' Gravesande's observations supported Leibniz's claim that the energy of a moving body is proportional to mv^2. Then she made the first (and still the only) translation of Newton's *Principia* into French, published posthumously in 1759, in which she showed how to derive the conservation of energy from its principles. Diderot, for his part, did not try to hide his admiration of Leibniz. In his *Encyclopédie* article 'Leibnizianism and the Philosophy of Leibniz', he wrote: 'Never can a man have read as much, studied as much, meditated more, and written more than Leibniz', concluding that 'if his ideas had been expounded with the colouring of Plato, the philosopher of Leipzig would have ceded nothing to the philosopher of Athens' (Diderot and d'Alembert 1751–2: vol. ix, 379). He then gave a full account of Leibniz's principles without attempting to criticize them (although in other articles he subjected the theological basis of Leibniz's philosophy to withering scorn). Diderot's political practice, moreover, is not so very different from Leibniz's, even if it was not through any direct influence. Neither philosopher was in favour of revolution, except as a last resort, when 'a prince can go to such excess, and place the well-being of the state in such danger, that the obligation to endure ceases' (Leibniz to Boineburg 1695: L 59). Both rather placed their faith in philosophers' ability to persuade benevolent rulers to adopt political reforms for the enlightenment of humanity and the betterment of their people, Leibniz with the Dukes of Hanover and Peter the Great, and Diderot with Catherine the Great: 'To whom should a philosopher address himself forcefully', Diderot wrote in *Pages against a Tyrant* (1769), 'if not to a sovereign?' (cited in Furbank 1993: 377).

In Germany, by contrast, Leibniz's philosophy did have a direct positive impact, largely through the mediation of Christian Wolff (1679–1754). Leibniz had helped his young compatriot to obtain a position as professor of mathematics and natural philosophy at the University of Halle in 1706, and Wolff had responded to Leibniz's explanations of his dynamics and metaphysics with some enthusiasm, although retaining an independence of mind on the issues. Wolff shared Leibniz's desire for improving the human condition through learning, and used his position to introduce many progressive reforms to university teaching in Germany to make it more practically efficacious. He was particularly taken with the Leibnizian ideal of reducing all philosophy to demonstrations given in a mathematical, deductive form – although where, as we have seen, Leibniz had a vision of logic far in advance of his time, Wolff insisted on giving his demonstrations in the driest imaginable Aristotelian syllogisms. Premises in one volume were justified with embarrassing triumphalism by cross-reference to conclusions of syllogisms in another, so that the whole system was a tangle held up only by its own bootstraps. It nevertheless proved astonishingly popular. Wolff also shared Leibniz's admiration for Chinese philosophy, although this almost cost him his life: in a public address in 1621 that drew massive crowds, he followed Leibniz both in arguing for the compatibility of freedom with determinism and in praising Confucius for producing a moral philosophy based on reason rather than revealed religion. But when Wolff's Pietist enemies persuaded Friedrich Wilhelm I that a deterministic ethics would make it impossible to prosecute deserting soldiers, the Prussian king commanded him to leave the state within forty-eight hours or be hanged. This affair became one of the chief *causes célèbres* of the Enlightenment, and contributed enormously to Wolff's fame and the spread of his ideas, and, by association, redounded to Leibniz's credit too.

For Leibniz, though, this association with Wolff was a mixed blessing. On the one hand, the combination of Wolff's influence and endorsement of many of his principles contributed to the spread of his ideas. On the other, with so little of his own work published and so much of Wolff's, the latter's philosophy came to be identified with his under the banner of Leibnizianism. Some of Wolff's theses seem to be straight out of Leibniz: there must be unities, since bodies are composites that are aggregates of them; these unities are simple substances; physical forces are grounded in substantial ones; and so forth. But there are some salient differences: in conscious opposition to Leibniz, Wolff claims that his simple substances are spatially united, so that they 'could also be said to be physical atoms'; moreover, they interact with one another, and it is by virtue of this dynamic interaction with one another that they are able to constitute a material continuum (Wolff [1737] 1964: 158). This rejection of Leibniz's non-interacting monads in favour of simple substances that were centres of force in a more straightforwardly realist sense was hugely influential on later thinkers, especially Euler, Maupertuis and Roger Boscovich (1711–87), and through them, eventually, on the inception of field theory.

The mention of Leonhard Euler (1707–83) brings us to Leibniz's Swiss legacy. For Euler's tutor was Leibniz's friend and correspondent Johann Bernoulli (1667–1748), who had learned the differential calculus from Leibniz with his elder brother Jakob. Both had made numerous applications of the calculus, especially in solutions to challenge problems, and quickly established themselves among Europe's leading mathematicians. When Jakob died of tuberculosis in 1705, Johann Bernoulli was named professor of mathematics at the University of Basel in his place. The first calculus textbook, published by Guillaume de l'Hôpital in 1696, was largely written by Johann Bernoulli, whom l'Hôpital had hired to teach him Leibniz's methods. By 1715, when he lent his public support to Leibniz in the priority dispute with Newton, Bernoulli had established Basel as a major conduit for Leibniz's ideas. There he had supervised the doctoral theses of his own son Daniel (with whom he subsequently developed as jealous a rivalry as he had had previously with Jakob), of his son's friend Euler, and also the theses of Johann Samuel König (1712–57) and Pierre-Louis Moreau de Maupertuis (1698–1759). Daniel Bernoulli (1700–82) maintained the family tradition begun by his uncle and father, and all three are known for important contributions to mathematics. But it is Euler who is widely regarded as one of the greatest and most prolific mathematicians ever to have lived, making seminal contributions not just to the development of mathematical analysis, but also to mechanics, fluid dynamics, optics and astronomy. The modern form of the differential and integral calculus is largely due to his success in combining Newton's method of fluxions with Leibniz's and Bernoulli's understanding of the calculus and use of differential equations. Among his numerous accomplishments, he developed Leibniz's logic diagrams, and also made a founding contribution to the development of Leibniz's Analysis Situs into modern topology.

The case of Maupertuis' relation to Leibniz is considerably more vexed. Despite joining Voltaire in his championing of Newton, he went to Basel to study the calculus with Johann Bernoulli, and with the latter's help, in 1733, he proved the oblate shape of the Earth proposed by Newton as against the prolate shape championed by Giovanni Cassini (1625–1712). Through an expedition to Lapland he was able to confirm this result experimentally, a triumph which catapulted him to fame. He gratuitously rubbed this in Cassini's face, alienated Bernoulli, ingratiated himself with du Châtelet, and then, after her death in 1740, surprised everyone by leaving for Germany at Frederick's invitation, to head up the Prussian Royal Academy of Sciences in Berlin. When he finally took up the post in 1746, he published a book arguing that his Principle of the Least Quantity of Action constituted the best proof of the existence of God, since it did not depend upon the Leibnizians' conservation of *vis viva*, or on their hypothesis that all matter is elastic. König noted that Leibniz had already proposed the Principle of Least Action in a letter of 1707 of which he had a copy, thus undermining Maupertuis' claim for its invention. Maupertuis, who had not noticed this when he approved König's paper for publication, challenged him to produce Leibniz's original letter, and when König was unable to do so, had the Academy declare the copy a probable forgery. Thus disgraced, König was forced to leave the Academy; he was quickly followed by Voltaire, who was utterly disgusted by the affair.

But there were other elements of Leibniz's thought in Maupertuis' mature writings, as König observed. Rejecting Leibniz's metaphysical points for physical ones, Maupertuis nonetheless endowed all matter with sensation and appetite, agreeing with Leibniz that they could not be explained purely mechanically. All matter is animate, Maupertuis claimed, with instinctual desires and aversions for matter of the same kind, by which are formed organisms of ever greater complexity. In these respects his thought constitutes a bridge (through Buffon) to Diderot's materialism. At the same time, though, Maupertuis took Leibniz's doctrine of the ideality of space and his characterization of the corporeal world as phenomenal, and gave them a purely phenomenalist interpretation: the world is built up from the phenomena as they appear to us, and space is no different from the phenomena of colour and tone in this respect. Arthur Schopenhauer (1788–1860), who regarded the ideality of space and the phenomenality of the corporeal world as 'Kant's most important and brilliant doctrine', not only noted that Maupertuis had expressed it 'already thirty years previously', but also cast doubt on its being original with Maupertuis himself (Schopenhauer, 1818, vol. II, ch. IV).

This brings us to what is without doubt one of the most important parts of Leibniz's philosophical legacy, although in my view one of the most unfortunate, German idealism. This began with Leibniz's early supporters. As d'Alembert reports in his *Encyclopédie* article on Divisibility, 'if one asks how monads, which are not bodies, can constitute bodies, the Leibnizians respond that they constitute only the appearance, and that matter does not exist outside our mind such as we conceive it' (Diderot and d'Alembert 1751–2: vol. IV, 1076). The major impetus to German idealism, however, came through the intervention of Immanuel Kant (1724–1804). Although in his early work he espoused a Wolff-inspired physicalist monadology, Kant perceptively discerned the profound difference between Wolff's interacting simple substances and Leibniz's isolated monads, immune from composition or any influence one on the other. Perhaps in response to interpretations such as Euler's, who supposed Leibniz's monads to be parts of bodies resulting from a 'limited division' (Euler 1843: 48–9), Kant asked: 'Is it really believable that Leibniz, the great mathematician, held that bodies are composed of monads?' Not if monads are immaterial, and material bodies are mere appearances to these perceiving substances. If all we experience are the phenomena, Kant reasoned, and reality consists in the agreement among these phenomena, as Leibniz said, then we are not entitled to say that we know anything of a reality beyond these appearances. Thus according to Kant, Leibniz's monads are denizens of 'the intelligible world, which is unknown to us'.[1] They do not constitute the physical world, but are 'supersensible beings' of which the human mind can have 'only [an] obscure intellectual intuition'. The 'sensible beings' of the physical world, on the other hand, Leibniz 'wishes . . . to be considered as . . . mere appearances in the strictest sense, dependent upon (specific, particular) forms of intuition'.

As the reader will observe, this picture of Leibniz as denying the knowability of a world beyond appearances contrasts with the picture drawn in chapter 5. There we saw Leibniz claim that one of the absolute general truths about the existence of things is that the phenomena themselves are appearances of things external to us, a truth which he believed he could prove through reason. The fact that we can learn about reality from the agreement of such appearances is for him underwritten by the pre-established harmony: the states of other monads coexistent with myself must have states that are completely compatible with mine. There will therefore be a harmony between what changes appear to each individual monad (in the changes of its representations of the rest of the universe) and what changes are occurring in other substances inside and outside its body, and therefore in the physical bodies and motions which those other substances and their changes constitute.

On Kant's interpretation, by contrast, although the representations the mind generates appear to be of bodies and motions external to it, the appearances of externality and change are produced in a priori intuition – space is the form of outer intuition, time of inner intuition. What things are in themselves we cannot know. Rejecting Leibniz's founding of his ontology in God, Kant replaced the pre-established harmony by one founded in an epistemological psychology: the objectivity of the external world is grounded in the way in which these representations must be constituted in our shared conceptual and perceptual apparatus. The sensible world is thus a construction by the mind from material given passively in our sensations using forms supplied by our cognitive faculties. Persuaded by Hume, and also by Leibniz's arguments in his *New Essays*, that the necessity characterizing mathematical and logical truths cannot be arrived at through induction from experience, and rejecting Leibniz's appeal to the divine mind to ground them, Kant situated their necessity in conditions governing the very possibility of experience. According to the 'empirical realism' of his first *Critique*, everything we know of reality is given in our perceptions as presented in our inner and outer intuition, whereas 'things-in-themselves' are intrinsically unknowable – Kant rejected the idea that they could be known through intellectual intuition. This was complemented by a 'transcendental idealism', according to which 'if we remove our own subject or even only the subjective constitution of the senses in general, then all constitution, all relations of objects in space and time, indeed space and time themselves, would disappear' (A42/B59–60).

Kant's attempt to reconcile the insights of Leibniz with empiricism in his Critical Philosophy became hugely influential, but initially it met with some sharp criticism. His positing of unknowable 'things-in-themselves' as mind-independent objects of sensations seemed to violate the very spirit and substance of the Critical Philosophy. This charge was brought against him by several contemporaries, but most notably by Johann Gottlieb Fichte (1762–1814). Also, Fichte objected, if all kinds of intellectual intuition were impossible, this would preclude the possibility of the ego's being present to itself, as required by Kant's doctrine of transcendental apperception, and also by his moral philosophy, where the ego is a moral agent that must be aware of itself. Fichte therefore dispensed with the unknowable things-in-themselves, but retained Kant's idea that the sensible world consists in our representations. The result was an idealism where all of reality, including what is not 'I', is constructed through the activity of an epistemic and moral agent.

A different version of idealism was proposed by Georg Hegel (1770–1831), who rejected Fichte's as 'subjective idealism', and offered a worldview in which reality is revealed by reason in an objective, historical process of dynamic unfolding toward knowledge of the Absolute. Consistently with his insistence that reason constitutes the essence of reality, he intellectualizes Leibniz's metaphysics (as had Kant before him), identifying the monad with its complete individual concept. For Hegel the monad is a self-determining entity which reflects the Absolute; and it does so by containing within its representations all its relations to everything else in the universe, as well as the law by which they succeed one another. These relations are internal to it, and the uniqueness of the point of view is what constitutes it as an individual. But, Hegel writes in his *Lectures on the History of Philosophy*, its existence in relation to others 'is only an appearance' (Hegel 1836: 470), and since the individual is determined by its relations to other beings, 'the same may be said of Being-for-itself' (470). So Leibniz's concept of substance falls asunder, Hegel claims, and is only stitched back together artificially by appeal to God to underwrite the harmony between all the representations. Still, 'the most important point in Leibniz is this intellectuality of representation', even if Leibniz himself did not succeed in carrying it to completion (470). Thus Hegel praises

Leibniz's account of individuation and the Principle of the Identity of Indiscernibles, but sees them as merely 'completing the system of Spinoza' (449). Where Spinoza had established the universality and oneness of substance, Leibniz's chief contribution to philosophy was to bring out 'the other side of Spinoza's philosophy, to wit, individuality, existence for itself, the monad, but monad regarded as thought – not as I, not the absolute Notion' (449). As for Leibniz's own positive philosophy, Hegel dismisses it as 'an artificial system, which is founded on a category of the understanding, namely that of the absoluteness of plurality, of abstract individuality' (473).

The young Bertrand Russell (1872–1970) was thoroughly immersed in this Hegelian philosophy, refracted through the neo-Hegelian thought of Hermann Lotze (1817–81) and F. H. Bradley (1846–1924). At a time when he was in the process of throwing over Hegelianism under the influence of his colleague G. E. Moore's common-sense realism, Russell fortuitously found himself required (by the departure of McTaggart to New Zealand) to teach a course on Leibniz's philosophy. This he mastered in short order in the summer of 1899, and his influential *Philosophy of Leibniz* was published the following year. Russell's book is rightly lauded for establishing Leibniz as a major philosopher in Anglo-American circles, as will be evident from the many references made to it above. He presented Leibniz's esoteric philosophy as an 'amazingly logical' derivation from a few simple premises, unfortunately flawed (like Hegel's) by its dependence on a subject–predicate logic. (In Italy, Giuseppe Peano, and in France, Louis Couturat, had meanwhile also discovered the amazing progress Leibniz had made in his unpublished papers on his characteristic, which inspired Peano's contributions to the axiomatization of arithmetic.) But what is not generally realized is the extent to which Russell's interpretation of Leibniz was still coloured by Hegel's. Thus his interpretation of Leibniz as 'eliminating relations', discussed in chapter 7, depended upon a conflation of the individual with its complete individual concept, and a conflation of the modifications that an individual may undergo with logical predicates.[2] This intellectualizes Leibniz's metaphysics as thoroughly as had Kant and Hegel, and is what leads Russell to saddle Leibniz with the Hegelian doctrine of internal relations (where external relations are only appearances) and the Kantian doctrine of the subjectivity of space, not to mention the alleged collapse of his philosophy into Spinozism.

Contemporary with Russell's rehabilitation of Leibniz, and also an object of his scorn, was a rival interpretation of the dynamical aspect of Leibniz's metaphysics as a needed correction of Kant. Hermann Cohen (1848–1919) maintained that Kant was right to locate objectivity in the conditions by which we represent objects in space and time, but wrong to see this in purely psychological terms. Our determinations of objects are conditioned by the scientific laws that apply to them, and these a priori laws are the principles of mathematics, and the fundamental laws of pure natural science. But as these laws change, so does our way of representing objects in space and time, resulting in a revisable a priori. Moreover, where Kant had connected the generation of magnitudes in intuition with sensation, Cohen appeals instead to Leibniz's dynamical account: extensive magnitudes, such as space, time and motion, are generated in intuition by the continuous activity of varying intensive magnitudes. Thus the varying infinitesimal magnitude dv produces the velocity v, and a curved line in space is produced by the integration of the varying line elements ds.

As may be appreciated, the relationship between the infinitesimal quantities of the calculus, which Leibniz regarded as fictions, and the monadic appetition or instantaneous tendency toward change which he regarded as all that is real in motion is one of the subtlest and most difficult points in his philosophy. Oblivious to this, and armed with Cantor's supposed refutation of infinitesimals, Russell's reaction is extreme: all mathematical quantities are constant, they do not vary in time; just as there are only external relations, so there are only extensive magnitudes; infinitesimals must be rejected.

In recent years, this tide has begun to turn. It began in the 1960s with Abraham Robinson's invention of Nonstandard Analysis, by which means he was able to establish rigorous definitions of infinitesimals in analysis. But despite being banished from calculus texts, Leibniz's differentials had always been used by applied mathematicians and engineers, and were a core concept in differential geometry. In recent years, with the advent of Category Theory – much more amenable to Leibniz's emphasis on transformations than the foundation for analysis supplied by set theory – they have been set on a firm foundation in which magnitudes are indeed allowed to vary.[3] This does not in itself validate all the metaphysical load that Cohen wanted them to carry, but it has at least increased respect for Leibniz's insights, as evidenced, for example, in Deleuze's philosophy.

I do not have the space here to trace all the other lines of influence of Leibniz on later philosophy which I have not already discussed above. But in closing, I will mention a few other areas in which appreciation of his insights has continued to grow in recent years. One is algorithmic information theory, where Gregory Chaitin (2006) credits him with being the source of all the leading ideas. This includes, of course, his discovery of binary arithmetic and recognition of its advantages for computing, an arithmetic which he claimed gave the true interpretation of the I Ching of the ancient Chinese king and philosopher Fuxi (GM vii 223–7). Another is the theory of fractals, where Benoît Mandelbrot credits Leibniz with anticipating many key concepts in the theory. Noting Leibniz's statement in *In Euclidis PROTA* (an attempt to improve upon Euclid's axioms for geometry), 'I have various definitions of a straight line. For example, a straight line is a line, any part of which is similar to the whole, and it alone, not only among lines but even among magnitudes, has this property' (GM v 185), Mandelbrot comments: 'This claim can be proved today' (Mandelbrot 1977: 419). In physics, Leibniz's losing the political battle of dominance with Newton has meant that Classical Mechanics is always equated with Newtonian Mechanics, based on the three laws for which Newton himself did not take credit. But the Leibnizian approach to physics based on symmetry and conservation principles and a least action principle has proved at least as fecund, with a line of development traceable through Maupertuis, Hamilton and Schrödinger to Schwinger and Feynman. Leibniz's relational approach to space, time and motion, which had already influenced Ernst Mach and informed some of the best work of the positivists, continues to inspire the approaches to quantum gravity of physicists such as Julian Barbour, Lee Smolin and Carlo Rovelli.

When all is said and done, the open-ended nature of Leibniz's way of doing philosophy has been remarkably successful in achieving his overarching ambition: to encourage further articulation and development of the 'seeds of thought', and above all to engender new discovery. But let us leave the last word to Denis Diderot: 'When one comes to one's senses and compares one's own small talents with those of a Leibniz,' he wrote in his article on Leibniz, 'one is tempted to throw away one's books and go and die peacefully in some forgotten corner' (Diderot and d'Alembert 1751–2: vol. ix, 379).

Notes

Chapter 1 Introduction

1 A similar interpretation was proposed by Cassirer, and more recently by Phemister (2005). An exception must be made, however, for Leibniz's correspondence with the Jesuit Des Bosses, in which he toys with a different conception of corporeal substance, where bodies are held together by a substantial bond (see chapter 5).
2 Benson Mates reports that Leibniz was likely mistaken about this etymology, and that 'the name probably derives from the Slavic Lipnice, which refers to a certain kind of grass that grows in river bottoms; variants on this appear as names of rivers and places all over Eastern Europe' (Mates 1986: 17).

Chapter 2 Logic, Language and the Encyclopaedia Project

1 Leibniz might have found the idea of the impossibility of a fastest motion in Hobbes, but his argument for it seems more indebted to Spinoza's exposition of *The Principles of Descartes' Philosophy* (Spinoza [1663] 1905: 69–74), which he likely read prior to a serious study of Descartes himself (see LoC li, 372, 407).

Chapter 3 Natural Philosophy and the Science of Life

1 The connection of Leibniz's views with those of Scaliger and Sennert is explored in Arthur 2006, Blank 2011 and Hirai 2012.

2 Scaligerian atomism was adopted by other natural philosophers, such as David van Goorle (1591–1612) in his *Exercitationes philosophicae* 1611 (published posthumously in 1620) and by Sébastien Basson (1592–1655) in his *Twelve Books of Natural Philosophy* (1621).

3 Leibniz coined the term 'organism', using it to mean, first, the condition of being organized, and then later a 'machine of nature' (see his letter to Lady Masham: GP iii 356; Nachtomy 2007: 216).

Chapter 4 Mathematical Philosophy

1 See Aristotle, *Metaphysics*, Θ 4, 47b; and especially the discussion by Ohad Nachtomy (Nachtomy 2007: 12–16).

2 By the identity of indiscernibles, it cannot be exactly the same Adam, but only a counterpart Adam indistinguishable from him in all relevant respects. The uniqueness of Adam or any other substance to one world is called 'super-essentialism': all its properties are true of it essentially. The connection of Leibniz's views on possible worlds with modern counterpart theory and possible world semantics is lucidly explained by Brandon Look (2013).

Chapter 5 The Reform of Metaphysics

1 From a dialogue engaging Malebranche's views, *Conversation of Philarète and Ariste* (1712, revised 1715: GP vi 579–94/L 623).

2 In his notes of 1678, Leibniz wrote: 'Ideas don't act, mind acts. The whole world is really the object of each mind, the whole world is perceived in some fashion by any mind. One world, and yet diverse minds. Mind is made not through the idea of the body, but because God considers the world in various ways, as I do the town' (A VI iv 1713).

3 Deleuze's term: he claims that 'Leibniz by *monad*, no less than Spinoza by *mode*, understands nothing other than an individual as an expressive center' (Deleuze 1992: 327).

4 Leibniz first formulated this in 1677–8:

> *Axiom: there is nothing in the intellect that was not first in the senses.* This axiom is false, as it is conceived. For at least the mind itself, and its properties, are in the intellect, and were never in the senses. It can be corrected in this way: Nothing is in a concept which was not in perception; or, we think about nothing to which something similar was not at least experienced by us. For it seems that perceptions are prior to simple concepts, and a concept is formed by memory of perceptions, omitting only this, that we also remember having perceived them already. (A VI iv 57)

Chapter 6 Dynamics: The Physics and Metaphysics of Action

1 I say 'correspond better' because the modern rendition of Newton's first law, $F = ma$, is not to be found in exactly that form in Newton's own work. He took the action of an external force to be proportional to the change of its motion, and followed his contemporaries in taking the quantity of motion to be proportional to mass and velocity in a given direction. The action of the force is understood to take place over a given time. For a continuously acting non-uniform force, however, the time interval has to be shrunk to an instant, and the change of velocity in a given time is the acceleration.

2 Cf. Newton's Corollary 3 of the *Principia*: 'The quantity of motion which is determined by adding the motions made in one direction and subtracting the motions made in the opposite direction, is not changed by the action of bodies on one another' (Newton [1687] 1999: 420).

3 See the discussion by Domenico Bertoloni Meli (Bertoloni Meli 1993: 19–23).

4 Newton also draws attention to this difficulty in Query 31 of his *Optics*, arguing that in order for motion to be conserved there must be active principles at work in the created universe (Newton 2004: 135–7).

5 In order to prove that the centre of gravity of several weights falling under gravity 'cannot rise higher than the place at which it was located at the beginning of its motion' (Hypothesis 1, Part IV, 108), Huygens had taken it to be 'beyond doubt' that this was so for a single heavy body.

6 For the more mathematically inclined the calculation is as follows. Assume two masses m_1 and m_2 with initial velocities of $\underline{u}_1$ and $\underline{u}_2$ and final velocities $\underline{v}_1$ and $\underline{v}_2$. Huygens assumes $\underline{u}_1 - \underline{u}_2 = \underline{v}_2 - \underline{v}_1$, or $\underline{u}_1 + \underline{v}_1 = \underline{v}_2 + \underline{u}_2$. Now according to the conservation of quantity of (directed) motion, $m_1\underline{u}_1 + m_2\underline{u}_2 = m_1\underline{v}_1 + m_2\underline{v}_2$, or $m_1(\underline{u}_1 - \underline{v}_1) = m_2(\underline{v}_2 - \underline{u}_2)$. Multiplying gives $m_1(\underline{u}_1^2 - \underline{v}_1^2) = m_2(\underline{v}_2^2 - \underline{u}_2^2)$, i.e. $m_1u_1^2 + m_2u_2^2 = m_1v_1^2 + m_2v_2^2$.

7 This criticism is repeated three decades later in a long footnote in Clarke's fifth letter to Leibniz, probably written by Newton, insisting on the correctness of the proportionality of force to velocity.

8 Here I have deleted an erroneous factor of 2 in the second term on the right (an error resulting from Leibniz's equating *a* with *L* at one point in the calculation), but which he corrected in 1706 after a protracted and confused exchange with Varignon. The result is equivalent to the correct modern formula for elliptical motion in polar coordinates.

9 As we shall see in chapter 9, Maupertuis regarded this letter as a forgery, but its authenticity has been established by Willi Kabitz (1913).

Chapter 7 The Philosophy of Space and Time

1 A caveat: here it needs to be appreciated that Einstein's relativity theory opposes the absoluteness of space and time in a different sense than

Leibniz's relational theory does: it makes their measures *relative to frame of reference*, thus opposing the classical assumption, made by Leibniz no less than Newton, that the time interval between two events would be invariant under a change of the frame of reference from which it was considered. Nevertheless, Einstein followed Leibniz and Mach in rejecting time and space as things existing independently of what is in them, and his rejection of the absoluteness of space and time in this sense was instrumental to his conceiving the Special Theory, and also to his search for a General Theory of Relativity.

2 In fact, despite profound differences in the theoretical contexts, Leibniz's denial that space is a substantival thing has much in common with the views of modern physicists such as Lee Smolin and Carlo Rovelli, who insist that there is *no background spacetime*. In keeping with the relativist tradition running from Leibniz though Mach to Einstein, Rovelli and Smolin maintain that things change and events occur in dynamic relations, but that the insistence on positing spacetime as a backdrop for this is holding up further progress toward a satisfactory synthesis of relativity and quantum theory.

3 There has been much good work on Leibniz's philosophy of relations in recent years. In this discussion I am depending heavily on the treatments by Massimo Mugnai (Mugnai 1992, 2012).

4 *Characteristica geometrica*, 1679 (Leibniz 1995b: 142ff.); see De Risi's magisterial discussion (2007: esp. 135ff. and 173–4).

5 Cf. what Leibniz wrote in a manuscript from 1680: 'the basis for measuring the duration of things is the agreement obtained by assuming different uniform motions (like those of different precise clocks)' (A VI iv 629 / LoC 275).

Chapter 8 Morals and Politics

1 Describing Georg Schuller as 'Leibniz's gopher' (2006: 188), Stewart concludes: 'whatever it was that happened on the day Spinoza died, Schuller was involved; and Leibniz was in the know' (213).

2 Here I am much indebted to a detailed study of Leibniz's 'perplexing cases' by Jorge Luis Fabra Zamora in an unpublished paper he has shared with me.

3 The quotations in this paragraph are from Hobbes's *The Elements of Law* (Hobbes [1640] 1969: 71–2), an early English draft of the Latin *De homine* (*On Man*) and *De cive* (*On Citizen*) which Leibniz read.

4 This is a different sense of voluntarism than that intended by Riley, when he says that 'Leibniz was, as a Christian, unavoidably a voluntarist' (PW 5); voluntarism in this sense means that justice must involve a voluntary act.

5 'What we have been saying would have a degree of validity even if we should concede [*etiamsi daremus*] that which cannot be conceded without

the utmost wickedness, that there is no God, or that the affairs of men are of no concern to him' (Grotius 1625: Prol. § 11; quoted from Miller 2011).

6 Of course, in one sense Hobbes did not deny this either, since the motivation for transferring one's rights to the sovereign is to live in a peaceable society. The point is that Gassendi and Leibniz regard the desire to do well by others as part of human nature, which Hobbes does not.

7 I am much indebted here to an excellent article by Ursula Goldenbaum. As she points out, Spinoza, whose *Tractaus theologico-politicus* Leibniz was studying at this time, 'also emphasized the pleasure we enjoy in our love of God as the basis for a possible reconciliation of striving for self-preservation with love and justice' (Goldenbaum 2009: 200).

8 Cf. Hobbes: 'we do not desire because we will. For will is itself an appetite; and we do not shun something because we will not to do it, but because now appetite, now aversion, is generated by those things desired or shunned, and a preconception of future pleasure or displeasure follows from those same objects' (*On Man*: Hobbes 1991: 45–6). Descartes also opposes a view of freedom of the will as indifference to alternatives (*Mediations* 4: AT vii 57–8/CSM 40).

9 Leibniz was one of the pioneers of Modal Logic, in which the axiom would be written: $\Diamond\Box p \rightarrow \Box p$ ('if it is possible that necessarily p, then necessarily p'). This axiom is still controversial.

Chapter 9 Leibnizian Posterity

1 Kant, 'On a Discovery According to Which Any New Critique of Pure Reason Has Been Made Superfluous by an Earlier One' (AK viii 248; quoted from Allison's translation given by Rutherford in his article 'Idealism Declined' in Lodge 2004: 232).

2 Thus the second premise Russell attributes to Leibniz runs: 'A subject may have predicates which are qualities existing at various times. Such a subject is called a *substance*' (Russell [1900] 1937: 4).

3 For an informed historical account see Bell 2006.

Select Bibliography

Modern Translations and Editions

Leibniz, G. W. (1969) *Philosophical Papers and Letters*, 2nd edn. Ed. and trans. Leroy Loemker. Dordrecht: D. Reidel. Cited as L.

Leibniz, G. W. (1981) *New Essays on Human Understanding*. Ed. and trans. Peter Remnant and Jonathan Bennett. Cambridge: Cambridge University Press. Cited as NE.

Leibniz, G. W. (1985) *Theodicy: Essays on the Goodness of God, the Freedom of Man and the Origin of Evil*. Ed. A. Farrer, trans. E. M. Huggard. La Salle, IL: Open Court. Cited as T.

Leibniz, G. W. (1988) *Political Writings*. Ed. and trans. Patrick Riley. Cambridge: Cambridge University Press. Cited as PW.

Leibniz, G. W. (1989) *Philosophical Essays*. Ed. and trans. Roger Ariew and Daniel Garber. Indianapolis and Cambridge, MA: Hackett. Cited as AG.

Leibniz, G. W. (1992) *De Summa Rerum: Metaphysical Papers 1675–1676*. Trans. with an introduction by G. H. R. Parkinson. New Haven: Yale University Press. Cited as DSR.

Leibniz, G. W. (1995a) *Philosophical Writings*. Ed. G. H. R. Parkinson, trans. Mary Morris and G. H. R. Parkinson. London: J. M. Dent; Rutland, VT: Charles Tuttle. Cited as MP.

Leibniz, G. W. (1998) *Philosophical Texts*. Ed. and trans. R. S. Woolhouse and Richard Francks. Oxford and New York: Oxford University Press. Cited as WFT.

Leibniz, G. W. (2001) *The Labyrinth of the Continuum: Writings of 1672 to 1686*. Selected, ed. and trans., with an introductory essay, by R. T. W. Arthur. New Haven: Yale University Press. Cited as LoC.

Leibniz, G. W. (2007) *The Leibniz–Des Bosses Correspondence*. Selected, ed. and trans., with an introductory essay, by Brandon Look and Don Rutherford. New Haven: Yale University Press. Cited as LDB.

Leibniz, G. W. (2008) *Protogaea*. Ed. and trans. Claudine Cohen and André Wakefield. Chicago and London: University of Chicago Press.

Leibniz, G. W. (2013) *The Leibniz–De Volder Correspondence*. Ed., trans. and introduction by Paul Lodge. New Haven: Yale University Press. Cited as LDV.

Further Reading

Adams, Robert M. (1994) *Leibniz: Determinist, Theist, Idealist*. New York: Oxford University Press. (An eloquently argued, uncompromisingly idealist interpretation of Leibniz's metaphysics.)

Antognazza, Maria Rosa (2009) *Leibniz: An Intellectual Biography*. Cambridge: Cambridge University Press. (The definitive biography of Leibniz. Anyone wishing to know more about the details of Leibniz's life and the setting of his ideas is highly encouraged to read this book, on which I have depended heavily.)

Bertoloni Meli, Domenico (1993) *Equivalence and Priority: Newton versus Leibniz*. Oxford: Clarendon Press. (A thorough and illuminating study of Leibniz's mathematical physics in contrast with Newton's, including translations of the *Tentamen* and other key texts.)

Brown, Stuart (1984) *Leibniz*. Minneapolis: University of Minnesota Press. (A fine introduction setting Leibniz's ideas in context, especially his debt to academic scepticism; my discussion of Leibniz's early Scholasticism is indebted to Brown's.)

Cassirer, Ernst ([1951] 1979) *The Philosophy of the Enlightenment*. Trans. Fritz Koelln and James Pettegrove. Princeton: Princeton University Press. (Although Cassirer's style is heavily Hegelian and neo-Kantian, he gives an engaging and perceptive reading that is particularly strong on Leibniz's influence on Enlightenment philosophy, especially in aesthetics.)

De Risi, Vincenzo (2007) *Geometry and Monadology*. Basel: Birkhäuser. (A scholarly *tour de force* expounding the mathematical development of Leibniz's Analysis Situs in connection with its phenomenological underpinnings.)

Eco, Umberto (1995) *The Search for the Perfect Language*. Oxford: Blackwell. (Erudite, exhibitionist and entertaining, this book on the origins of modern ideas about language is great for setting Leibniz's views in their historical context.)

Garber, Daniel (2009) *Leibniz: Body, Substance, Monad*. Oxford: Oxford University Press. (A careful exposition of the development of Leibniz's thought, arguing for an evolution from a corporeal substance metaphysics to a later idealism.)

Jolley, Nicholas (2005) *Leibniz*. Oxford: Routledge. (Like Brown's this is also an excellent introduction that presents Leibniz as an idealist, beginning with his monads; especially strong on Leibniz's ethics.)

Mates, Benson (1986) *The Philosophy of Leibniz: Metaphysics and Language*. Oxford: Oxford University Press. (A monograph study of Leibniz's philosophy which is especially strong on his philosophy of language, and to which I am indebted for much biographical detail.)

Mugnai, Massimo (in press) 'Universal Language, *Ars Characteristica*, Logical Calculus, and Natural Language', in Maria Rosa Antognazza (ed.), *The Oxford Handbook of Leibniz*. Oxford: Oxford University Press. (A succinct and accurate account of Leibniz's thought on logic and language, on which I have depended heavily in chapter 2.)

Nachtomy, Ohad (2007) *Possibility, Agency, and Individuality in Leibniz's Metaphysics*. Dordrecht: Springer. (A wonderfully clear exposition of the importance of possibility in Leibniz's system; also highly recommended for its detailed treatments of Leibniz on substance, aggregates, nested individuals and free will, which support the interpretations I give here.)

Phemister, Pauline (2005) *Leibniz and the Natural World*. Dordrecht: Springer. (A cogent reading of Leibniz as synthesizing idealism and materialism in positing corporeal substances as the real metaphysical constituents of the universe.)

Phemister, Pauline (2006) *The Rationalists: Descartes, Spinoza and Leibniz*. Cambridge: Polity. (A very readable comparison of the views of these three great thinkers, even-handedly pointing out their main points of agreement and difference.)

Russell, Bertrand ([1900] 1937) *A Critical Exposition of the Philosophy of Leibniz*, 2nd edn. Cambridge: Cambridge University Press. (Russell's study established Leibniz as a philosopher of the first rank in the English-speaking world, concentrating on the formal aspects of his philosophy that had previously been unappreciated.)

Rutherford, Donald (1995) *Leibniz and the Rational Order of Nature*. Cambridge: Cambridge University Press. (A treasure trove of insight into Leibniz's analysis of concepts and its development from its origins in Bisterfeld to the complete concept theory of the 1680s.)

Smith, Justin E. H. (2011) *Divine Machines: Leibniz and the Sciences of Life*. Princeton: Princeton University Press. (A comprehensive study of Leibniz's medical and biological thought, including translations of key texts in the appendices.)

Primary Sources

Aristotle (1984) *The Complete Works of Aristotle*, 2 vols. Revised Oxford translation, ed. Jonathan Barnes. Princeton: Princeton University Press.

Bisterfeld, J. H. (1657) *Philosophiae primae seminarium*, Lyon.

Bisterfeld, J. H. (1661) *Opera (Bisterfeldius Redivivus)*, 2 vols. The Hague: A. Vlacq.

Boyle, Robert (2000) *The Works of Robert Boyle*. Ed. Michael Cyril William Hunter and Edward Bradford Davis. London: Pickering and Chatto.

Condillac, Étienne Bonnot de (1798) *Traité de systèmes*. Paris: Ch. Houel.

Dalgarno, George (1661) *Ars signorum* (*Art of Signs*). London: T. Hayes.

Descartes, René (1964–76) *Oeuvres de Descartes*, 12 vols. New edition. Eds Ch. Adam and P. Tannery. Paris: J. Vrin. Cited as AT.

Descartes, René (1984–5) *The Philosophical Writings of Descartes*, vols 1 and 2. Eds John Cottingham, Robert Stoothof and Dugald Murdoch. Cambridge: Cambridge University Press. Cited as CSM i, CSM ii.

Descartes, René (1991) *The Philosophical Writings of Descartes*, vol. 3. Eds John Cottingham, Robert Stoothof, Dugald Murdoch and Anthony Kenny. Cambridge: Cambridge University Press. Cited as CSMK.

Diderot, Denis and Jean Le Rond d'Alembert (eds) (1751–2) *Encyclopédie ou Dictionnaire raisonné des sciences, des arts et des métiers, par une Société de Gens de lettres*, 17 vols. Paris: Briasson, David, LeBreton, Durand.

Euler, Leonhard (1843) *Lettres à une Princesse d'Allemagne*. Paris: Charpentier.

Gassendi, Pierre (1658 [1964]) *Opera Omnia*, 6 vols. Stuttgart-Bad Canstatt: Friedrich Frommann.

Grotius, Hugo (1625) *De iure belli ac pacis libri tres*. Paris: Buon.

Hegel, G. W. F. (1836) *Geschichte der Philosophie* (Werke, Bd 15, ed. Karl Ludwig Michelet), vol. 3, part 3. Berlin: Duncker und Humblot.

Hobbes, Thomas ([1640] 1969) *The Elements of Law*. Ed. with a preface and critical notes by Ferdinand Tönnies. London: Frank Cass & Co. Ltd.

Hobbes, Thomas (1668) *Opera philosophica omnia*, vol. 1: *De corpore*. Amsterdam: Johannes Blaeu.

Hobbes, Thomas (1991) *Man and Citizen*. Ed. with an introduction by Bernard Gert. Indianapolis and Cambridge, MA: Hackett Publishing Company.

Huygens, Christiaan (1673) *Horologium Oscillatorium*. Paris: F. Muguet.

Kant, Immanuel (1910–) *Gesammelte Schriften*. Ed. Akademie der Wissenschaften. Berlin: Reimer (later DeGruyter). Cited as AK.

Leibniz, G. W. (1710) *Théodicée: Essais de Théodicée sur la bonté de Dieu, la liberté de l'homme et l'origine du mal*. La Salle, Ill.: Open Court. Cited as T.

Leibniz, G. W. (1768) *Opera omnia . . .* , 4 vols. Ed. Louis Dutens. Geneva: Fratres de Tournes. Cited as D.

Leibniz, G. W. (1840) *Opera philosophica quae exstant Latina Gallica Germanica omnia*, ed. Joannes Eduardus Erdmann. Berlin: G. Eichler.

Leibniz, G. W. (1846) *Historia et Origo calculi differentialis a G. G. Leibnitzio conscripta*. Ed. C. I. Gerhardt. Hanover.

Leibniz, G. W. (1849–63) *Leibnizens Mathematische Schriften*. Ed. C. I. Gerhardt. Berlin and Halle: Asher and Schmidt; reprint edn: Hildesheim: Georg Olms, 1971. 7 vols. Cited as GM.

Leibniz, G. W. (1857). *Nouvelles lettres et opuscules inédits de Leibniz*. Ed. Alexandre Foucher de Careil. Paris: Auguste Durand.

Leibniz, G. W. (1875–90) *Die Philosophische Schriften von Gottfried Wilhelm Leibniz*. Ed. C. I. Gerhardt. Berlin: Weidmann; reprint edn: Hildesheim and New York: Georg Olms, 1978. 7 vols. Cited as GP.

Leibniz, G. W. (1903) *Opuscules et fragments inédits de Leibniz*. Ed. Louis Couturat. Paris: Alcan; reprint ed. Hildesheim: Olms, 1966. Cited as C.

Leibniz, G. W. (1923–) *Sämtliche Schriften und Briefe*. Ed. Akademie der Wissenschaften der DDR. Darmstadt and Berlin: Akademie-Verlag. Cited as A.

Leibniz, G. W. (1948) *Textes inédits*. Ed. Gaston Grua. Paris. Cited as Grua.

Leibniz, G. W. (1991) 'Phoranomus; seu de Potentia et Legibus Naturae' (July 1689). Ed. André Robinet, *Physis*, 28(3): 429–541; 28(23): 797–885.

Leibniz, G. W. ([1675–6] 1993) *De quadratura arithmetica circuli ellipseos et hyperbolae cujus corollarium est trigonometria sine tabulis*. Ed. and commentary by Eberhard Knobloch. Göttingen: Vandenhoek & Ruprecht.

Leibniz, G. W. (1994) *La réforme de la dynamique*. Ed., presentation, trans. and commentaries by Michel Fichant. Paris: J. Vrin.

Leibniz, G. W. (1995b) *La caractéristique géometrique*. Text established, introduced and annotated by Javier Echeverría; trans., annotated and postface by Marc Parmentier. Paris: J. Vrin.

Malebranche, Nicolas ([1674–5] 1980) *The Search after Truth*. Trans. T. M. Lennon and P. J. Olscamp. Columbus: Ohio State University Press.

Newton, Isaac ([1687] 1999) *The 'Principia': The Mathematical Principles of Natural Philosophy*. Trans. I. B. Cohen and Anne Whitman. Berkeley: University of Califormia Press.

Newton, Isaac (2004) *Philosophical Writings*. Ed. Andrew Janiak. Cambridge: Cambridge University Press.

Ockham, William (1984) *Quæstiones in Libros Physicorum Aristotelis, Opera Philosophica et Theologica*, vol. 6, ed. Stephan Brown. St Bonaventure: Franciscan Institute.

Scaliger, Julius Caesar (1557) *Exotericarum exercitationum liber Libri XV de subtilitate ad Hieronymum Cardanum* [*Exotericarum*] (i.e. 'Fifteen Books of Exoteric Exercises on Subtlety, for Hieronymus Cardan'). Paris: M. Vascosani.

Schopenhauer, Arthur (1818) *Die Welt als Wille und Vorstellung*. Leipzig: F. A. Brockhaus.

Sennert, Daniel (1619) *De chymicorum cum Aristotelicis et Galenicis consensu ac dissensu* (i.e. 'On the Agreement and Disagreement of the Chemists with Aristotelians and Galenists, Book I'), Witterberg: Zachariah Schurer.

Sennert, Daniel (1651) *Hypomnemata Physica*. Venice edn, Francis Baba.

Spinoza, Baruch ([1663] 1905) *The Principles of Descartes' Philosophy*. Ed. and trans. H. H. Britan. La Salle: Open Court.

Spinoza, Baruch (1882) *Opera*. Ed. J. van Vloten and J. P. N. Land. The Hague: Martin Nijhoff.

Stahl, Georg Ernst and G. W. Leibniz (1720) Negotium otiosum . . . Halle: Literis Orphanotrophei.

Steno, Nicolaus ([1669] 1916) *The Prodomus of Nicolaus Steno's Dissertation Concerning a Solid Body Enclosed by a Process of Nature within a Solid*. Ed. J. G. Winter. London.

Voltaire ([1733] 1994) *Letters Concerning the English Nation*. Ed. Nicholas Cronk. Oxford: Oxford University Press.

Voltaire (1879) *Oeuvres Complètes de Voltaire*. Paris: Garnieres Frères.

Wilkins, John (1668) *Essay towards a Real Character and a Philosophical Language*. London: John Martyn.

Wolff, Christian ([1737] 1964) *Cosmologia Generalis*. Hildesheim: Olms.

Secondary Sources and Other References

Arthur, R. T. W. (1985) 'Leibniz's Theory of Time', pp. 263–313 in Kathleen Okruhlik and James Robert Brown (eds), *The Natural Philosophy of Leibniz*. Dordrecht: Reidel.

Arthur, R. T. W. (2006) 'Animal Generation and Substance in Sennert and Leibniz', pp. 147–74 in Justin E. H. Smith (ed.), *The Problem of Animal Generation in Modern Philosophy*. Cambridge: Cambridge University Press.

Arthur, R. T. W. (2013) 'Leibniz's Theory of Space', *Foundations of Science*, 18(3): 499–528.

Bell, John (2006) *The Continuous and the Infinitesimal*. Milan: Polimetrica.

Bergson, Henri (1911) *Creative Evolution*. Trans. Arthur Mitchell. New York: Henry Holt and Co.

Blank, Andreas (2011) 'Sennert and Leibniz on Animate Atoms', pp. 115–30 in Justin E. H. Smith and Ohad Nachtomy (eds), *Machines of Nature and Corporeal Substances in Leibniz*. Dordrecht: Springer.

Borges, Jorge Luis (1964a) *Labyrinths*. Ed. Donald A. Yates and James Irby. New York: New Directions Books.

Borges, Jorge Luis (1964b) 'The Analytical Language of John Wilkins', pp. 101–5 in *Other Inquisitions, 1939–1952*. Trans. Ruth L. C. Simms. Austin: University of Texas Press.

Broad, C. D. (1975) *Leibniz: An Introduction*. Cambridge: Cambridge University Press.

Chaitin, Gregory (2006) 'The Limits of Reason', *Scientific American*, March: 74–81.

Deleuze, Gilles (1992) *Expressionism in Philosophy*. Trans. Martin Joughin. New York: Zone Books.

Deleuze, Gilles (1993) *The Fold: Leibniz and the Baroque*. Foreword and trans. Tom Conley. Minneapolis: University of Minnesota Press.

Foucher de Careil, Alexandre (1854) *Réfutation inédite de Spinoza par Leibniz*. Paris.

Furbank, P. N. (1993) *Diderot: A Critical Biography*. London: Minerva.

Goldenbaum, Ursula (2009) 'It's Love! Leibniz's Foundations of Natural Law as the Outcome of his Struggle with Hobbes' and Spinoza's Naturalism', pp. 190–201 in Mark Kulstad, Mogens Laerke and David Snyder (eds), *The Philosophy of the Young Leibniz*. Stuttgart: Franz Steiner Verlag.

Hess, Heinz-Jürgen (1978) 'Die unveröffentlichen naturwissenschaftlichen und technischen Arbeiten von G. W. Leibniz aus der Zeit seines Parisaufenthaltes', pp. 183–217 in *Leibniz à Paris 1672–1676*, vol. 1. Wiesbaden: Franz Steiner Verlag.

Hirai, Hiro (2012) 'Living Atoms, Hylomorphism and Spontaneous Generation in Daniel Sennert', pp. 77–98 in Gideon Manning (ed.), *Matter and Form in Early Modern Science and Philosophy*. Boston and Leiden: Brill.

Jolley, Nicholas (ed.) (1995) *The Cambridge Companion to Leibniz*. Cambridge: Cambridge University Press.

Kabitz, Willi (1913) 'Über eine in Gotha aufgefundene Abschrift des von S. König in seinem Streite mit Maupertuis und der Akademie veröffentlichten, seinerzeit für unecht erklärten Leibnizbriefes', *Sitzungsberichte der Königlich Preussischen Akademie der Wissenschaften*, II: 632–8.

Levey, Sam (2005) 'Leibniz on Precise Shapes and the Corporeal World', pp. 69–94 in Donald Rutherford and J. A. Cover (eds), *Leibniz: Nature and Freedom*. Oxford: Oxford University Press.

Lodge, Paul (ed.) (2004) *Leibniz and His Correspondents*. Cambridge: Cambridge University Press

Look, Brandon C. (2013) 'Leibniz's Modal Metaphysics', *The Stanford Encyclopedia of Philosophy*. Ed. Edward N. Zalta. http://plato.stanford.edu/archives/spr2013/entries/leibniz-modal/.

Maat, Jaap (2004) *Philosophical Languages in the Seventeenth Century: Dalgarno, Wilkins and Leibniz*. Dordrecht: Kluwer.

Mandelbrot, Benoît (1977) *The Fractal Geometry of Nature*. San Francisco: Freeman.

Mercer, Christia (2001) *Leibniz's Metaphysics: Its Origins and Development*. Cambridge: Cambridge University Press.

Miller, Jon (2011) 'Hugo Grotius', *The Stanford Encyclopedia of Philosophy*. Ed. Edward N. Zalta. http://plato.stanford.edu/archives/fall2011/entries/grotius/.

Mugnai, Massimo (1992) *Leibniz' Theory of Relations* (*Studia Leibnitiana Supplementa 28*). Stuttgart: Franz Steiner Verlag.

Mugnai, Massimo (2001) *Introduzione alla filosofia di Leibniz*. Turin: Einaudi.

Mugnai, Massimo (2012) 'Leibniz's Ontology of Relations: A Last Word?', pp. 171–208 in Daniel Garber and Donald Rutherford (eds), *Oxford Studies in Early Modern Philosophy*, vol. 6. Oxford: Oxford University Press.

Nachtomy, Ohad (2009) 'Leibniz and *The Logic of Life*', *Studia Leibnitiana*, Band XLI, Heft 1: 1–20.

Nachtomy, Ohad (2011) 'Leibniz on Artificial and Natural Machines: Or, What it Means to Remain a Machine to the Least of Its Parts', pp. 61–80 in Justin E. H. Smith and Ohad Nachtomy (eds), *Machines of Nature and Corporeal Substances in Leibniz*. Dordrecht: Springer.

Pross, Addy (2011) 'Toward a General Theory of Evolution: Extending Darwinian Theory to Inanimate Matter', *Journal of Systems Chemistry*, 2(1): 1–14.

Rescher, Nicholas (1967) *The Philosophy of Leibniz*. Englewood Cliffs, NJ: Prentice-Hall.

Rescher, Nicholas (2003) *On Leibniz*. Pittsburgh: University of Pittsburgh Press.

Russell, Bertrand (1923) 'Vagueness', *Australasian Journal of Psychology and Philosophy*, 1(2): 84–92.

Russell, Bertrand ([1946] 1972) *A History of Western Philosophy*. New York: Simon and Schuster.

Schneewind, J. B. (1990) *Moral Philosophy from Montaigne to Kant*. Cambridge: Cambridge University Press.

Stephenson, Neal (2003–4) *The Baroque Cycle*, 3 vols. New York: Harper Collins.

Stewart, Matthew (2006) *The Courtier and the Heretic*. New York: W. W. Norton.

Electronic Resources

An extremely useful source is Gregory Brown's site *Leibnitiana* (http://www.gwleibniz.com). This site has links to Leibniz Societies around the globe, to Leibniz journals, to available translations and encyclopedia articles, and contains various pages of Leibniz-related miscellany.

On-line translations of many of Leibniz's works are available in Jonathan Bennett's *Some Texts from Early Modern Philosophy* (http://www.earlymoderntexts.com/), and also in Lloyd Strickland's site *Leibniz Translations* (http://www.leibniz-translations.com/index.html).

Index